*Inequality in an Age
of Decline*

America, 1940

Hopper, Edward
Gas. (1940)
Oil on canvas, 26¼ x 40¼".
Collection, The Museum of Modern Art, New York
Mrs. Simon Guggenheim Fund.

America, 1979

Wide World Photos, *Los Angeles Times*

PAUL BLUMBERG

Inequality in an Age of Decline

New York   Oxford
OXFORD UNIVERSITY PRESS
1980

Library of Congress Cataloging in Publication Data

Blumberg, Paul.
Inequality in an age of decline.

Includes index.
1. Equality.   2. Social mobility—United
States.   3. United States—Economic conditions—
1971–   I. Title.
HM146.B59   305.5   80-16047
ISBN 0-19-502804-X

Acknowledgment is made for permission to reprint the following materials:

Excerpt from *The Price* by Arthur Miller. Copyright © 1968 by Arthur Miller and Ingeborg M. Miller, Trustee. Reprint by permission of Viking Penguin Inc.
Tennessee Williams, *Cat on a Hot Tin Roof*. Copyright © 1955 by Tennessee Williams. Reprinted by permission of New Directions.

In an age when family matters less—
for my uncles,
who eased the loss
and became friends and teachers, too

Contents

Preface

The America we have always known is disappearing before our eyes. What we have been witnessing lately seems nothing less than the transformation of an entire society in an incredibly brief time. In its broadest outlines, this transformation is based on the crisis of the American economy and the associated weakening of American power around the world. How can one speak of a crisis in what is the world's largest and richest economy? When an object is falling from a great height, one can focus either on its altitude or on its rate of descent. In this book I have chosen to concentrate on the latter; after all, an object's rate of fall, not its current altitude, represents its future.

In recent years, with the deepening woes of U.S. capitalism, economic news has moved from the financial page to the front page and often to the headlines. The crisis of American capitalism, in fact, has become one of the central events of our time. Every age throws to the surface those whose training, talent, or sensitivity equips them to solve the problems, fight the battles, or explain the world. In the 1960s, during the legal struggle for civil rights, lawyers seemed to occupy a strategic place. Today, with the right tools and sufficient vision, economists could become the chief explainers of our age.

The implications of recent economic events are enormous and are reverberating throughout American life. In no area, however, has the economic crisis had more impact than upon the American class structure which is now undergoing a fundamental upheaval. During the long postwar era, some of America's most distinguished social analysts, as well as the most influential sections of the media, described an America of rising affluence and growing equality, trends which they expected to continue indefinitely, culminating in a capitalism which was classless, harmonious, and abundant. I have dealt at length with what I call this theory of class convergence in Chapter 1 because it for so long dominated both the conventional wisdom and social theory.

Now, however, all these optimistic postwar predictions are collapsing. Today America faces not rising living standards and growing equality but stagnating living standards and growing inequality (Chapters 2 and 5). In the 1970s the United States appeared to be reaching an historic turning point. The American economy has always been special, different, exceptional. But now we are coming to the end of American economic exceptionalism and approaching what may be the gradual Europeanization of the American class system. Just a few short years ago the rosy predictions by America's leading social scientists of affluence and equality seemed plausible; today they sound naive, outmoded, and like exercises in intellectual wishful thinking.

The crisis of American capitalism seems based, at least in part, on several developments discussed in Chapter 4: the "permanent war economy" which, as Seymour Melman so cogently argued, has since the end of World War II drained enormous economic and human resources away from productive investment and depleted vast sectors of the civilian economy; the rapid international diffusion of technology which increasingly neutralizes the traditional American advantage; and the ability of newer industrial nations to leapfrog the U.S., which, however ironic and premature it may seem, is now becoming an aging industrial power.

For the long postwar period, the U.S. was rich enough to afford both guns and butter; huge military expenditures were compatible with rising living standards. Now, however, as America becomes a poorer country, the arms race on the same postwar scale can be pursued only by making deep inroads into already languishing public services and social programs, and into private living standards as well.

The economic crisis has more than economic consequences, however. An age of scarcity and economic decline is now threatening some of the moral and ideological underpinnings of American civilization (Chapter 6). Growing scarcity is undermining that aspect of American national character which was shaped by the nation's long heritage of abundance. Economic decline is eroding traditional American optimism and faith in continuous progress. Stagnating living standards and growing inequality are straining the credibility of historic American notions of classlessness. And the new austerity is making it more difficult for Americans to find meaning in their lives in ways that have been patterned for them by the corporation and mass advertising—in privatized material consumption. It is clear that a major challenge for America in the coming years will be to redefine its national goals and values in terms of new economic realities.

In a society long used to rising affluence and international dominance, stagnating living standards and the decline of American power carries the potential for increased social conflict at home and growing belligerence abroad. And yet my hope, expressed in the final chapter, is that domestic conflict and international belligerence arising from America's current crisis will be offset by stabilizing influences emerging from what seems to be a gradual enrichment of democracy and civility in American life.

Writing a book about a timely subject carries both risks and rewards. The rewards lie obviously in its relevance to the events of the day; the risks are that one can simply go on analyzing new data forever and never finish. Lest this work become an ongoing, unpublished chronicle of trends rather than a completed book, I decided to carry the analysis only through the end of the 1970s. Nonetheless, the trends I traced to the end of the seventies have continued and in some cases even accelerated in the early days of the new decade. Inflation has soared even beyond the peaks of the 1970s. Workers' real earnings have not merely stagnated but have fallen. Housing costs which continue to squeeze young first-time buyers out of the market have raised a cry among parents hardly even comprehensible during most of the postwar era: "Where will our children live?" The pace and severity of plant closings have increased. And suddenly, out of nowhere, the industry that more than any other has symbolized American economic supremacy for generations, automobiles, finds itself in its deepest crisis ever. While Detroit's current predicament may ultimately be remedied by its reluctant but imperative and long overdue conversion to small-car production, the present situation may also portend a permanent decline of the U.S. auto industry. Indeed, in the most symbolic event of the new decade, in 1980, for the first time, Japan will produce more automobiles than the United States. But if America is not automobiles, what is it? The answer may become more clear in the days ahead.

Many people have given intellectual and moral support to me during the writing of this book, and to them I am very grateful. Of the ideas developed here, many grew out of long walks and talks with my friend Conrad Miller. His intellectual stimulation in these spirited conversations helped to focus and organize my own thoughts. Economist Arnold Cantor of the Research Department of the AFL-CIO read an early draft and offered many helpful suggestions. My uncle Bernard Karsh of the University of Illinois—sociologist, pilot, mechanic, all-around fixer, and general Renaissance man—read the manuscript and made many useful observations. Irving Howe helped place an excerpt from Chapter 2, "White-Collar Status Panic," in *The New Republic* and offered a generous comment on the article. His words are always a spur to ambition. To my uncle James Perlman of San Francisco State University I owe a general rather than a specific debt—for sensitizing me at a very early age to social and political ideas that have stayed with me through my adult life. My uncle Carl Shier, international rep for the UAW, kept his famous "care packages" and newsletters coming from the labor front. Dean Savage provided his usual bibliographic wizardry. Steven Cohen and other colleagues at Queens College offered much informal help at the office and over the lunch table. The staff at the New York office of the Bureau of Labor Statistics provided valuable assistance by phone and in person on many occasions. Pearl Sigberman and her excellent staff in the Word Processing center at Queens College typed the manuscript. Laura Gramm took time out from a busy schedule to proofread the galleys. I owe special thanks to those who made my association with Oxford University Press such a gratifying one: my editor, Susan Rabiner, who with equal measures of skill, efficiency, and encouragement guided the manuscript through its voyage; her assistant, Shelley Reinhardt; copy editor Cheryl Trobiani; and Helena Schwarz in publicity. From Berkeley my family gave their customary transcontinental encouragement and reassurances of the essential family tie. Ruth Blumberg's historic trip to New York allowed me to take a much-needed break and to see New York anew through the eyes of a tourist. I owe thanks also to my son, Ira, who was always understanding when I could not spend as much time with him as I wished. Although far away, Marvin Rosen and Johanna Fortuin are always a help and always here in spirit. Finally, I owe thanks to friends for their indulgence on those many occasions when I could not join them and who realized that I had nothing to lose but my chains to the typewriter.

Introduction:
The End of the
American Century

The 1970s were not kind to the United States. At the beginning of that decade, only a handful of prophets foresaw that the structure of postwar American international hegemony was going to crumble. By the end of the decade, even the most casual viewer of the television news realized that American power was no longer what it once was and that if America was still first, it was more and more merely first among equals.

If it is true that human beings age at an uneven pace—going for long periods with no perceptible change only to age quickly in a relatively brief time, then perhaps the same is true of nations: the United States, which swashbuckled its way through the postwar decades with no visible signs of wear, suddenly in the 1970s aged and wore very perceptibly. Evidence of America's economic and political decline began to accumulate slowly in the early 1970s, but by the end of the decade events cascaded down one upon another in a dizzying torrent, and it seemed that each morning's newspaper brought fresh testimony of America's diminished economic position abroad and the waning of the political and military influence that it had exercised with such self-confidence since the end of World War II. The most extraordinary transformations of the American condition, both domestic and international, which might normally have taken decades, were telescoped into a few years.

In the 1950s British playwright John Osborne, reflecting on the

decline of Britain in his play *Look Back in Anger,* sardonically
and a bit enviously called this the "American century," a term
coined earlier by Henry Luce and a view hardly anyone at the time
would have cared to dispute. Yet little more than two decades
later, it is obvious that we are, in Andrew Hacker's words, at the
end of the American era. Whether the decline of American supremacy in the 1970s was more aptly symbolized by the bang of
the Vietnam War or the whimper of once-mighty American industries crying for protection from foreign competition, it is certain
that we now live in a world far different from the one in which we
have lived since the end of World War II. In a period of such rapid
social change, the American "century" has lasted little more than
30 years.[1]

U.S. hegemony rose out of the ashes of World War II. While the
war devastated both victors and vanquished in Europe and Asia,
the United States emerged from the war untouched and triumphant. The Europe-centered system of international power had
collapsed, and the United States and the Soviet Union stepped into
the vacuum. But while both were termed superpowers, there was
no question that the military and economic might of the United
States was supreme. Indeed, the postwar Pax Americana was
based on America's clear-cut military superiority and its overwhelming economic and technological strength, which in turn generated huge trade surpluses and financed its immense international
obligations and which provided the foundation for the firm dollar-
based international monetary system.

But for many reasons U.S. hegemony was unstable, and in fact
contained the seeds of its own destruction. American power rested
upon the reconstruction of Europe and Japan, in order to
strengthen the political and military alliance against the Communist bloc. But to promote its international political interests the
United States often undermined its long-term economic interests.
Thus, the U.S. opened up an enormous market to Japan while
tolerating Japanese restrictions on U.S. investment and trade; and
the U.S. not only provided Europe with massive economic aid following World War II but encouraged the formation of the European Common Market which would, in some cases, discriminate
against American imports.[2] It was inevitable, therefore, that the

economies of Europe and Japan, rebuilt with substantial U.S. aid and support, would eventually become competitors of the United States. And indeed that has now happened. With postwar reconstruction complete by the 1960s, Europe and Japan, once merely America's dependent junior partners, have emerged as full-scale economic rivals.

The American economy has faltered. It was plagued during the 1970s by an unprecedented inflation initially generated in the late 1960s by the deficit spending of the Vietnam War; a prompt tax increase to finance an unpopular war was impossible. Upon this was superimposed the energy chaos beginning in 1973, followed by record unemployment rates in the mid-1970s, producing the strange conjunction of high inflation and high unemployment—*stagflation*. Suddenly in the 1970s the Keynesian fine-tuning of American capitalism—resting upon government fiscal and monetary policy—began to break down. When the American economy weakened, its huge trade surpluses disappeared. The balance-of-payments problem, which first appeared as early as 1958, became progressively worse as the economy earned insufficient foreign exchange to pay for its enormous international commitments—a far-flung network of military bases, extensive foreign aid, growing imports, the Vietnam War, and the foreign investment of U.S. multinational corporations. With the hemorrhage of monetary reserves, the U.S. dollar, the postwar international currency Gibraltar, began to crumble, culminating in its devaluation in 1971 and 1973 and its astonishing plunge afterwards.

Meanwhile, the Organization of Petroleum Exporting Countries (OPEC), which had tried unsuccessfully to organize an oil embargo during the Six-Day War in 1967, succeeded six years later in a world where U.S. power had retreated significantly. As the power of OPEC increased, so did America's international vulnerability. By the late 1970s it was clear that the U.S. was losing control over its oil supply to a remote, highly unstable, and increasingly hostile region of the world. And despite brave talk of energy independence during the 1970s, the U.S. found itself year by year becoming more dependent on OPEC oil, with potentially catastrophic consequences for America's economic well-being and physical security.

In the early 1950s the CIA, with the help of Iranian army officers, easily disposed of Iranian nationalist leader Mohammed Mossadegh and restored the Shah. But a quarter of a century later, America watched from the sidelines as the Shah's government collapsed before an enormous revolutionary wave. America was losing the will or the ability to defend its favorite despots around the world. Of course American power is still vast, but the world has become more complex, and it is more difficult than ever to exercise that power.

At the same time, Soviet military power—nuclear and conventional, strategic and tactical, quantitative and qualitative—has continued to increase remarkably. Just as Europe and Japan have reached near economic parity with the United States, so Soviet and Warsaw Pact forces have reached near military parity with the United States. In the early 1960s the celebrated missile gap with the Soviet Union turned out to be political rhetoric and public relations. But in the late 1970s there was no question that Soviet military power was, in fact, rapidly closing on the U.S. How perplexing that the United States, after spending some $2 trillion on defense since World War II, channeled through what is supposedly the world's most efficient economic system, should find itself barely abreast of the Soviet Union.

If an aspiring writer wished to set her novel against a background of American power in decline, she might have fabricated the following events to create an appropriately gloomy mood. The value of the dollar sinks unbelievably abroad. The price of gold soars. In the first year of this fictitious decade, domestic oil production peaks and then begins to fall. While the price of imported oil mounts ever higher, scarcities develop. Intermittently, lines appear at gasoline stations, foreshadowing a drama in the years ahead almost too frightening to contemplate. A book entitled *How to Prosper During the Coming Bad Years* remains on the best-seller list for over a year. A major American automobile company nearly goes under, with symbolic parallels to the British economy and its moribund automobile industry. A president is forced to resign. America withdraws from a war against a small Asian nation. For the first time in decades, the United States becomes an onlooker at major international events as China, Vietnam and Cambodia tangle in military conflict over what is suddenly entirely Communist turf. For the first time since World War II, a strengthened and emboldened Soviet army occupies a country outside its satellite empire. Two national symbols of mainstream American culture and American values—Norman Rockwell and John Wayne—die.

"A contrived and highly implausible scenario," the critics would say.

On and off during the disturbing events of the 1970s, nostalgia seemed to dominate the national mood, as Americans turned fondly back to the memories of the old songs of the forties and fifties, the old fashions, the old movies, the old radio shows, the old heroes, the old wars. There may be meaning in this national nostalgia, for is it not reasonable to assume that societies, like human beings, turn nostalgic after their best days have passed? In the confusion of the present, Americans seem more than ever to long for the good old days.

ECONOMIC DECLINE AND SOCIAL CLASS

In the early 1960s President Kennedy spoke of America on a New Frontier. By the 1970s America was, indeed, on a new frontier, but one radically different from the one Kennedy had in mind. It was a frontier of economic crisis unlike anything America had ever experienced before: unprecedented inflation, high unemployment, a precipitously declining dollar, enormous trade deficits, the rapid erosion of the U.S. technological lead, declining productivity growth, and loss of control over vital energy sources. While America had experienced some of these problems before (unemployment, inflation), their simultaneous combination was entirely new.

Despite the importance of these developments, there has been little examination of their effect upon the American class structure. Yet such an examination is crucial. America has more unsolved economic problems now than at any time since the Great Depression; and here, as in all things, problems which are not solved begin to dominate. Thus, we have entered an age of economic determinism with a vengeance, in which the concept of the economic substructure may take on new meaning. The central fact of our time may indeed be the decline of American economic hegemony, and that decline is having an enormous impact upon the American class structure. The old postwar assumptions about social class in America are now collapsing, for changed economic and social circumstances demand new analysis and new theory. But in order to understand these changing conditions, one must place them in the context of the dominant theories about the American class structure that prevailed during the long postwar era.

CHAPTER ONE

Theories of Class in Postwar America

ANTECEDENTS

In the postwar discussion of social class in America, sociologists, critics, and other commentators split roughly into two camps. In the first were those who supported what I have called a theory of *class convergence*. Convergence theorists argued essentially that unremitting egalitarian trends in American society were steadily reducing inequality and that the gap between classes had so significantly narrowed over the years that it was doubtful whether American society could any longer be profitably understood in terms of the traditional concepts of social class. Arrayed against the convergence theorists were those who argued a view that I have termed *class stability*. Stability theorists contended that despite postwar changes, class differences had not diminished and the traditional inequalities characteristic of a class society continued with no significant trend toward growing social and economic equality.

The postwar debate over social class in America seemed new because the data and even some of the concepts (e.g., the notion of postindustrial society) derived from America's postwar experience. Yet the roots of the debate over inequality go back as far as the Colonial period to two central and related elements of the American heritage: the tradition of classlessness and the tradition of abundance.

The tradition of classlessness is fundamental to American history. In fact its components are so well known they need only be mentioned here: the absence of a feudal heritage and an hereditary aristocracy; the founding of the republic in a revolt against aristocratic monarchy; the egalitarian thrust of the Declaration of Independence and the Constitution; the triumph of Jeffersonian republicanism over Hamiltonian federalism; the egalitarian impact of such presidents as Andrew Jackson and Abraham Lincoln; the pervasiveness of the Horatio Alger myth of unlimited mobility, for native and immigrant alike; the frontier tradition and the ease, unpretentiousness, and informality of American national character.

This egalitarian tradition affected not only American society but American sociology as well, the practitioners of which were often led to play down the importance of class in this country. Although the founders of American sociology—Lester Ward, William Graham Sumner, Albion Small, Franklin Giddings, Charles Cooley, E. A. Ross—treated social class to one degree or another, they nonetheless "gave voice to class theories which were, in the final analysis, highly colored by the 'classlessness' of the American scene."[1] In fact, the tradition of classlessness narcotized thinking about social class for decades, and American sociology entered the 1920s "with little class research in progress, a minimum of theoretical consideration of the precise meaning of the term, and practically no recognition of the class framework as a major area of investigation within the discipline of sociology."[2]

From the beginning, America was also known as a land of unique abundance. As early as 1605, a British play suggested what was to be the prevailing view of America for centuries thereafter. Describing the wealth of Virginia, a character in the drama exclaims:

I tell thee, gold is more plentiful there than copper is with us. . . . Why, man, all their dripping pans are pure gold; and all their chains with which they chain up their streets are massy gold . . . and for rubies and diamonds they go forth on holidays and gather 'em by the seashore to hang on their children's coats.[3]

Among the direct antecedents of the postwar debate over inequality was the early controversy over the failure of American socialism and the question of American "exceptionalism," issues that go back to Marx and Engels. Thus Engels, in a letter to an American reformer in 1886, writes a bit like a contemporary convergence theorist as he explains the historic forces which had inhibited the development of working-class consciousness in America:

For America after all was the ideal of all bourgeois; a country *rich, vast, expanding* with purely *bourgeois* institutions unleavened by feudal remnants or monarchical traditions and without a permanent and hereditary proletariate [sic]. Here everyone could become, if not a capitalist, at all events an independent man, producing or trading, with his own means, for his own account. And because there were not, *as yet,* classes with opposing interests, our—and your—bourgeois thought that America stood *above* class antagonism and struggles [italics in original].[4]

Yet Engels naturally believed this condition was temporary, and in the same year he wrote, ". . . even in America the condition of the working class must gradually sink lower and lower."[5] And he later argued that although American working-class consciousness had been delayed, "Once the Americans get started it will be with an energy and violence compared to which we in Europe shall be mere children."[6]

In his well-known essay written in 1906, *Why Is There No Socialism in the United States?,* the German economist Werner Sombart, assessing the housing, diet, and dress of American workers, argued that the American working class lived entirely as well as the German middle class.[7] In his celebrated passage explaining the failure of American socialism, Sombart stated simply that, "All socialist utopias have come to grief on roast beef and apple pie." *

---

* Less well known is the final page of Sombart's essay: "However, my present opinion is as follows: *all the factors that till now have prevented the development of Socialism in the United States are about to disappear or to be converted into their opposite, with the result that in the next generation Socialism in America will very probably experience the greatest possible expansion of its appeal* [italics in original]."

In many respects, therefore, the postwar debate over inequality is a continuation of an historic dialogue over social class and abundance in American society. Moreover, any analysis of this postwar debate must recognize its ideological foundations. Because social class is linked with the distribution of income and wealth, with mobility, poverty, and power—issues not only charged politically but inextricably entwined with some of the most sensitive values of American capitalism—the issue "whither inequality" is as much an ideological question as it is a scientific one.

It is impossible, for example, to understand the intensity of the debate over the functional theory of social stratification, initiated by Kingsley Davis and Wilbert E. Moore, without understanding the political and ideological roots of that debate.[8] In their modest sociological essay published in 1945, Davis and Moore argued that social and economic inequality are both functional and indispensable. Davis and Moore attempted to explain how society regularly manages to induce people to get out of the house and onto the job. Without some incentive to leave a warm bed, to fight the commuter rush, to work all day every day in dreary factory or office, few persons would do it, and the wheels of society would quickly grind to a halt. Davis and Moore argued that the elements of social class—money, status, power, and the rest—were society's prime motivating instruments with which society could, with a minimum of additional coercion, manage to get most people to perform obediently and conscientiously on the job. Why can't everyone be given roughly equal rewards for working, thus maintaining a relatively classless arrangement? Simply because all jobs are not equal; they are not equally important or equally difficult, nor do they require the same amount of training and sacrifice to master. In order to fill the most important, difficult, and responsible jobs with the most appropriate persons, rewards and incentives must be unequal. For society's proper functioning, therefore, Davis and Moore argued, social class is an indispensable social tool.

When Davis and Moore published their essay, they had no notion they were launching what was to be the longest and most heated postwar controversy in sociology. And in the years following publication of their article, the authors were undoubtedly perplexed at the passions it stirred, for they thought they were merely making a dispassionate contribution to the school of functionalism in contemporary social science. In only one narrow sense, however, was the debate between academic functionalists and anti-functionalists. Because the subject was whether large social-class differences were necessary in contemporary society, the debate inevitably became a controversy between the political right (defending gross inequality) and the political left (attacking inequality).[9] On the surface the debate was formulated in a social science framework, but politics was never far below the surface. The sociological debate over whether inequality is functional and necessary in human society highlighted one amusing fact about research in the field of social stratification: more often than not, the only consistently perfect correlation in social-class research is between the "findings" of the sociologist and his politics.

The same ideological roots are at the foundation of the postwar debate over the future of class in America. Not far below the surface in the argument between convergence theorists and stability theorists lie the political differences between writers of the center and right, on the one hand, and writers of the left, on the other. This will become obvious in the following section in which I have sketched the outlines of these two opposing theories, each of which purports to explain basic social-class trends in America since the end of the Second World War.

CLASS CONVERGENCE

Class convergence theory dominated postwar America. That dominance rested upon the strength and influence of its two major supporters: first, the mass media, which popularized and disseminated the idea; second, America's most prestigious social scientists, who provided its theoretical underpinnings.

In popularized form, class convergence theory was actually the "official" ideology of postwar America, and the gospel of classlessness was spread via television, newspapers, and the major news magazines. Most supporters of convergence theory, both popular and academic, were exponents of what I have called the *Time* magazine *Weltanschauung:* the enthusiastic celebration of American material achievements, a view in which postwar America soared onward and upward in every social and economic dimension and in which America was fast becoming a middle-class society of modern consumers. In its most exaggerated form, convergence theory was simply a Chamber of Commerce cheering section, a ringing tribute to the American way of life. At its best and most reasonable, it was a balanced but optimistic appraisal of American living standards which grew out of the unusually prosperous postwar experience.

Probably the purest popular expression of the class convergence position can be found in a volume on American living standards compiled by the Editors of *Fortune* magazine in the mid-1950s entitled *The Changing American Market*.[10] The book provides an unusually complete picture of the exuberant outlook of the early postwar period, which from our present troubled perspective seems naive, almost childishly hopeful, and completely oblivious of the hazards of economic life in America in the final decades of the twentieth century.

The Editors of *Fortune* captured the spirit of their age, describing the American economy as a virtual cornucopia yielding an endless bounty of material wealth to a population increasingly affluent and homogeneous. Their book is a rapturous tribute to the material achievements of American capitalism, which had created the first middle-class society on earth in which want, poverty, inequality, and discrimination were vanishing quickly. The celebratory mood of the book is revealed in the chapter headings alone: "The Rich Middle-Income Class"; "The Lush New Suburban Market"; "The Insatiable Market for Housing"; "The Fabulous Market for Food"; "The Wonderful Ordinary Luxury Market". And while Americans lived well today, tomorrow's prospects were "resplendent" and "exhilarating."

All of the prevailing assumptions of the 1950s—which now lie in ruins—are here. American technology is the wonder of the world. The U.S. economy is "of course" the most productive on earth. The entire world "marvels at," "envies," "fears," and "is baffled by" the American standard of living and the economy that produced it. The *Fortune* magazine world of the 1950s was a world of narrow-visioned ethnocentrism in which American economic, political, and military might were thought to be invincible and almost part of the natural order of things. It was a world of absolute optimism untempered by the possibility of shortages of energy or resources, or the possible slippage of American power. It was a world of unbridled belief in continuous progress fueled by the "increasing richness" and "astounding productivity" of the American economy, as well as by the unique drive, energy, and genius of the American people.

The underlying theoretical foundation for the class convergence model brought together various elements, including affluent society theory, end-of-ideology theory, and postindustrial society theory. The most widely read works that helped create the intellectual climate for the class convergence world view were probably David Riesman's *The Lonely Crowd,* William H. Whyte's *The Organization Man,* John Kenneth Galbraith's *The Affluent Society,* and to a lesser extent, Daniel Bell's *The End of Ideology* and later *The Coming of Post-Industrial Society.* An array of lesser known books, essays, and articles by such writers as Robert Nisbet, Peter Drucker, Irving Kristol, Kurt Mayer, Raymond Aron, Harold Wilensky, and others buttressed these works.[11] Although these writers did not all share an identical political position—ranging from the moderate liberalism of Riesman and early Galbraith through the neo-conservatism of Bell and Kristol to the undisguised traditional conservatism of Nisbet—in their writings on social class most tended to be boosters rather than critics of American society, and most applauded the affluence and the new economic equality they saw about them.

On the issue of equality American conservatives, whether new or old, face an uncomfortable dilemma. Historically, conservatives have not only been defenders of tradition and heritage, but have been the prime exponents of the social virtues of inequality. In modern times, however, inequality is a doctrine that is increasingly difficult to defend. If the history of the Western world since the Enlightenment can be seen as a monumental struggle between the conservative ideology of inequality and the liberal/radical ideology of equality, then surely the latter is winning out. The American and French Revolutions, the victory of popular democracy, the spread of socialist and Marxist movements—all represent the triumph of the idea of equality. Thus, modern conservatives find it politically embarrassing and indeed almost impossible to advocate simple and direct inequality, elitism, and privilege. Especially in America the historical tradition which conservatives, as conservatives, seek to preserve is one which is overwhelmingly egalitarian.

Contemporary American conservatives have attempted to resolve this dilemma in the following fashion. Generally, they have resigned themselves to the kind of economic equality achieved through the impersonal workings of the marketplace. This kind of equality and class convergence, in fact, demonstrates the wealth, efficiency, and social justice of capitalism. Conservatives, by advertising the equitably shared abundance that capitalism produces and the ways in which that system facilitates equality of opportunity and social ascent, defend the present order of things with the paradoxical claim that it yields the very objectives that egalitarians desire. At the same time, however, contemporary American conservatives have shown a traditional disdain for programs of equality designed by government which involve social engineering such as that represented by wars on poverty, redistributive legislation, affirmative action, and the like. Contemporary conservatives see this kind of equality, achieved (or imposed) by the state, as either a threat to liberty (the traditional basis of conservative opposition to equality) or as a menace to merit, standards, order, and authority.[12]

Generally speaking, the postwar class convergence model might be illustrated as follows:

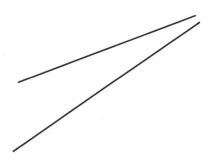

What is suggested by convergence theory is that all strata of the population are generally moving upwards in the acquisition of a varied mix of social and economic characteristics. The lower strata, however, are moving upwards more quickly than the higher strata, thus rapidly closing the gap between themselves and those above. The diagram is intentionally oversimplified in order to concentrate on overall patterns. It thus leaves open the questions of precisely which and how many strata are moving upwards and at what rate and the exact mix of social and economic characteristics involved.

The basic premise of convergence theory is that a combination of economic, social, and political forces in the postwar world has increased the affluence of huge sectors of the population, reduced poverty, diffused education, homogenized life styles, and expanded citizenship and has thus substantially reduced the importance of social class in American society. Convergence theorists anticipated a continuation of these trends which would lead both to further reductions of class differences and to a corresponding decline in the power of social-class analysis to explain contemporary social life.

Probably the single most sophisticated brief statement of the convergence position appeared in Robert Nisbet's essay, "The Decline and Fall of Social Class," published in the late 1950s.[13] Nisbet argued that the concept of social class, while historically useful and applicable to American society until early in the 20th century, was now "nearly valueless for the clarification of the data of wealth, power, and social status in [the] contemporary United States. . . ." The concept of social class had simply been rendered obsolete by the egalitarian social and economic events of our time. According to Nisbet, the doctrine of social class is artificially kept alive by nostalgic leftists who, out of misplaced allegiance to Marx, continue to cling to outmoded ideas of class and class conflict. He argued that class analysis is to mid-twentieth century sociology roughly what the Ptolemaic system was to sixteenth century astronomy: both systems could explain their worlds only with increasingly tedious methods and cumbersome reasoning. As class differences continue to narrow, defenders of the faith must use statistical gymnastics to highlight trivial differences among groups.

Writing in 1963, sociologist Kurt Mayer found himself in fundamental agreement with Nisbet. Mayer observed that while complete classlessness is found in a few nonliterate societies living close to the level of subsistence, and perhaps in the Israeli kibbutzim, there are no advanced industrial societies which are classless. But, Mayer said, "This poses the fascinating question whether a classless society would be possible in a complex, highly developed industrial society. We shall argue that the answer is yes, and indeed that American society is currently travelling along this road at least part of the way." [14]

What specific social and economic events of our time have made social class theoretically irrelevant? What changes in American society permitted convergence theorist Harold Wilensky to argue that "among the concepts that have done the most to mislead us in our search for an understanding of social reality are 'class' and 'class consciousness.' "? [15] Condensing an enormous literature into a short space, one may summarize the essential arguments of the postwar convergence theorists.

Affluence and Poverty

As noted, convergence theorists argued that the postwar period was one of continuously increasing benefits for the American people. For the Editors of *Fortune,* the central fact of the postwar American economy was the "rise of a huge new moneyed middle-income class" whose importance was impossible to exaggerate. This development, *Fortune* argued, "could be construed in no less portentous a word than revolution."

Whatever one's approach to social class, it must be granted that the income of the American people did rise substantially in the postwar era. In the years between 1947 and 1978, real gross family income doubled, from $8,850 to $17,650 (in 1978 dollars), and the proportion of affluent families earning over $25,000 annually (again in 1978 dollars) rose from only 5.5 percent in 1955 to 28 percent in 1978. Convergence theorists expected these trends to continue. In the mid-1960s, futurist Herman Kahn, reflecting the optimism of the age and extrapolating from the income growth that had already occurred, forecast that between

1965 and the end of the century, real per capita income would triple, rising from about $3,500 in 1965 to over $10,000 (in 1965 dollars) by the year 2000. He predicted, moreover, that by the turn of the century this level of affluence would be achieved in the framework of a four-day work week and a 39-week work year.

Convergence theorists believed that in addition to the impressive rise in absolute living standards, there had been a radical redistribution of income from the end of World War I at least to the end of World War II, with a sharply reduced proportion of income shares going to the highest earners. Their source for this claim was Simon Kuznets's influential work, *Share of Upper Income Groups in Income and Savings.*[16]

Before the 1960s convergence theorists paid little attention to poverty in the United States. Thus, in *The Affluent Society* Galbraith recognized the persistence of case and insular poverty but argued that in America poverty "can no longer be presented as a universal or massive affliction. It is more nearly an afterthought."[17] And in their 300-page analysis of the mid-1950s American standard of living the Editors of *Fortune* devoted only a page and a half to poverty, and they made short shrift of it at that. They noted that in the mid-1950s there were some 12 million family units which had a cash income of less than $2,000 annually. This is a group one might naturally consider poor, but *Fortune* dismissed most of these families as pseudo-poor. Half of the 12 million units were really unattached individuals who had much lower living costs than larger family units and who often supplemented their income with "savings and gifts." Another 2 million were farm families who received "a great deal of non-cash income." Finally, they argued, not all the remaining low-income families had low income every year. Many were just temporarily down and out as a result of strikes, illness, layoffs, or because they simply "had a bad year."[18] By this sleight of hand, the Editors of *Fortune* were virtually able to define poverty out of existence.

By the early 1960s, however, when Michael Harrington published *The Other America* and President Johnson launched his War on Poverty, convergence theorists found it difficult to ignore widespread poverty in the United States. Retreating to a more defensible position, their argument then became that while poverty was a larger problem than heretofore recognized, the dynamism of the American economy was quickly reducing both the absolute number and the proportion of poor persons in the U.S. Thus they cited census data which showed that from the end of the 1950s to the late 1970s the number of persons living below the government's official poverty line declined from 40 million to 25 million, or from 22 percent to 12 percent of the population. Some audacious convergence theorists of the 1970s managed to define poverty out of existence once again, this time claiming that the tremendous increase in income-in-kind going to low-income groups since the 1960s (food stamps, Medicaid, etc.) had reduced the actual poor population in the U.S. to virtual insignificance.[19]

The "Standard Package"

According to convergence theorists, the great postwar rise in income permitted a growing number of Americans of all strata to acquire what David Riesman once called the standard package of goods and services provided by an affluent society. Consequently, ownership of an enormous array of consumer durables such as dishwashers, air conditioners, washing machines, clothes dryers, color televisions, home freezers, and a potpourri of exotic appurtenances, as well as automobiles and, most important, private homes has trickled down the social structure.[20] The United States is, in fact, the first and only industrial country in the world to include as part of its national goal a single-family home for every family. And, as most Americans are home owners, the nation has moved close to fulfilling that goal.

Yesterday's luxuries have become today's necessities. As the definition of the standard package is constantly enriched and revised upwards, goods once possessed only by the rich are now widely distributed throughout the class structure. The Editors of *Fortune* declared that one of the most important social phenomena in all of history is "the ability of a great and growing number of Americans to buy what were considered luxuries by their fathers and even by themselves only a generation ago. Luxury has reached the masses. . . . He who understands what has happened to the so-called luxury market products in the U.S. understands not only the

American market but the sweep and drive of the forces that have made the U.S. great."[21]

Although the rich are still able to consume on a more lavish scale than the rest, the broad mass of the population increasingly enjoy the standard package common to all, rendering the excess consumption of the rich socially irrelevant. As Raymond Aron wrote some years ago, ". . . the general increase in wealth has narrowed the gap between different modes of living. If the basic needs . . . are provided for in an approximately similar way, what real difference is made by great fortunes or huge incomes?"[22] In a similar vein, *Fortune* argued that as the luxury market spreads inexorably downward, the difference between the consumption of the rich and the rest of the population becomes not qualitative but merely quantitative, e.g., the *size* of one's boat. And in an essay titled "Abundance for What?" written in 1957, David Riesman forecast a time not too far distant when Americans, so satiated with the material abundance about them, would reach a condition of utter "wantlessness."[23]

For a number of thinkers—Hobbes, Malthus, Sartre, and others—scarcity, especially material scarcity, is a fundamental cause of human conflict. Men, degraded and enslaved by an unremitting struggle to grasp stingy nature's grudging gifts, are thrust into battle with other men to secure for themselves a prosperity that cannot be equitably enjoyed. Hobbes believed that competition for scarce goods—for property and the good life, the "convenient Seat," as he called it—was responsible for most of the quarrels of men in society as well as for the grim condition of man in the state of nature. In *The German Ideology* Marx argued that a harmonious communist society could not be built on an economic foundation of scarcity, for by socializing scarcity one would only generalize want, and with unsatisfied economic needs and the competition among people that this produces, "the struggle for necessities would begin again and all the old crap would revive." Indeed, it is not surprising, as Daniel Bell notes, that for most utopian thinkers and socialists the abolition of scarcity and establishment of a society of abundance is a fundamental prerequisite for a society of social peace and justice.[24]

Postwar convergence theorists believed that America was rapidly building the material preconditions for the abolition of scarcity and the creation of a society of abundance. For the first time in history, they argued, leisure and consumption were replacing work and production as the main preoccupations of life for the mass of citizens. Ironically, it was capitalist America that was about to make Engels's celebrated leap from the kingdom of necessity to the kingdom of freedom.

On the frontier of this society of abundance were the new postwar suburbs, America's classless kibbutzim: homogeneous, casual, unpretentious, and sociable. In Park Forest and Levittown convergence theorists saw "the shape of the egalitarian future," in David Riesman's phrase. In his travels in Suburbia (capitalized by the Editors of *Fortune* to signify its importance as the locus of a new way of life), William H. Whyte found a common belief among suburban residents, one which he presumably shared, that in the economy "America has at last found something very close to the secret of perpetual motion." He speaks also of the "beneficent society" and the "benevolent economy" which had nurtured and coddled the suburban generation. Although not all people who arrived in suburbia were middle class, that was soon remedied. In his essay "Classlessness in Suburbia," Whyte observes, "People may come out of the new suburbs middle class; a great many who enter, however, are not."[25] The suburbs, in other words, provided a kind of basic training for middle-class life. Raw (working-class) recruits were taken in and systematically acculturated to the new middle-class mold.

Economic Transformation

Convergence theorists argued that vast industrial and occupational changes in this century had upgraded the entire work force and had further narrowed class differences. Among these major changes were: the shift from goods to services; the white-collar revolution; the disappearing proletariat; and the shift from property to expertise.

The enormous increase in industrial and agricultural productivity in our century—fewer workers able to produce more goods—altered the industries in which people work and the occupations they pursue. In advanced industrial society, employment shifts from goods-producing sectors (agriculture, mining, manufacturing) to service-producing sectors (communication and transportation, trade, finance, insurance, professional services such as health and education, and government employment).* From the drudgery of working with things, people move to industries which offer the presumed ease and glamour of working with other people. At the turn of the century, the service-producing sectors employed only three out of ten workers; today the proportion is nearly seven out of ten.

The growth of productivity radically reduced the need for farmers and urban production workers. On the other hand, the vast size and scale of corporate and government bureaucracies created jobs for a huge army of white-collar clerical employees to carry on the functions of coordination, record-keeping, and communication essential in large-scale enterprises. Moreover, the complexity and sophistication of the modern economy required the training of large numbers of professionals and technical workers. As a consequence, the occupational structure of American capitalism has been transformed. Since the turn of the century the proportion of farmers in the labor force has fallen dramatically, from 38 percent to a mere 3 percent today, while the number of white-collar professionals, technicians, managers, sales workers and clerical employees has soared. In 1900, white-collar workers constituted only about 18 percent of the labor force; by 1980 they comprised over 50 percent and are continuing to grow. In 1956, when the number of white-collar workers surpassed the number of blue-collar workers for the first time, some convergence theorists (equating white collar with middle class) enthusiastically announced that in the literal demographic sense America had become the first middle-class society in history.

As one of the prime features of emerging postindustrial society was the "centrality of theoretical knowledge," convergence

* The shift from "primary" activities (agriculture and mining) to "secondary" (manufacturing) to "tertiary" (services), first observed by economist Colin Clark in 1940, was elaborated by Daniel Bell and others and became a theoretical cornerstone of contemporary theories of postindustrial society.

theorists pointed to the crucial function and explosive growth of a professional-managerial class. In an essay written in 1958 on America's alleged new middle-class majority, Peter Drucker announced that "During the past two or three years, professional, technical, and managerial people have become the largest group in the American working population. . . . It is this salaried middle class that has now become our largest working group, larger in fact than the blue-collar people, the machine operators."[26] Drucker's assertion that professionals, technicians, and managers were now the largest group in the labor force was based on some statistical legerdemain, as we shall see later, but it neatly conveyed the class convergence mood that America was soon going to be a country where nearly everyone was somehow a highly trained white-collar employee.

Accordingly, convergence theorists took no little pleasure in arguing that Marx's political vanguard, the industrial working class, was becoming both demographically and sociologically obsolete and was, in fact, destined for the trash heap of history. Drucker expressed the typical view when he wrote that "already the machine operators represent the past rather than the future."[27] And Daniel Bell prophesized that

. . . by the end of the century the proportion of factory workers in the labor force may be as small as the proportion of farmers today [4 percent when Bell wrote]; indeed the entire area of blue-collar work may have diminished so greatly that the term will lose its sociological meaning as new categories, more appropriate to the visions of the new labor force, are established. Instead of the industrial worker, we see the dominance of the professional and technical class in the labor force. . . .[28]

Many convergence theorists thought that the driving force behind the growing obsolescence of the factory worker was advanced technology, specifically automation. Drucker's optimistic vision was typical of the postwar view that automation was destined to revolutionize the nature of work in modern society. "The essence of work," Drucker wrote, "is the replacement of manual labor, whether skilled or unskilled, by knowledge. . . . Automation requires such knowledge as is brought to work by the logician, the mathematician, the psychologist, the chemist, the engineer, the economist—a whole host of highly educated people where formerly we employed manual workers."[29] And while convergence theorists argued that automation would transform most workers into technicians or better, they also observed that those who remained blue-collar workers were becoming much more highly skilled. Over the decades, for example, census data seemed to suggest that within the working class the percentage of unskilled workers was declining, while the percentage of semiskilled and skilled workers was increasing.

Convergence theorists also argued that at the top of the social structure class differences had eroded. With the alleged separation of ownership and management in the modern corporation—the "decomposition of capital," as Ralf Dahrendorf called it—property ownership is increasingly irrelevant to the exercise of social and economic power. Replacing property as the kingpin in modern society is knowledge, technical competence regardless of property ownership. And the "technostructure" is far more open and accessible to intelligent and ambitious middle-class men—and women—than the institutions of property ever were.

Cultural Uplift and Homogenization

Convergence theorists argued that the dominant social and technological forces in contemporary society systematically erode distinctive class subcultures and create a common culture shared by all Americans. Sociologist Harold Wilensky wrote:

> . . . modern society tends toward cultural standardization—a widespread sharing of beliefs, values and tastes, crosscutting groups and categories. The forces at work are well known: popular education and mass literacy; high rates of social and residential mobility; the emergence of national markets and a national politics, both making use of nationwide media of mass communication and entertainment.[30]

Education played a particularly complex role. Not only did it serve as a melting pot, absorbing persons of diverse class backgrounds into a common cultural tradition, but it also provided training for an increasingly sophisticated economy and at the same time permitted an enormous amount of social mobility.

Convergence theorists celebrated the postwar explosion of higher education for both its homogenizing cultural effects and for its role in promoting social mobility. Exponents of class convergence began to think of education, like everything else in postwar America, as a permanent growth industry, where the nation's need for more schools, more colleges, and more teachers was virtually limitless. Peter Drucker wrote in 1958:

Today . . . we cannot get enough educated people. . . . [W]e realize that our economic progress, our defense strength and our political position in the world depend more and more on constantly increasing the supply of higher educated people both in quantity and in quality. . . . In the past the question has always been: How many educated people can a society afford? Today it is increasingly: How many people who are not highly educated can a society afford?[31]

With the top of the occupational structure expanding so rapidly, convergence theorists expected that the ever-increasing numbers of graduates would continue to be able to secure jobs commensurate with their training and expectations.

Convergence theorists pointed out that higher education was no longer merely a badge of upper-class position, as it had often been prior to the twentieth century, but was the primary vehicle of social ascent. In a society in which corporate bureaucracy replaced the nepotism of petty bourgeois capitalism and civil service tests replaced political patronage, technical competence attained through formal education and certification became a fundamental basis for social position. The shift from ascription to achievement, from inheritance to merit, from "particularism" to "universalism" became the foundation of upward social mobility for able men and women regardless of social origins. Convergence theorists might have extended their argument by noting that at every Ivy League college today prep school graduates form a shrinking minority of the student body and have lost the dominance they enjoyed prior to World War II.

Many convergence theorists spoke of a postwar cultural explosion in the United States—one writer likened postwar America to the beginning of the Periclean Age in Greece. Convergence theorists attributed the steadily growing audience for dance, theater, and classical music to the expansion of higher education; for convergence theorists the cultural explosion involved a cultural upgrading of all strata of the population.

Convergence theorists also argued that the mass media—movies, newsmagazines, radio, and television—have been a major force in eroding class subcultures and homogenizing cultural tastes. Television especially, with its amazing influence and dispersion, was seen as the great unifier. In a study of the television viewing habits of men of diverse occupational backgrounds, for example, Harold Wilensky concluded that

The engineers and executives, middle mass, and the underdogs on relief are quite similar in their TV viewing habits. Television, again, appears to be a powerful force for cultural standardization, since these groups included men making more than $100,000 and others who have been unemployed for years.[32]

Embourgeoisement

A central tenet of the class convergence model is the theory of the embourgeoisement of the working class, a notion which contains both economic and cultural elements. Throughout the twentieth century, blue-collar workers have been narrowing the income gap between themselves and the white-collar employees above them.[33] Convergence theorists argued that as workers have become more affluent and as education, the media, and other forces relentlessly homogenized the culture, manual workers themselves have become absorbed into the enormous American middle class. Kurt Mayer expressed this position well:

The rising standard of living has made many elements of a middle-class style of life, such as home ownership, suburban living, paid vacations, and highly valued consumer goods, available not only to white-collar employees but also to large numbers of manual wage earners. Nor has this trend been confined to material status symbols. The economic leveling has been accompanied by a visible "democratization" of behavior patterns. The gap in formal education which has traditionally set the wage worker sharply apart from the white-collar employee has been reduced considerably. . . . The rise in educational achievement, combined with increasing exposure to the mass media of communication, has induced large numbers of people at the lower social levels to adopt behavior patterns which differ little from those of the higher status circles. . . .[34]

Thus, Mayer concluded that ". . . the traditional dividing line between manual workers and white-collar employees no longer holds, because large segments of the working class now share a 'white-collar' style of life and many also accept middle-class values and beliefs."[35]

Many others agreed. Characterizing this white-collar/blue-collar blend, Burleigh Gardner of the Warner school of social stratification had spoken decades earlier of the "middle majority" and W. Lloyd Warner himself had written about the "level of the common man," encompassing in this term both lower middle-class clerical, sales, and small businessmen and the "upper lower" or working class proper. Wilensky's concept of the middle mass is also based on the view that the increasing similarity of most manual workers with intermediate white-collar workers has all but erased the social distinctions between them; he argued that a more fundamental cleavage now lies, not between white-collar and blue-collar workers, but between these two groups considered together and the poor beneath them.

Class Consciousness and Class Struggle

Convergence theorists never accepted the view that American workers were class conscious on any meaningful level; after all, that is what American exceptionalism is all about. Whether it was because of Sombart's roast beef and apple pie, the immigrant character of American labor and its ethnic diversity, or the ideology of classlessness, convergence theorists simply did not see class consciousness as a salient component of American working-class thinking. Attempts to understand the behavior of American workers in class terms were merely exercises in Marxist wish fulfillment. If pressed, convergence theorists might grant that American workers were *job* conscious—as labor historians John R.

Commons and Selig Perlman had argued—but they did not think the collective awareness of workers went much beyond that.

Convergence theorists were less likely than ever to accept the possibility of working-class consciousness in the jubilant postwar era, when workers were presumably riding the elevator to the middle class. Throughout the postwar period they challenged studies that purported to demonstrate substantial class consciousness among American workers. For example, convergence theorists were critical of Richard Centers's pioneering study of class consciousness conducted shortly after World War II.[36] Centers, a Marxist of sorts, rejected the studies of class consciousness done periodically by Gallup and other polling organizations which simply asked respondents to place themselves in the upper, middle, or lower class. When 80–90 percent of respondents chose the middle class, the media proclaimed America a middle-class society.

Centers argued that such polls distorted social reality. Workers, he claimed, do not think of themselves as upper class, and, because the term is stigmatizing, neither do they think of themselves as lower class. Rather, American workers think of themselves as just that, as working people, as workers. Centers designed a study in which a national sample of a thousand white men were asked to place themselves in one of the following forced-choice categories: upper class, middle class, working class, and lower class. With the question structured this way, Centers discovered that American workers were suddenly very aware of class. Over half of his respondents (51 percent) said they were in the working class and only 43 percent placed themselves in the middle class. And of the blue-collar workers in his sample, 77 percent said they were in the working class.

Convergence theorists rejected all such forced-choice methods of studying class consciousness. Because small differences in the phrasing of questions or in terminology yield large changes in response, they argued, studying "class consciousness" in this way does not so much measure actual class consciousness as create it artificially, usually reflecting the biases of the investigator.[37]

Even those convergence theorists who did not dispute Centers's methods claimed that whatever high levels of class consciousness might have existed in the 1940s no longer characterize the more prosperous, educated, and homogeneous society of the 1960s and 1970s. More recent studies by Charles Tucker and by Robert Hodge and Donald Treiman, which claimed to be near replications of Centers's study, have found substantial reductions in working-class identification.[38] Tucker, for example, found that identification with the working class among all respondents dropped from 51 percent in Centers's 1945 study to 31 percent in his own 1963 study; among blue-collar respondents, working-class identification declined from 77 percent in Centers's study to 45 percent in his own. To convergence theorists, such data supported the thesis of the gradual embourgeoisement of the American working class.

Convergence theorists believed not only that postwar prosperity had precluded any incipient subjective class consciousness among American workers but also that the postwar era had sharply diminished objective class conflict. Exponents of the celebrated end-of-ideology theory argued that the modern class struggle and its ideological manifestations, which had marked Western society since the industrial revolution, were coming to an end. Summarizing this position, Seymour Martin Lipset declared in 1960 that "the fundamental problems of the industrial revolution have been solved."[39] The working class had gained the franchise; trade unions had been accepted and peaceful collective bargaining had safely regulated and "encapsulated" remaining class differences; conservatives had reluctantly accepted the basic features of the welfare state; and the democratic left had realized that nationalization was not the panacea once imagined but was fraught with dangers which communist totalitarianism had amply demonstrated. In short, ideological issues in the West had dried up, and the political issues which now divided left and right were simply questions of a little more or a little less welfare state legislation or economic planning.

In fact, with the alleged decline of class conflict, some prominent industrial relations specialists went so far as to predict the eventual "withering away of the strike" itself![40] They argued that as living standards had risen, class lines had blurred, collective bargaining had been institutionalized, and employers felt earnest "solicitude" for their workers, rather than the hardhearted indifference they had felt earlier. Employers often "welcomed" unions as part of the enterprise, and workers, they said, "do not hate their jobs and their bosses as passionately as they formerly did." All these things meant that the strike was on the way out. As Arthur Ross and Paul Hartman wrote in 1960, "Management and labor have outlived this instrument [the strike] just as the European Socialist movement has largely outlived the issue of public ownership."[41]

Citizenship

Advocates of class convergence theory also argued that in the United States and other Western democracies political as well as economic inequality had been reduced. Most postwar convergence theorists supported pluralist rather than elitist models of power. In their exploration of power in America they employed such concepts as veto groups (Riesman), countervailing power (Galbraith), and other terms that connoted the diffusion rather than the concentration of political power and that denied any inevitable connection between economic and political power.

Convergence theorists argued that political reforms over many generations had diminished the effects of economic inequality. The most convincing case for this thesis was undoubtedly made by British sociologist T. H. Marshall in his celebrated essay, *Citizenship and Social Class*.[42] Tracing major political reforms in England since the 18th century, Marshall argued that class differences in the modern world have been progressively diminished by the steady expansion in the number of persons entitled to the rights of full citizenship and by the enrichment of the concept of citizenship itself. Developing consecutively in the eighteenth, nineteenth, and twentieth centuries, civil citizenship granted myriad political liberties associated with the American Bill of Rights; political citizenship granted the franchise and the right to run for political office; and social citizenship, which is still evolving, has conferred the ever-growing panoply of benefits associated with the modern welfare state. If there has been an undeclared war since the eighteenth century between the inequality generated by the economic system and the equality associated with political democracy and the extension of citizenship, then, convergence theorists argue, the forces of inequality are clearly in retreat. "[I]t may be," Marshall concluded, "that the inequalities permitted . . . by citizenship do not any longer constitute class distinctions in the sense in which that term is used for past societies."[43]

CLASS STABILITY

Those opposed to convergence theory argued that the great class inequality characteristic of American life had *not* diminished in the postwar period; thus class and class relations retained their fundamental stability. Those who supported the theory of class stability, or some variation of it, tended to be on the political left and were usually cast in the role of critics rather than boosters of American society. Among writers whose work falls into this tradition are S. M. Miller and Frank Riessman, Herbert Gans, Richard Hamilton, Andrew Levison, Brendan and Patricia Sexton, Richard Parker, Maurice Zeitlin, Lillian Rubin, and numerous others who have written on the postwar class structure in America. Although they focused their attention on the English rather than the American class structure, British sociologists John Goldthorpe and David Lockwood have also made significant contributions to class stability theory.[44]

Most stability theorists—except the most dogmatic radicals—granted that living standards increased for most persons in the postwar era; indeed, it would be difficult to deny that. Yet, while conceding that the rising tide has raised all ships, stability theorists have pointed out that the lavish yachts are still just as far above the creaky rowboats as ever. Using another metaphor, one writer has said that to understand class in America one must bear in mind ". . . the image of a deeply unequal society that is moving up an inclined plane of increasing benefits for most, but exhibiting little if any reduction in its overall degree of stratification inequality. . . ."[45] Indeed, the class stability model is perhaps best illustrated by such an inclined plane:

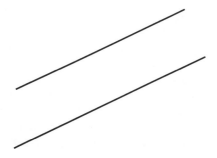

According to stability theorists, during the postwar period all strata of society have been moving upwards but at approximately the same rate, so that the higher strata have been able to maintain the same distance between themselves and those below. While everyone appears to be better off in an absolute sense, the lower strata are making no relative gains on the higher strata and thus class differences are not narrowing.

Aside from their other disagreements, there is an underlying difference in the time orientation of convergence theorists and stability theorists. Convergence theorists celebrated the status quo by comparing the present to the past and saying how far we have come. Stability theorists criticized the status quo by comparing the present with a more ideal future and saying how far we have yet to go. Convergence theorists, for example, argued that compared to twenty years ago poverty in America had been significantly reduced. Stability theorists, on the other hand, observed the enormous amount of poverty that existed compared to an ideal future where poverty might be eliminated. Thus, convergence theorists pointed to the past as the major reference point (a common conservative orientation), while stability theorists looked to the future (a common radical orientation).*

* For example, Seymour Martin Lipset has often pointed out not how much inequality remains in America but how much more egalitarian America is today than it was a century ago.

Despite increasing postwar affluence, stability theorists argued that the distribution of both income and wealth was extraordinarily unequal and that there had been no significant movement in the entire postwar period towards a more equitable distribution of either. Although analysis of income distribution is extremely complex and conclusions differ depending on the data used, the methods of analysis employed, and the assumptions made, most scholars agree that "there has been remarkable stability in the overall distribution of cash income since the end of World War II."[46] While government spending over the years has tended to have a redistributive effect, this has been virtually negated by the declining redistributive effect of taxes. According to census data, which undoubtedly underestimate the actual concentration of income,* over the entire postwar period families in the top 20 percent of income earners received 41–43 percent of total gross income, while the bottom 20 percent received only 4–5 percent. The most affluent 10 percent earned nearly 30 percent of total income, which is more than the entire lower 50 percent received.

Paul Samuelson's well-known metaphor on income inequality in the United States remains as vivid and as accurate as ever (with perhaps an adjustment in altitude to allow for recent inflation): "If we made an income pyramid out of a child's blocks, with each layer portraying $1,000 of income, the peak would be far higher than the Eiffel Tower, but almost all of us would be within a yard of the ground."[47] In major U.S. corporations the income ratio of the top executives to the lowest paid production workers continues to be approximately 100:1. The highest paid corporate executives in the United States in recent years have earned in excess of $800,000 annually in salary and bonus alone, excluding additional compensation in stock options and other lucrative forms of remuneration.[48] Thus, a top corporate executive earns far more in one year than a unionized blue-collar worker makes in an entire lifetime of toil.

The distribution of wealth remains even more concentrated than income. While the top 1 percent of income earners accounts for 7–8 percent of total income, the richest 1 percent of American

---

* See p. 89.

families owns a far larger share of America's wealth: 51 percent of all privately held corporate stock, 36 percent of all bonds, 92 percent of the value of all trusts, and 25 percent of all net worth. These concentrations have remained essentially unchanged since 1945.[49]

The British socialist John Strachey once observed that the persistence and magnitude of income and wealth concentrations in capitalist society—despite all the efforts of democratic forces, reform legislation, transfer payments, and trade unions to reduce them—suggests that capitalism has strong, inherent tendencies to generate and perpetuate enormous inequalities.[50]

In the postwar period, convergence theorists emphasized the absolute gains in income for all groups while stability theorists stressed the freeze in the relative distribution of income and wealth. While the income pie has grown inexorably, the lower strata continue to receive the same small relative share. Certainly the importance of absolute gains cannot be discounted, but relative deprivation remains a powerful social irritant. The pleasures derived from a rising standard of living may sour with the realization that one is not gaining on those beyond and that as one proceeds the horizon recedes. In Europe the impressive postwar affluence of the French, Italian, German, British, and Scandinavian working classes has neither conservatized those groups nor led to the anticipated decline of the political left. Prosperity does not guarantee social peace or personal contentment. While the 1960s was America's most affluent decade it was also a decade of unprecedented social unrest, suggesting that relative deprivation may be as formidable a motive for social upheaval as absolute deprivation. Although blacks in the United States were better off absolutely in the 1960s than ever before in American history, their sensed social and economic deprivation relative to whites proved explosive.

Stability theorists also argued that absolute living standards had been exaggerated by enthusiastic convergence theorists and that a standard of living which is enjoyed only by the upper middle class and above, no more than 20–25 percent of the population, was portrayed as the standard common to most workers. The myth of the working-class millionaire has gained widespread currency in this country. The way to make a fortune—it is often asserted by the popular wisdom and reinforced by the media with a mix of envy, praise for the system, and resentment—is to become a plumber. Stories abound of workers earning astronomical incomes. Nonetheless, while we willingly pay lawyers at least $60 an hour, psychiatrists $75 an hour, and doctors $25 for a ten-minute visit (a rate of $150 an hour), we begrudge our mechanic or other craftsman 10 percent of those fees. In any case, it should be understood that while workers' income has unmistakably risen in the postwar period, that affluence is almost always overstated in the general zeal to congratulate the system and temper labor's greed. In the inimitable prose of new journalist Tom Wolfe:

In America truck drivers, mechanics, factory workers, policemen, firemen, and garbagemen make so much money—$15,000 to $20,000 per year is not uncommon—that the word "proletarian" can no longer be used in this country with a straight face. So one now says "lower middle class." One can't even call working men "blue collar" any longer. They all have on collars like Joe Namath's or Johnny Bench's or Walt Frazier's. They all have on Qiana sport shirts with elephant collars and 1940s Airbrush Wallpaper Flowers Buncha Grapes and Seashell designs all over them.[51]

Tom Wolfe notwithstanding, as late as 1976 only 14 percent of all blue-collar *families* earned $25,000 or more, compared to 60 percent of the families of self-employed professionals. At the beginning of that decade the University of Michigan's Survey Research Center found that the median American family had liquid assets of only $800 in 1970. And in that year, when individual corporate stock ownership was more widely distributed than ever before or since—stock ownership declined after 1970—74 percent of American families did not own a single share of stock, either directly, through an investment club, or through mutual funds.

Stability theorists argued that substantial middle-class salaries *began* where top blue-collar salaries *ended*. In 1978 a middle-aged unionized steelworker could earn $20,000 (assuming a 52-week year with no layoffs or shutdowns); and a 50-year-old highly skilled union printer who had worked for decades at a metropolitan newspaper could earn upwards of $19,000. But in the same year *starting* salaries for 23-year-old graduates of the Harvard Business School were $26,000, and *starting* salaries for 24-year-old law school graduates hired as first-year associates by large Wall Street and Park Avenue firms were $28,000, with a few companies paying up to $33,000. And from there, the ladder disappears into the clouds.[52]

While convergence theorists spoke of the nearly universal distribution of the "standard package" in postwar America, stability theorists urged caution. Some consumer goods—radios, televisions, refrigerators, and so on—have obviously filtered down and become part of the household of nearly every family. Yet it is simply untrue, as Raymond Aron said of Western society, that the basic needs are provided for in an approximately similar way. It is absurd, for example, to say that housing, one of the most basic needs of all, is met in an approximately equal way for most Americans. And there continue to be substantial inequities in the distribution of innumerable consumer durables and home furnishings as well.[53]

Stability theorists might well have argued also that whatever *quantitative* gains in living standards were made in the postwar period were more than offset by the *qualitative* deterioration in American life. The spreading decay of the central cities, the disintegration of public services, the crisis of legitimacy in major political, economic, and social institutions, engendering a spirit of anomie and social conflict, the climate of fear and the siege mentality that pervades the urban mindscape—all these more than counterbalance the ability of urban dwellers to afford a few more privatized toys and trinkets in the last generation.

Convergence theorists made some curious interpretations of trends in the American occupational structure, usually in order to convey the impression that the top was expanding rapidly and the bottom contracting rapidly, leading to general improvement and progress. Perhaps their strangest prediction concerned the imminent disappearance of the working class. Table 1, however, tells a different story.

In the first seventy-nine years of this century, the proportion of manual workers in the U.S. labor force fell little more than two

Table 1. OCCUPATIONAL DISTRIBUTION OF THE EMPLOYED LABOR FORCE, 1900 AND 1979
(In Thousands)

	MEN Percentage		MEN Number		WOMEN Percentage		WOMEN Number		TOTAL Percentage		TOTAL Number	
	1900	1979	1900	1979	1900	1979	1900	1979	1900	1979	1900	1979
WHITE-COLLAR WORKERS	17.6%	41.3%	4,166	23,241	17.8%	64.3%	949	25,694	17.6%	50.9%	5,115	48,935
Professional & technical workers	3.3	15.3	800	8,630	8.2	16.5	434	6,590	4.3	15.8	1,234	15,220
Managers & administrators (nonfarm)	6.8	13.9	1,623	7,809	1.4	6.3	74	2,503	5.8	10.7	1,697	10,312
Sales workers	4.6	6.1	1,079	3,425	4.3	6.6	228	2,647	4.5	6.3	1,307	6,073
Clerical workers	2.8	6.0	665	3,378	4.0	34.9	212	13,942	3.0	18.0	877	17,331
BLUE-COLLAR WORKERS	37.6	46.3	8,924	26,042	27.8	14.6	1,477	5,817	35.8	33.1	10,401	31,859
Craft & kindred workers	12.6	21.4	2,985	12,038	1.4	1.8	76	726	10.5	13.3	3,062	12,764
Semiskilled operatives	10.4	17.4	2,456	9,791	23.8	11.4	1,264	4,543	12.8	14.9	3,720	14,332
Unskilled nonfarm laborers	14.7	7.5	3,482	4,215	2.6	1.4	137	548	12.5	4.9	3,620	4,762
SERVICE WORKERS	3.1	8.5	740	4,783	35.5	19.9	1,886	7,945	9.0	13.2	2,626	12,728
FARM WORKERS	41.7	3.9	9,880	2,214	19.0	1.2	1,008	486	37.5	2.8	10,888	2,698
Farmers & farm managers	23.0	2.3	5,451	1,278	5.8	.2	311	99	19.9	1.4	5,763	1,376
Farm laborers & foremen	18.7	1.7	4,429	936	13.1	1.0	697	387	17.7	1.4	5,125	1,322
TOTAL	100.0%	100.0%	23,711	56,280	100.0%	100.0%	5,319	39,941	100.0%	100.0%	29,030	96,220

SOURCES: Computed from U.S. Bureau of the Census, *Historical Statistics of the United States, Colonial Times to 1970, Bicentennial Edition*, Part I (Washington, D.C., 1975), pp. 139–40; *Employment and Earnings* 26 (June 1979), pp. 35–36. Percentages may not add to 100 due to rounding. All subtotals do not add to totals due to minor errors in government data.

percentage points, from 35.8 percent to 33.1 percent, hardly a precipitous decline. In absolute numbers, there were three times as many manual workers (31 million) in 1979 as there were at the turn of the century (10 million), an enormous increase. It is true, of course, that both the number of white-collar workers and their proportion of the labor force have grown tremendously. Yet white-collar growth has come about not through a reduction of the urban working class but through a sharp contraction of agricultural labor. In fact, the number of male blue-collar workers has increased not only absolutely but also as a proportion of all working men. Thus, working-class men comprised only 37 percent of the male labor force in 1900 but 46 percent in 1979. While it may be true that the number of production workers per se is declining, the overall size of the American working class is growing, and as a proportion of the total labor force has pretty much held its own for the first eight decades of this century. The American working class is alive and well and living in Detroit, Chicago, Houston, Birmingham, and Los Angeles.

As noted, however, white-collar occupations have been increasing far more rapidly than blue-collar occupations. And convergence theorists rejoiced in the mid-1950s when census figures revealed that for the first time the number of white-collar workers exceeded the number of blue-collar workers. Even without recourse to the theory of working-class embourgeoisement, convergence theorists argued that since white-collar workers were all presumably middle class, America had become a middle-class society.

This claim, however, was based on a bit of statistical sleight of hand, and among those who challenged it, Andrew Levison most effectively laid the claim to rest.[54] While it is true that the number of workers formally classified as white collar now far exceeds the number classified as blue collar, *service workers* (not to be confused with those workers in service *industries*)—barbers, hairdressers, elevator operators, bootblacks, bartenders, waiters, guards, doormen, and the like—most of whom closely resemble blue-collar workers in income, occupational status, education, and working conditions, were conveniently omitted from the class convergence equation. Levison demonstrated that when service workers are properly included in the working-class category (as they were before 1950), when such "white-collar" workers as grocery stock clerks, shipping clerks, baggagemen, bus and train dispatchers, messengers, peddlers, and newsboys are more accurately reclassified as working class, and when the occupational distribution of the *male* labor force is considered (for men still largely determine the class position of their families), it becomes apparent that there is still a working-class majority in the United States.

The white-collar revolution in the twentieth century, which carried white-collar employees from under a fifth of the labor force in 1900 to over half today, could be more accurately termed a white-*blouse* revolution. Since 1900, millions of married women have entered the labor force for the first time, not primarily as blue-collar workers but as part of the army of low-level clerical, sales, and semiprofessional workers who fill the needs of the giant corporate and government bureaucracies that developed in this century. Thus, while the female labor force is overwhelmingly white collar, the male labor force, a generation after America presumably became a middle-class society, is still predominantly blue collar and service.

Convergence theorists argued that mechanization, automation, the white-collar revolution, and the shift from goods to services were all ushering in a world of enhanced worker skill. This argument seemed to be easily verified by a casual glance at trends in occupations during this century that revealed the decline of agriculture, a fall in the number of unskilled manual workers and a rise of semiskilled and skilled workers, and the enormous increase of white-collar employees.

The belief that a postindustrial society had upgraded workers' skills was so widely accepted that many stability theorists granted much of the argument as well. In his justly acclaimed *Labor and Monopoly Capital,* however, Harry Braverman reassessed the issue of skill and argued that mechanization plus the organization of production according to principles of scientific management had reduced or destroyed the skills of millions of workers.[55] Although social scientists with an urban bias hailed the decline of agriculture (significantly, agriculture is listed at the bottom of the census classification), Braverman reminded his readers that the shift from agriculture to industry eliminated millions of highly skilled and versatile farmers and transformed most of them into urban workers with a much lower and narrower range of skills. Braverman described the process whereby innumerable skilled crafts were destroyed by the introduction of machines and by the progressive fragmentation of tasks and the endless subdivision of labor. (Automobiles, after all, were originally built exclusively by all-around, highly skilled craftsmen.) The slight growth in the craft category, Braverman argued, is illusory. While genuine craft has been destroyed, "many of the possessors of partial skills continue to carry the label of craftsmanship." Moreover, the craft category has been swelled by a growing number of mechanics and repairmen; 27 percent of all craft workers in 1977 were mechanics, who, Braverman argued, do not "conform to traditional standards of craftsmanship and represent . . . an ever slighter level of technical capacity and training." [56]

The most universally misunderstood trend in the labor force has been the celebrated movement of unskilled laborers into the semi-skilled category, which was widely held to be a confirmation of the convergence doctrine that modern industry upgrades the skill of manual workers. But this important theoretical conclusion was based upon embarrassingly unexamined assumptions, and Braverman's revelations pulled the props out from under this crucial bit of received wisdom. Before the 1930s the Bureau of the Census divided the working class into only two categories: skilled craftsmen and laborers. In the 1930s, however, Alba Edwards, father of the modern occupational classification scheme at the Bureau of the Census, determined to distinguish two groups within the laborer category: those who operated machinery, such as machine tenders, watchers, feeders, and so on, and those who did not. The former came to be called semiskilled operatives and the latter, unskilled laborers; but the distinction between semiskilled and unskilled was not based on actual measurement of skill. According to Edwards's modification of the census classification, any worker who utilized machinery on the job was called semiskilled, no matter how simple, routine, or repetitive the job or how brief the training (typical assembly-line labor, for example). The consequence of this modification was that, with the growing mechanization of modern industry, an increasing number of workers were automatically classified as semiskilled and a decreasing number as unskilled. The turn-of-the-century teamster was retroactively classified unskilled while his mid-century counterpart, the truck driver, was classed as semiskilled. Thus, the frequently noted upgrading of the American working class from unskilled to semiskilled was merely an artifact of an arbitrary census classification, not the consequence of a genuine increase in manual skill.

Finally, according to Braverman, social scientists possess not only an urban bias but a white-collar bias as well. They assume that any kind of white-collar position, including routinized clerical and retail sales positions, represents a higher degree of skill and training than any kind of manual work. Only armed with this unwarranted assumption can convergence theorists claim that the shift to all forms of white-collar work signifies an upgrading in the skill of the American worker.

Within the white-collar groups, however, convergence theorists stressed the dynamic expansion of professional and technical workers particularly. In a postindustrial society based on the "centrality of theoretical knowledge," the growth of professional and technical workers was obviously crucial. And it is true that professional and technical workers, both male and female, have increased tremendously in our century. At the end of the 1970s there were ten times as many male professionals and fourteen times as many female professionals as at the turn of the century. Accordingly, Daniel Bell has written that "the central occupational category in the society today is the professional and technical. Growth in this category has outdistanced all other major occupational groups in recent decades." [57]

Yet it is a mistake to imagine that this group consists solely, or even primarily, of high-paid, glamorous, or highly technical jobs on the frontier of postindustrial society. For example, five professional occupations—primarily low-paid, low status, and female-dominated—comprise over a third of all professionals: schoolteachers (nursery school, primary and secondary), librarians, social workers, nurses, and dieticians. Schoolteachers alone make up nearly one quarter (22 percent) of all professionals in the country.[58]

On the other hand, those professionals we associate with a technologically advanced postindustrial society—scientists, engineers, science and engineering technicians, and computer specialists—comprise only 20 percent of all professionals and only 3 percent of the entire labor force. The traditional high-status occupations of law and medicine make up under 9 percent of all professionals and barely 1 percent of the labor force. Combining postindustrial professionals, high-status professionals in law and medicine, and college and university faculty at all institutions yields under one third of all professionals or less than 5 percent of the entire working population.

Men, of course, continue to dominate the best professional jobs. Yet men in the postindustrial occupations such as scientists and engineers comprise under one third of all male professionals and less than 5 percent of the entire male labor force. All men working in the leading postindustrial sectors, in addition to law, medicine, and college faculty, comprise under half (47 percent) of all male professionals and merely 7 percent of the male labor force. It is quite clear, therefore, that convergence theorists have exaggerated the magnitude of upper-level professional occupations, however considered.

Finally, stability theorists might argue that whatever expansion of the professions has occurred is being offset by deteriorating social and economic conditions in many fields: overcrowding due to the glut of college graduates competing for positions; growing underemployment; rising secular unemployment; routinization and subdivision of tasks; and financial cutbacks in state and local government due to widespread fiscal crisis.[59]

While Bell writes that the expansion of professional and technical occupations has created a society based on the "centrality of theoretical knowledge," one might just as easily argue that the prime characteristic of postindustrial society is the "centrality of theoretical ignorance." In advanced society technical specialists learn more and more about less and less, developing Veblen's trained incapacity to understand anything outside their narrow sphere of technical expertise. At the same time, the typical production worker knows less and less about more and more, as technology soars beyond his capacity to understand. And the typical citizen is hopelessly ignorant of the everyday material environment that impinges upon his existence—television, radio, the automobile, nuclear power, the computer—as well as about the processes underlying even the basic provisioning of life—the growing of food, construction of shelter, etc. In this sense contemporary "postindustrial man" is far more ignorant of his workaday environment than the most ignorant savage ever was.[60]

What of the dream that automation would eliminate the working class and produce a nation of professionals and technicians? Automation failed to fulfill the glowing expectations of convergence theorists for two reasons. First, automation enthusiasts vastly underestimated the costs and the technical difficulty of introducing automated processes throughout the economy. Despite hopes, by the late 1960s only about 1.5 percent of American workers were employed in automated industries, and another 4.5 percent were working in industries that had introduced some automation. At the current state of the technological art, most industries simply do not lend themselves to the kind of automation once envisioned. In short, automation did not and is not expected to sweep through the American economy as early postwar writers had predicted.

Second, it is a mistake to assume a priori, as did many automation enthusiasts, that advanced technology and automation necessarily increase the skill requirements of workers. These writers basically confused the skill which is necessary for those *few* who invent, design, and maintain sophisticated equipment with the skill necessary for the *many* who operate this equipment. It obviously took enormous ingenuity to invent the Xerox machine, but chimpanzees could be trained to push the operating button; in fact, simplicity of operation is part of its beauty. Many years ago, after exhaustive studies of automated factories, James Bright learned that as machines become more complex, the skill that the worker needs to operate the machinery increases up to a point. Beyond that point, however, as machines take over more and more of the work, the skill that the operator requires often declines.[61] A fully automated camera with automatic aperture, shutter speed, and even automatic focus—in short, an "idiot box" as it is appropriately called—requires far less skill to use than a non-automated, manually controlled camera that requires the user to have knowledge of shutter speeds, lens openings, depth of field, and to use judgment to adjust the camera accordingly.*

Observing the top of the class structure, stability theorists rejected the popular view developed a half century ago by Adolph A. Berle and Gardiner C. Means that in the development of the modern corporation control of the firm passed out of the hands of the formal owners and that a new class of managers—bureaucrats, technocrats, salaried experts—now holds the reigns of economic power. Freed from the narrow constraints of proprietorship and thereby from an exclusive concern with profits, modern salaried managers are supposedly able to redirect corporate policy toward broader economic and social goals such as corporate stability, public service, and community involvement. According to this view, the modern corporation is a "soulful corporation" which acts responsibly, not only toward its own stockholders but also toward its workers, consumers, and society at large.[62]

Anti-Marxist convergence theorists always found the theory of the separation of ownership and control attractive because it permitted them to argue that the capitalism of Marx's day had metamorphosed into something far more civilized; the ugly duckling had become a lovely swan. While there is some truth to the theory in the sense that the great mass of small individual shareholders have little or no influence upon the management of the corporation, stability theorists argued that the thesis represented a vast distortion of corporate reality. First, the separation of ownership and control has been exaggerated; depending upon how "control"

---

* One reason the Egyptian army did so well in the Yom Kippur War against Israel—better than they had ever done before—was that they had acquired much of the military hardware of the automated battlefield, such as anti-tank and anti-aircraft missiles, which *reduced* the level of military skill necessary for effective action. The automated sophistication of this equipment was such that even illiterate, poorly trained peasants could push the right buttons and hit the target.

is defined, a large proportion of America's leading corporations are still controlled by proprietary—i.e., ownership—interests.[63] Second, even though the modern manager may not have the same personal incentive for profit as a previous owner-manager, his performance will likely be judged by others in terms of the profitability of the enterprise, especially if profits consistently suffer. Finally, the widespread use of the stock option since 1950 as a tax-avoidance compensation device for top managers, rewarding them with the opportunity to purchase enormous amounts of their company's stock usually at substantial discount, has created a class of managers in U.S. corporations who, in fact if not in theory, have accumulated huge stockholdings and thus have an immense ownership interest in the companies they manage.[64]

As we have seen earlier, convergence theorists argued that rising levels of formal education among all social strata in the postwar era supplied the economy with the increasingly trained manpower it required, promoted cultural homogeneity, and facilitated social mobility via the ladder of educational achievement. Stability theorists, however, were more skeptical. In the educational system they saw a prime example of how theoretically egalitarian institutions are subverted by a class society.

The educational system nominally offers perfect equality of opportunity. In theory, success in school depends solely upon intelligence, effort, and merit unrelated to social background. Yet through an insidious mix of economic and cultural forces, the class system is able to transform this nominally egalitarian institution into an instrument of class privilege. Consider. Students from higher socioeconomic levels consistently earn better grades and have higher educational aspirations than others. Because neighborhoods are segregated by class and because attendance is based on the neighborhood school principle, schools tend to be segregated by class. (The upper class, of course, insulates itself completely, with a few token exceptions, at exclusive prep and boarding schools.) Even within each public school, students of different social classes are tracked into different programs and have vastly different educational experiences. College attendance is based virtually as much on social-class background as on inteligence test scores and ability; even at the highest ability levels, students from the middle and upper classes are far more likely to attend college and to graduate than students from the working and lower classes. Although Ivy League colleges are no longer as exclusively "preppy" as they once were, it is still true that the majority of working- and lower-class youth do not attend college, and among those who do, most are tracked, for both economic and cultural reasons, into junior colleges or lower ranking four-year schools. Junior colleges foster the illusion of equality of opportunity for all, while at the same time channeling lower strata students into terminal degrees or technical and vocational programs. With the illusion of equality of opportunity institutionally secure, the blame for "failure" is conveniently shifted away from the system and onto the individual.

Table 2, which shows the pattern of increasing college enrollment by social class over the decades, nicely illustrates the class

Table 2. SOCIAL-CLASS ORIGINS OF COLLEGE ENTRANTS, 1920–1970

Social Class	Percentage of Each Class Attending				
	1920[a]	1940[b]	1950[c]	1960[c]	1970[c,d]
Upper and upper-middle	40%	70%	75%	80%	88%
Lower-middle	8	20	38	45	64
Upper-working	2	5	12	25	40
Lower-working	0	0	2	6	15
% of total age group entering college	6	16	22	33	47

SOURCE: Robert J. Havighurst and Bernice L. Neugarten, *Society and Education,* 4th ed. (Boston: Allyn and Bacon, 1975), Table 5.2, p. 93.

[a] Estimated from scattered data.

[b] Estimated on the basis of several studies of the occupations of fathers of college students.

[c] Composite figures from several studies of social class and college attendance.

[d] Figures for 1970 were given by Havighurst and Neugarten for males and females separately. These totals were obtained by averaging figures for male and female enrollment and may involve very minor inaccuracies.

stability principle of an inclined plane up which all classes are moving at the same time that the traditional distances are maintained. Although the working class (especially the "upper working class") has increased its rate of college attendance in the last two generations, the upper and middle classes have increased their share as much or even more. And, as noted, the quantitative differences are reinforced by qualitative differences, since the upper and middle classes attend better and more prestigious educational institutions.

Thus, as education has become a major road to occupational success in the twentieth century, the educational system has been effectively appropriated by the upper strata and transformed into an instrument which tends to reproduce the class structure and transmit inequality. The educational system demonstrates that in a class society oases of egalitarianism are difficult to maintain. Instead of homogeneity and equality, the American educational system unintentionally fosters heterogeneity and inequality.[65]

We have seen that convergence theorists believed the great expansion of higher education after World War II reflected the demands of an advanced society for more highly trained workers. That view was generally accepted until the 1970s when two things occurred. First, studies began to show that aside from a fairly narrow band of professional occupations, a worker's level of formal education did not seem to be related to his ability to perform his job. In his influential work, *Education and Jobs: The Great Training Robbery,* Ivar Berg summarized a number of studies which indicated that more highly educated workers did not have higher productivity, lower absenteeism and turnover, or greater job satisfaction and higher promotion rates than workers with less education.[66] Often, in fact, there was an inverse relation between educational level and job performance. Berg argued, moreover, that educational achievement had already "exceeded requirements in most job categories." Obviously there was something wrong with the class convergence notion that more and better educated workers were essential for the technologically sophisticated postindustrial economy. The second important fact about education and jobs in the 1970s was that the enormous growth in college enrollment created a huge reservoir of graduates who were unable to obtain jobs commensurate with their expectations. The growth of higher education did not now seem like an automatic and coordinated response to the educational needs of the economy. It seemed more like total anarchy.[67]

In preparation for the general postwar competition for jobs, young people attended college in record numbers. Employers accordingly raised their educational requirements, not so much because they needed more highly educated workers but because of the availability of a huge pool of educated labor. The college diploma, then, became not so much a badge of occupational competence as a screening device whereby upper- and middle-class youth could command positions by the display of this educational passport. Meanwhile, the use of the diploma as an admission ticket to desirable jobs effectively barred the way to working- and lower-class youth who lacked the white-collar union card. Where occupations were once transmitted from father to son by inheritance, now the transmission was effected by possession of the college diploma.[68]

Ironically, however, by the 1970s the system began to break down because there were simply too many people with credentials and not enough positions. Inflation devalued the coin, and the once-exclusive coin—the college diploma—began to become nearly as worthless, especially in the social sciences and humanities, as a high-school diploma a generation earlier. It must be noted that the kind of unexamined postwar optimism of which Peter Drucker's earlier-cited remarks are typical—the view that "we cannot get enough educated people" and that the economy could absorb an infinite number of college graduates and make full use of their training—helped lay the intellectual groundwork for our present dilemma. Millions of college graduates realized in the 1970s, after having been inspired by a generation of prophets, that they were part of a growing underemployed college-educated mass all trying to make their way in an economy that was rapidly proving itself incapable of providing them with the limitless professional, technical, and managerial jobs they had been told to expect.

While the expansion of higher education has had an enormous impact upon American society in other ways (see Chapter 6), it is nonetheless true that the easy connection between higher education and good jobs promised by convergence theorists during the hopeful 1950s and 1960s had collapsed by the 1970s, creating serious social and psychological problems for a mass of disillusioned college graduates.

Convergence theorists argued that education and the media, especially television, were homogenizing cultural tastes and dissolving class lines and class culture. On the other hand, Herbert Gans's sophisticated analysis of cultural tastes suggested just the opposite.[69] Only simple societies are culturally homogeneous, he argued; modern societies create and sustain "esthetic pluralism." There are an enormous variety of "taste cultures" in America, from Bach to rock, from *Partisan Review* to the *Enquirer,* and Gans argued that "taste publics" which partake of these taste cultures are fundamentally based on social class. Gans described five postwar taste cultures in the United States: high culture, upper-middle culture, lower-middle culture, low culture, and quasi-folk low culture. Because each level of taste culture normally requires a certain minimum formal educational level for its understanding and appreciation and because class is based in part on education, there is still a close correspondence between class and various taste cultures.

Many convergence theorists argued that there had been a genuine flowering of high culture in the United States in the postwar period. Stability theorists, with reservations, agreed. Although one must be cautious when writing from the perspective of New York City, there is evidence, as one New York critic wrote in 1979, that "dance, opera, theater, concert and art events across the country are drawing crowds undreamed of a decade ago. . . ." America does seem to be coming of age culturally and is beginning to shake loose from its cultural inferiority complex vis-à-vis things European. Dance critics speak of the "dance explosion." Art museums often seem as crowded as sporting events. Fans stand in line overnight for tickets to a rare concert by pianist Vladimir Horowitz. Even a city like Los Angeles is taking on cultural pretensions. What is even more remarkable than the cultural programming on public television is that it has an American audience. The "Live from Lincoln Center" series, presenting the best of opera, ballet, and symphonic music live on TV for the first time, reaches audiences of 4 to 9 million, small by commercial network standards but huge considering the program content and the reputed Philistine tastes of the American public. Classical music, sometimes presented in a variety of uniquely informal American formats—the New York Philharmonic rug concerts, free concerts in the park, the Mostly Mozart series—are drawing larger audiences than ever. The new informality—a kind of Bach in bell bottoms—is demystifying classical music without vulgarizing it and yet widening its appeal. America, which had its rock music superstars and its folk music superstars, now has its classical music superstars who are often worshipped as hysterically as the others. Internationally renowned conductors and performers, who, with modern air travel, are now able to appear regularly on two or three continents, are becoming genuine culture heroes to a segment of American society: Jean-Pierre Rampal, Herbert von Karajan, Isaac Stern, Georg Solti, Leonard Bernstein, Andre Previn, Daniel Barenboim, Pinchas Zukerman, James Galway, and many, many others. While America had classical music heroes earlier in the century, what is different about the current period is that, aided by records, TV appearances, and the jet plane, never have so many stars been revered by so many fans. Opera and ballet have their own superstars, as, of course, does the theater.

Convergence and stability theorists did not differ so much about whether there had been a growth of high culture in the United States, but about both the extent and the class nature of the audience. As we have seen, convergence theorists implied that cultural taste was becoming homogenized and that class was becoming irrelevant to culture preference. Stability theorists, on the other hand, argued that the growing audience for high culture came basically from expanded college-educated groups within the middle and upper classes. Those convergence theorists who argued that Americans increasingly shared a common culture regardless of class overlooked the fundamental fact that among audiences for high culture in the United States—symphony concerts, chamber music, opera, ballet, and the legitimate theater—the American working class is almost totally absent.

In 1976 *Playbill* magazine, which is distributed to all patrons of New York Broadway theaters, sponsored a study of the New York theater audience. Between summer 1976 and summer 1977 the survey team interviewed a purportedly random sample of some 8,500 patrons attending 27 plays at New York's legitimate theaters. The plays included not only serious drama which might be expected to draw a rarified audience but light comedies and such popular musicals as *A Chorus Line, Annie,* and *I Love My Wife,* as well as such revivals as *Guys and Dolls* and *Fiddler on the Roof.* The extraordinarily high concentration of New York theatergoers among upper-level white-collar professionals and managers and the scanty representation not only of blue-collar and service workers but of lower white-collar clerical and sales employees, as well, casts grave doubt on the facile assumptions about cultural class convergence and the homogenization of culture in the United States (see Table 3).*

Table 3. OCCUPATIONS OF BROADWAY THEATER-GOERS, 1976–1977

(Percentages)

Professionals, managers, and executive sales	71.8%
Clerical and retail sales	7.0
Craftsmen, foremen, and operatives	5.4
Service workers and other manual workers	5.6
Housewives	1.9
Students, retired, and others not employed	8.3
TOTAL (N = 8,432)	100.0%

SOURCE: "Who's Who in the Audience: A Study of the New York Theatregoing Market" (New York: *Playbill* magazine, 1978).

* The suspiciously sparse representation of housewives suggests a possible bias in the sample to get a maximum number of "upscale" individuals in order to sell space to *Playbill's* advertisers. Description of the sampling technique is inadequate to determine this one way or another. Nonetheless, other studies confirm that blue-collar workers comprise a minuscule proportion of all theatergoers. In a 1979 survey of Broadway theater attendance in the New York City metropolitan area, for example, only 3

In 1978 New York City's 24-hour-a-day classical music radio station, WNCN, surveyed the 11,000 subscribers to their monthly program guide, *Keynote.* Of those responding to the survey, fully 80 percent were college graduates and 42 percent held postgraduate degrees, suggesting an extraordinary overrepresentation of highly educated, upper strata persons among WNCN's classical music supporters.

It is true, however, as some convergence theorists argued, that certain kinds of TV programming, movies, pop music, and sports do appeal to a broad mass of the population, cutting across class lines. After all, persons who attend James Bond films are not homogenous as to class background, nor are all those who watch professional football games or listen to Frank Sinatra records. Gans argued that this does not represent a kind of class convergence of culture. Rather, he said, some forms of culture, sport, and entertainment contain multiple elements and are sufficiently complex so that each taste public is able to extract from them something which appeals to its distinctive esthetic taste.

Most class stability theorists with their feet on the ground did not claim that American workers were propelled by a Marxian class consciousness, but neither did they agree with convergence theorists who argued that class consciousness among American workers was virtually absent. In another context, Freud observed that in individual psychology forbidden thoughts emerge in disguised form, in dream symbolism and in accidental slips of the tongue and pen. Within the framework of the American tradition of classlessness, social class is America's forbidden thought, its dirty little secret that cannot be expressed openly and directly but emerges via subterranean paths and in masquerade. Most Americans avoid social-class terminology in ordinary conversation, and in that sense there is little overt class expression and class concern.

percent of all theatergoers were blue-collar workers, while well over half were professional, technical, managerial, or sales workers; two thirds of the theatergoers had attended college, while only 5 percent had less than a high school education. See *A Study of the New York Audience for the Broadway Theatre,* prepared for the League of New York Theatres and Producers, Inc. (January 1980).

There is widespread awareness of inequality, especially since the War on Poverty of the 1960s, but an uncomfortable reluctance to acknowledge that it constitutes a social-class system. Sociologist Stanislaw Ossowski characterized this ideology, common to both the U.S. and the U.S.S.R., as one of "nonegalitarian classlessness."[70]

Although explicit class terms are generally avoided on the level of everyday discourse, American thought and language is suffused with thinly masked but universally understood euphemisms which carry concrete expressions of social class, social distance, and social mobility: high society; upper crust; higher ups; the other side of the tracks; making good; rags to riches; social climber; moving up in the world; keeping up with the Joneses; poor but honest; white trash; ne'er do well; and dozens more. In fact, social class is the essence of what most Americans mean when they speak of personal success or failure. Moreover, Americans recognize and can use the language of social class when presented with it, and, when directly asked, most acknowledge that there are social classes in America which are economically based. Also, when asked to choose, most Americans can place themselves fairly accurately within the class structure; i.e., there is a close correspondence between the objective class position of most persons and their subjective awareness of it, as measured by forced-choice studies. There is little support among Americans for a class conflict model of society, however. And it is true that class identification, *as such,* does not seem to be a salient and conscious aspect of most Americans' sense of who and what they are.[71]

In support of their argument against class awareness, convergence theorists cited studies by Tucker and by Hodge and Treiman which suggested a sharp postwar drop in working-class identification in the United States. Stability theorists referred instead to a more comprehensive study of class awareness in which E. M. Schreiber and G. T. Nygreen conducted an analysis of seven election studies done between 1952 and 1968 by the University of Michigan's Survey Research Center.[72] In these studies the wording of the questions on social-class identification more closely resembled the wording of the questions in Richard Centers's 1945 study than any other study. From the original Centers investigation in

1945 to the election studies of the late 1960s there was very little change in the class identification of American men. In each of the seven postwar election studies, just as in the Centers study, over 50 percent of the entire sample of men identified themselves as working class and, despite rising blue-collar income and increasing educational levels, over 75 percent of manual workers continued to place themselves in the working class. Contrary to what convergence theorists have argued, in the postwar period there has apparently *not* been a falloff in forced-choice identification with the working class.

In larger historical terms, it must not be forgotten that between the period of the great railroad strikes of the 1870s and the great sit-down strikes of the 1930s, American labor history was more violent than in any other country in the industrial world. In fact, the egalitarian tradition here may have actually intensified the struggle, as American workers were less likely than workers elsewhere to defer to their employers.

In addition, American class consciousness is genuine enough to manifest itself politically in virtually every election. Although its strength varies depending upon the election and the issues, there is in America a persistent class vote.[73] Certainly, as Harold Wilensky observed, not all workers are consistently class-conscious voters for the left party; one expects political variation within the working class according to race, religion, union membership, and other characteristics. Nonetheless, in almost all elections, the collective working-class vote is substantially more Democratic than the votes of either upper- or lower white-collar workers. Michael Harrington has argued that the growing postwar alliance of the American labor movement with the Democratic party has created an "invisible," mass social democratic movement of the left supported by the bulk of unionized workers. Although the vocabulary of American labor is, by reason of American history, not anticapitalist, much of the concrete economic and social program of the AFL–CIO constitutes "socialistic aims . . . phrased in capitalistic rhetoric." Harrington elaborates:

There is in the United States today a class political movement of workers which seeks to democratize many of the specific economic powers of capital but does not denounce capitalism itself. It champions . . . the political economy of the working class—but not socialism. And its impact upon the society is roughly analogous to that of the social democratic parties of Europe.[74]

While this may be one part Harrington's wishful thinking, it is probably two parts reality.

In short, stability theorists argued that working-class consciousness in America has been pushed just beneath the surface by the ideological traditions of equality, classlessness, and democracy, giving the *illusion* of its absence. Yet it emerges in masquerade, clothed in American dress, and to be properly understood must be placed in the context of the American experience.

As may easily be inferred from the foregoing, stability theorists thoroughly reject the notion of working-class embourgeoisement. They do so even though the highest paid blue-collar workers may presently earn more than some white-collar clerical, sales, and low-level professional workers. Even granting the claim that blue-collar workers are more prosperous than ever before in American history, it is important to recognize that affluence is not necessarily embourgeoisement. Stability theorists argue this for both economic and cultural reasons. First, the fundamental *class* position of the worker remains unchanged, despite rising income. Second, what John Goldthorpe and his colleagues discovered about affluent British workers applies equally well to their American counterparts. From their highly regarded study designed to test the embourgeoisement thesis, Goldthorpe *et al* concluded that "the acquisition by manual workers and their families of relatively high incomes and living standards does not, on our evidence, lead to widespread change in their social values and life-styles in the direction of 'middle-classness'. . . ."[75]

Income and possessions are obviously important components of social class; indeed I shall discuss crucial trends in earnings in the following chapter. Yet income and possessions are only part of class. In the controversy over whether workers have become middle class, adherents of the stability model argued that convergence theorists placed too much emphasis on the sphere of *consumption* and too little on the sphere of *production*.[76] In modern society class is still determined by one's role in the production process and the nature of one's work. Despite rising levels of affluence, the basic class position of workers remains the same. Workers still sell their physical labor or manual skill to an employer in return for a wage. They have virtually no ownership rights and, even in unionized firms, have little control over the process of production outside the job area.

While convergence theorists wrote about the affluence of the working class—the "Detroit middle class" as the Editors of *Fortune* called it—they said too little about the price manual workers must pay for this modest affluence. For convergence theorists, most of whom are middle-class academics, writers, or journalists, the problems of work may indeed be solved and the problems of leisure and consumption foremost. But for the working class, regardless of income, the problems of work remain. Blue-collar jobs are, for the most part, physically hard, exhausting, boring, psychically unrewarding, and/or dangerous. The American working class has been called an "endangered species," not because it is being automated out of existence, as convergence theorists forecast, but because of on-the-job threats to life and limb. Each year 100,000 workers die of work-related accidents or disease, 400,000 are disabled, and 6 million are injured on the job.[77] Virtually all of these dangers afflict blue-collar workers exclusively. Office work may not pay very well, but it is relatively safe.

Popular studies report that most blue-collar workers are "satisfied" with their jobs. Yet, when blue-collar workers are asked, only about one quarter say they would go into the same line of work if they had a chance to begin over again (compared to about 50 percent for all white-collar workers and 80–95 percent for high-level professionals). Also, Marx's treatise on the alienation of factory labor, written over 135 years ago, is still a central theoretical and empirical point of departure for contemporary industrial sociologists studying work satisfaction.

Andrew Levison argued that blue-collar workers continue to labor in a strict authoritarian climate of rules and regimentation unknown in a white-collar setting. Although white-collar workers are supervised, there is no one in the white-collar world comparable to the industrial foreman in the exercise of arbitrary authority, especially in nonunion plants. Blue-collar workers still suffer higher rates of unemployment and more job insecurity than white-collar workers and face more limited opportunities for advancement. Manual workers are not promoted from the factory floor to the executive suite or even into the office; that is obviously not the corporate recruitment pattern. There is a virtual caste line dividing the manual work of the factory and the nonmanual work of the office.

Men born into the working class usually end up there. In their well-known study of occupational mobility in the U.S., Peter M. Blau and Otis Dudley Duncan found that only 37 percent of men born into blue-collar homes became white-collar workers (mainly low-level clericals, professionals, or small businessmen). On the other hand, nearly 70 percent of the sons of white-collar workers became white-collar workers themselves.[78] For blue-collar workers getting ahead thus normally means collective, pecuniary mobility (via the union contract) rather than individual occupational mobility.

Finally, postwar studies of occupational prestige demonstrated that despite rising blue-collar income, the public continues to hold manual work in low esteem. Affluence does not remove the stigma that afflicts those who work with their hands.* The enormous college enrollment following World War II testifies to the desire of American youth to escape that stigma, regardless of the demand for and the wages of even skilled manual workers. "Even your grandfather was better than a carpenter," Willy Loman cried in Arthur Miller's *Death of a Salesman,* censuring his son Biff who longed to escape the white-collar rat race.

---

* Definitions of what constitutes a "manual" job and what constitutes a "nonmanual" job are purely arbitrary, determined more by social convention than by physical reality or logic. There is no one whose job is more manual, in the literal sense, than a typist. Yet in official statistics as well as in the public mind, a typist is considered a nonmanual worker. The Office carries with it the mystique and aura of clean work, mental work, and nonmanual work, even if it is none of those things, just as the Factory carries the opposite image. A surgeon is also a manual worker in the most literal sense of the word, but for obvious reasons would never be considered so.

While convergence theorists claimed that class lines had been blurred by affluence, early postwar stability theorists such as Bennett Berger and William M. Dobriner found that even in suburbia—quintessential middle-class turf—manual workers retained their distinctive values and behavior.[79] And in an influential postwar essay, S. M. Miller and Frank Riessman wrote that "even at the same income level (even a relatively high one) wage earners have different tastes, style, and modes of reaction than middle-class people."[80] In areas where a few externals of blue-collar behavior did begin to resemble white-collar patterns, stability theorists asserted that this common behavior had different social meanings for the working class than for the middle class. Thus, while home ownership for the middle class was often a validation of status, for workers it more often represented independence from landlords; and while higher education for the children of manual workers was intended more strictly as vocational preparation for a trade, for the middle class it possessed larger status significance.[81]

In an ambitious secondary analysis of data from twenty postwar Gallup Polls and three National Opinion Research Center surveys, Norval D. Glenn and Jon P. Alston found substantial cultural differences between blue- and white-collar workers on a broad range of issues including political values and participation, attitudes toward marriage, family and childrearing, leisure-time interests, religious practices, and the like.[82] While no enormous chasm separated white- and blue-collar workers and the authors suggested that perhaps too much had been made of the distinction between these two groups, nonetheless they stressed that the manual/nonmanual cleavage was the most significant among the eight occupational groups they studied. And skilled manual workers, who according to the embourgeoisement thesis might be considered most likely to be absorbed into the middle class, were clearly closer to the rest of the working class in most values and behavior than to lower-level white-collar workers. Glenn and Alston conclude, "The findings of this study indicate that skilled manual workers . . . are more appropriately considered part of the working class than of the 'middle class' or of a 'middle mass.'"[83]

Indeed, the University of Michigan election surveys conducted throughout the 1950s and 1960s, noted earlier, showed that despite the growing homogenization of upper blue-collar and lower white-collar living standards, there was still a sharp difference in the social-class identification of these two groups. Thus, for example, in these studies only about 26 percent of skilled manual workers considered themselves middle class as compared to 54 percent of clerical and sales workers. And even the highest paid, highest educated blue-collar workers were far less likely to consider themselves middle class than comparable white-collar workers.[84]

In his intensive interviews with affluent, skilled workers in Providence, Rhode Island, on the other hand, Gavin Mackensie concluded that craftsmen actually had little in common with the bulk of the less skilled and less affluent workers beneath them; but neither had they been absorbed into the middle class. Mackensie argued that affluent, skilled craftsmen should be seen as comprising a separate stratum altogether, between the mass of workers below and the middle class above; in short, they form an autonomous "aristocracy of labor," long ago recognized by Samuel Gompers and the old American Federation of Labor.[85]

Research in the early postwar period found that manual workers differed in many important ways from most nonmanual workers in their leisure-time interests and cultural orientation. Early studies found that working-class leisure was organized around the home and that workers spent much time puttering around the house and garden, fixing the car, and in unplanned, informal visiting with kin. Compared to nonmanual groups, workers read fewer books, attended fewer movies, and showed little interest in classical music, art, lectures, and the like.[86]

These patterns continued into the 1970s. Although Lillian Rubin's sensitive study of fifty white working-class families in the San Francisco Bay area found some changes in working-class values and behavior compared to the previous generation, much distinctively blue-collar culture remained.[87] The men in Rubin's study engaged in traditional patterns of working-class leisure: bowling, motorcycle riding, beer drinking after work (but not so much any more in the evening away from the family), casual rather than formal visiting with friends, neighbors and extended kin, and vacations close to home with boats or campers. Consistent with earlier studies, these workers participated hardly at all in community affairs or in formal organizations of any type. And here as in virtually all studies of blue-collar leisure, workers had very few friendships and very little association with white-collar people at any level.[88]

Again, the findings of John Goldthorpe and his associates in their pioneering study of the affluent British worker seem applicable here despite the differences between the American and British class structures. The British workers they studied were affluent (by traditional working-class standards), but they were not bourgeois. Although they enjoyed a material living standard higher than ever before, they continued to be almost totally isolated from middle-class society, from primary group contact with middle-class people as well as from the world of middle-class organizations and associations. Not only were they segregated from the middle-class world, neither did they aspire to it. Material affluence had not made these workers middle class as much as it had created among them a kind of privatized world of personal consumption, or what the authors called a "civilization of individual consumers."

In one sense, of course, the embourgeoisement controversy between convergence theorists and stability theorists can be seen merely as a political or intellectual game. Americans live in a country with a considerable degree of consensus and unity and share a common core of values, language, culture, and behavior. At the same time, class inequality creates certain differences. The game is played accordingly: those who support the embourgeoisement thesis for political or intellectual reasons stress the broad areas of similarity between manual and nonmanual workers; those who have a political or intellectual interest in opposing the embourgeoisement thesis emphasize the existing differences. Since so many studies make comparisons in percentage differences between manual and nonmanual groups, a substantial range of differences can either be called important or unimportant (the "fully" or "only" game) depending on the bias of the investigator.

Radicals who do see a blurring of class lines and a convergence between lower white-collar workers and the working class are more likely to see the process in terms of the proletarianization of the lower middle class rather than the embourgeoisement of the working class, a leveling down rather than a leveling up. They argue that during this century the lower reaches of new middle-class salaried workers have lost much of their economic advantage over wage workers, and, for a variety of reasons, are rapidly losing their status advantages as well: the enormous increase in their numbers, thus diminishing their exclusiveness; the influx of women, blacks, and other minorities into their ranks; the decline of their early twentieth-century educational monopoly; the increasing size, bureaucratization, and automation of the office, creating an impersonal and factory-like atmosphere; the increasing subdivision and routinization of clerical labor together with diminished responsibility on the job; rising rates of lower middle-class unemployment; lower job security, reduced promotional opportunities, and declining job satisfaction.[89] These traditional assaults on lower white-collar status have been recently joined by another—that vast mass of college-educated workers unable to find jobs commensurate with their training or expectations, creating a huge reserve of underemployed (and occasionally unemployed) graduates.[90] This controversy over whether the lower ranks of the new middle class will remain middle class, both economically and in terms of their class identity, or will be proletarianized objectively and/or subjectively, goes back not merely to C. Wright Mills in the 1950s and Lewis Corey in the 1930s, but reaches back at least to Karl Kautsky and the early Marxist debate over revisionism.[91]

Finally, in this postwar debate over social class, stability theorists issued a challenge to T. H. Marshall's provocative thesis. While granting some long-term historical validity to Marshall's argument that expanded citizenship had diminished social-class differences, the instincts of stability theorists told them that the effects of citizenship had been insufficient to warrant abandoning the central Marxian insight into the innumerable ways in which economic power continues to be translated into political power, even in an age of universal citizenship and political democracy.[92]

Of the two alternate models of the postwar American class structure discussed here, the reader will infer that my own sympathies tend to lie more often with the stability theorists. Yet both models are deficient as complete explanations because neither sufficiently takes into account the legitimate arguments of the other side. Stability theorists, in their zeal to find fault with postwar America and in an effort to exercise the traditional role of intellectuals as social critics, underestimated the importance of the unprecedented affluence enjoyed by vast numbers of the American people and a certain inevitable homogenization which such affluence creates. Without joining the great American celebration or adopting the *Time* magazine *Weltanschauung,* one can nevertheless say that in postwar America never had so many lived so well for so long.

Convergence theorists, on the other hand, in their rush to congratulate and to cheer on the system, played down the enormous inequalities of income, wealth, status, and power that remained in American society and ignored the persistence of class privilege and inequality of opportunity. Their eagerness to praise the system blinded otherwise perceptive intellectuals to the huge numbers of poor in our midst. And their wish was such a prolific father to their thoughts that it spawned a set of sanguine predictions about the future which within just a few years proved to be embarrassing and even ridiculous. America was on the verge of achieving a classless society. The age of scarcity was coming to an end in our time. The working class was becoming extinct. Strikes were withering away. Automation held limitless promise to enhance job skill and satisfaction. College graduates would continue to enjoy vast job opportunities at the top. Political ideology was obsolete and unnecessary.

We can see now that convergence theorists were truly prisoners of their age. They assumed that postwar American power and prosperity were natural and permanent. Their predictions, made with rose-colored glasses firmly in place, were based on simple extrapolations into the future of optimistic postwar trends. These men were unable to imagine that there could be a tunnel at the end of the light.

But now the postwar era has ended. Whatever the strengths and weaknesses of convergence and stability theory, as we enter an era of diminishing American economic and political power, these partially correct postwar theories of the American class structure must now yield to new models which describe the emerging American reality. And that reality is far more somber than the exuberant theory of class convergence and darker even than the limited optimism of class stability. It is to these new models that we turn in the following chapters.

CHAPTER TWO

Stagnation:
Up the Down Escalator

"Well, in *our* country," said Alice, still panting a little, "you'd generally get to somewhere else—if you ran very fast for a long time, as we've been doing."

"A slow sort of country!" said the Queen. "Now, *here,* you see, it takes all the running *you* can do to keep in the same place. If you want to get somewhere else, you must run at least twice as fast as that!"

WORKING FOR WAGES: THE NEW AMERICAN TREADMILL

While the theories of class convergence and class stability differ on almost every detail, they share one fundamental premise. Both agree that absolute living standards in the United States have increased continuously in the postwar period. For convergence theorists, the rise in living standards confirms their faith in the inexorable tendency of the American economy to produce unlimited material advance. Indeed, the belief that living standards will continue to rise indefinitely is the foundation upon which the entire theory of class convergence rests. And stability theorists, who argue that the postwar era has not narrowed class differences appreciably, believe nonetheless that despite continuing inequality, American society continues to move up that inclined plane of increasing benefits for most persons. True, as we have seen, there are social and cultural aspects of both theories which retain their relevance, but the assumption of increasing affluence is undeniably fundamental. Indeed, it is fundamental not only to theorists but to the great mass of the American people themselves.

It is this crucial assumption of increasing affluence which recent trends now call into serious question. While growing affluence may have prevailed during the long postwar era, the decisive end of that era in the early 1970s has weakened America both domestically and internationally and carries serious implications for facile assumptions about the affluent society. Theories of class convergence and class stability, which dominated the entire postwar epoch, must now give way to two new theories of class development in America: class stagnation and class divergence.

Contrary to the expectations of both convergence and stability theorists, the living standards of the American people, considered as a whole, have stagnated for more than a decade. Moreover, the current situation is in its duration without precedent in the entire postwar era. In its economic dimension, the recent pattern of inequality in American society can be pictured roughly as two parallel horizontal lines:

Contrary to the model of class convergence, the lower strata are not narrowing the gap between themselves and those above; and contrary to the models of both class convergence and class stability, the American population is no longer moving up an inclined plane of increasing benefits for all. In terms of the model of class stagnation which fits much of the data in the last decade or more, living standards in the U.S. have ceased to grow significantly and the great inequality characteristic of American society continues unchanged.

In what follows I shall be considering primarily the economic dimension of class but we shall see that these economic events have the most far-reaching social implications for the American class structure, as well as for the nature and quality of American life itself.

Let us consider first the data on weekly earnings regularly collected by the Bureau of Labor Statistics (BLS).[1] This information is gathered through monthly surveys of the payroll records of nearly 150,000 private nonfarm business establishments in the United States and represent the earnings of some 59.5 million American workers (in 1979), or nearly two thirds of the employed labor force. All agricultural workers and government employees, executives, managers, supervisors at all levels, and the self-employed are excluded from these payroll surveys. All blue-collar production workers and white-collar nonsupervisory employees are included. These surveys, then, cover the great mass of the American working class in private industry, as well as most salaried white-collar employees.

Table 4 and Figure 1 show the average weekly earnings of these workers from 1947 through 1979. Examining first the entire postwar period, we see that the income of American workers has risen enormously in the three postwar decades: gross income increased nearly fivefold, from $45 a week in 1947 to $219 in 1979, and spendable (after tax) earnings of married workers with three dependents increased only slightly less rapidly, from $44 to $194. Naturally, these current dollar measurements are inflated, and they seriously exaggerate the actual gains. But genuine gains have been made. In constant (1967) dollars, which measure real purchasing power, the average spendable weekly earnings of American workers rose from nearly $67 in 1947 to a bit under $90 at the end of the 1970s.

The BLS data also underestimate the actual earnings as well as the gains of many American workers in some important ways. First, the figures exclude all fringe benefits (health and other forms of insurance, employer pension contributions, etc.), which have increased for most workers over the years. Second, the BLS data provide an average of the weekly earnings of all workers, part-time as well as full-time. As part-time workers are a slowly grow-

Table 4. GROSS AND SPENDABLE WEEKLY EARNINGS OF PRODUCTION OR NONSUPERVISORY WORKERS ON PRIVATE NONAGRICULTURAL PAYROLLS, 1947–1979

Year	Gross Average Weekly Earnings (Current Dollars)	Spendable Average Weekly Earnings, Workers with Three Dependents[a] (Current Dollars)	(1967 Dollars)
1947	$45.58	$44.64	$66.73
1948	49.00	48.51	67.28
1949	50.24	49.74	69.66
1950	53.13	52.04	72.18
1951	57.86	55.79	71.71
1952	60.65	57.87	72.79
1953	63.76	60.31	75.29
1954	64.52	60.85	75.59
1955	67.72	63.41	79.06
1956	70.74	65.82	80.86
1957	73.33	67.71	80.32
1958	75.08	69.11	79.80
1959	78.78	71.86	82.31
1960	80.67	72.96	82.25
1961	82.60	74.48	83.13
1962	85.91	76.99	84.98
1963	88.46	78.56	85.67
1964	91.33	82.57	88.88
1965	95.45	86.63	91.67
1966	98.82	88.66	91.21
1967	101.84	90.86	90.86
1968	107.73	95.28	91.44
1969	114.61	99.99	91.07
1970	119.83	104.90	90.20
1971	127.31	112.43	92.69
1972	136.90	121.68	97.11
1973	145.39	127.38	95.70
1974	154.76	134.61	91.14
1975	163.53	145.65	90.35
1976	175.45	155.87	91.42
1977	189.00	169.93	93.63
1978	203.70	180.71	92.53
1979	219.91	194.82	89.49

SOURCES: U.S. Department of Labor, Bureau of Labor Statistics, *Employment and Earnings, United States, 1909–78* (Washington, D.C., 1979); *Employment and Earnings* (March 1980).

[a] Spendable earnings are derived by subtracting estimated Social Security and Federal income taxes from gross earnings.

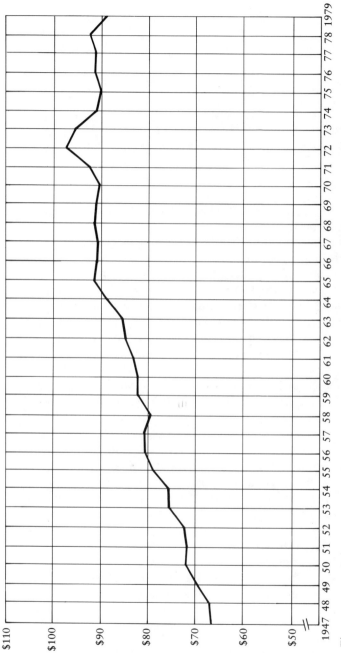

Figure 1. SPENDABLE AVERAGE WEEKLY EARNINGS OF WORKERS WITH THREE DEPENDENTS IN CONSTANT (1967) DOLLARS, 1947–1979

SOURCE: Figures in Table 4.

ing share of the labor force (rising from 15 percent in 1955 to 22 percent in 1977), this increasingly underestimates the earnings of full-time workers.[2] Third, these data naturally include women workers as well as men. As the earnings of women are lower than those of men, and as female labor force participation has grown (from 28 percent of the labor force in 1947 to 41 percent in 1977), the earnings of men are increasingly understated.[3] Finally, these income figures are averages for all workers and do not reveal the "life cycle" increases that individual workers receive as they advance through their careers. Especially for workers in their twenties and thirties, career-related raises exceed the average income gains for all workers.

On the other hand, the BLS data overstate the growth of income of American workers in at least two ways. First, in computing take-home pay, the BLS deducts all federal taxes but no state and local taxes, which have increased sharply in recent years (see pages 72–3 below). Second, in deducting federal income tax to arrive at spendable earnings, the BLS apparently makes smaller deductions from workers' gross income than is provided by government guidelines supplied to employers, and the gap between the two has been widening.[4]

With these qualifications in mind, it is clear nonetheless from Table 4 and Figure 1 that the overall earnings of American workers in the past thirty years have moved undeniably upwards, validating the assumptions of virtually all postwar writers on social class. The most recent picture, however, is both significant and alarming. From 1947, when the Bureau of Labor Statistics first began to report wage data for production workers in all private, nonfarm employment, until 1965, the real income of American workers rose steadily. Then, in a dramatic change after 1965, the rising income curve flattened out. Slight gains made in 1972 and 1973 were subsequently lost, and by the mid-1970s real weekly wages were no higher than in the mid-1960s. Then, by the end of the 1970s, under the impact of surging inflation, real wages fell to their lowest point in a decade and a half.

A comparison of two fourteen-year periods, 1951–65 and 1965–79, highlights these striking changes (see Table 5 below). Between 1951 and 1965, workers' weekly earnings in current dollars increased from $55 to $86; and in constant dollars, measuring

Table 5. SPENDABLE WEEKLY EARNINGS OF WORKERS
WITH THREE DEPENDENTS

	1951	*1965*	*1979*
Current Dollars	$55.79	$86.63	$194.82
Constant (1967) Dollars	$71.71	$91.67	$89.49

real purchasing power, wages and salaries rose 28 percent, from
$71 to $91. In the following fourteen-year period, however, from
1965 to 1979, the picture changed drastically. Although at the end
of the 1970s the average worker brought home over twice what he
brought home in the mid-1960s ($194 compared to $86), inflation
completely leveled these gains, and workers found themselves
worse off than they were a decade and a half earlier. It is clear
that for the last fifteen years many American workers, like Alice in
Wonderland, have been running fast and getting nowhere.

Moreover, a close examination of postwar wage trends reveals
that since the end of World War II there has been a sharp decade-
by-decade decline in the *rate* at which spendable earnings have
grown, a development that, with a nod to Marx, might be called
the "falling rate of affluence." Thus, Table 6 shows that between
1947–57, real spendable earnings grew over 20 percent, between
1957–67 they rose only 13 percent, and from 1967–77 spendable
earnings increased only a little over 3 percent.

Table 6. THE "FALLING RATE OF AFFLU-
ENCE" FOR AMERICAN WORKERS

Decade	*% Increase over Decade in Real Spendable Weekly Earnings for Workers with Three Dependents*
1947–1957	+ 20.4%
1957–1967	+ 13.1%
1967–1977	+ 3.3%
1969–1979	− 1.7%

SOURCE: Computed from figures in Table 4.

One might argue that the falling rate of affluence and the stagnation of income revealed by BLS data in recent years are simply
consequences of the increasing participation of low-paid women
and part-time workers in the labor force and that the inclusion of
these growing numbers of workers drags down the average figures.[5] It is true that the increasing labor force participation of
these groups leads to a growing underestimation of the income of
male full-time workers, but this could not account mathematically
for the sharply falling *rate* of income growth. What could reduce
the rate of growth in income is not the proportion of a particular
low-paid group in the labor force, but the growth of that proportion. It is true that the labor-force participation of women and
part-time workers has increased since 1965, after which income
stagnated. But women and part-timers had also increased their
labor-force participation *before* 1965 and, in fact, throughout the
postwar period. The growth in the labor-force participation of
women has been stable at least since the 1950s, rising about .4
percent annually, and the growth of part-time workers has been
only slightly less stable. Since the increases for both groups have
been fairly steady, this could not have accounted for the sharp
reduction in the rate of income growth since the mid-1960s.[6]

While BLS income data for all workers begins in 1947, their
data on production workers in manufacturing extends back to
1939. Although there are relatively few part-time or female production workers in manufacturing, income trends for the mainly
full-time male production workers in manufacturing are similar to
those for all workers, showing a large increase in earnings over the
decades but a falling rate of income growth (see Table 7). While
manufacturing workers have made larger nominal gains than most
workers in the last decade and a half, we see here once again, this
time over a forty-year period, the operation of the falling rate of
affluence. In each succeeding decade, the spendable earnings of
manufacturing workers have risen at a decreasing rate.

Although the official BLS figures show real spendable earnings
of all workers down about 2 percent from 1965 to 1979, the actual situation is undoubtedly worse. As noted, the BLS spendable
income figures are derived by deducting only federal income taxes
and Social Security taxes from gross income. Because of wide

Table 7. THE "FALLING RATE OF AFFLU-
ENCE" AMONG PRODUCTION WORKERS IN
MANUFACTURING

Decade	*% Increase over Decade in Real Spendable Weekly Earnings for Workers with Three Dependents*
1939–1949	31.8%
1949–1959	22.6
1959–1969	11.6
1969–1979	5.0

Source: Computed from U.S. Department of Labor,
Bureau of Labor Statistics, *Employment and Earnings,
United States, 1909–78* (1979); *Employment and Earnings*
(March 1980).

regional variations, the BLS does not deduct state and local taxes
in its national computations. Yet state and local taxes have risen
much faster in recent years than federal taxes. By the end of the
1970s, state and local income taxes were four times higher than a
decade earlier; in the late 1960s states and localities took in taxes
only about 10 percent of what the federal government claimed,
but by the late 1970s state and local income taxes had risen to
over 16 percent of the federal government's total.

Moreover, in the 1980s wages will come under continuing assault, for Social Security taxes are scheduled to rise sharply
throughout the decade. In 1980, for example, the maximum Social
Security tax on an employee was under $1,600 annually, but this
is scheduled to rise to over $3,000 by 1987. Clearly, unless work-
ers' gross earnings rise to offset these additional taxes, spendable
earnings will decline even further during the 1980s.

POSTINDUSTRIAL SOCIETY BLUES

While the figures presented here show that the "average" worker's
income has stagnated for more than a decade, such averages con-

ceal an enormous amount of variation. An average, after all, gen-
eralizes the experience of those who fall above and below it.
Among the variations, there is, first, variation by industry. Table 8
shows these industrial differentials in wages and wage trends since
1948.

Recall first that postindustrial society enthusiasts speak with
glowing optimism about the growth of occupations in the tertiary
sector. As jobs in the goods-producing sector—agriculture, mining, construction, manufacturing—decline, presumably glamorous
and high-paying jobs in the service-producing sector expand. Unfortunately, the postindustrial sector is surrounded by a mislead-
ing aura which suggests that employees in these industries are
primarily professionals, managers, technicians and high-status
white-collar workers of all kinds. But a moment's thought is sufficient to realize that the mass of employees in "finance" are bank
tellers, not bank presidents; that the majority of employees in retail trade are low-paid salespeople, not chief executives of Macy's
or Gimbels; that the bulk of employees in insurance are clerical
workers, not company executives or six-digit-income insurance
agents. Thus, despite the paroxysms of praise for postindustrial
occupations, one must observe that it is precisely in this postindustrial sector—especially finance, insurance, real estate, trade, and
services *—that average pay is lowest, unions are weak or absent,
low-paid part-time and female workers are most common, and the
falling rate of affluence is most pronounced, often culminating, as
in the case of trade and finance, in actual BLS-reported declines in
real earnings in the 1970s. For too long postindustrial theorists
have conditioned us to see the tertiary sector in twenty-first century science-fiction stereotypes which bear little relation to reality.

Table 8 reveals that mining is the only industry in which workers have enjoyed rising rates of income growth during the entire
postwar period. Manufacturing workers, though subject to the

* Service industries comprise a miscellaneous group including business
services (such as advertising); repair services (automobile and television
repair); personal services (laundries, barber and beauty shops, hotel and
motel services); entertainment and recreation services (theaters, motion
pictures, bowling alleys); and professional services (such as medical, legal,
private educational, and engineering services).

Table 8. NET SPENDABLE AVERAGE WEEKLY EARNINGS OF PRODUCTION OR NONSUPERVISORY WORKERS WITH THREE DEPENDENTS, BY INDUSTRY, 1948–1978, SELECTED YEARS

(In 1967 Dollars)

Industry	1948	1958	1968	1978	Part-time Workers as % of Total (1977)	Women as % of Total (1976)
MINING	$87.17	$99.54	$117.58	$141.58	11%	7%
% increase over previous decade	n.a.[a]	14.2%	18.1%	20.4%		
CONTRACT CONSTRUCTION	$86.82	$106.82	$134.34	$136.54	17	7
% increase over previous decade	n.a.	23.0%	25.8%	1.6%		
MANUFACTURING	$72.55	$86.87	$102.45	$110.02	12	29
% increase over previous decade	n.a.	19.7%	17.9%	7.4%		
TRANSPORTATION & UTILITIES	n.a.	n.a.	$114.72	$130.20	13	22
% increase over previous decade	n.a.	n.a.	n.a.	13.5%		
WHOLESALE & RETAIL TRADE	$56.02	$67.53	$75.33	$72.64	33	24–47[b]
% increase over previous decade	n.a.	20.5%	11.6%	– 3.6%		
FINANCE, INSURANCE & REAL ESTATE	$62.45	$75.23	$87.01	$82.63	16	55
% increase over previous decade	n.a.	20.5%	15.7%	– 5.0%		
SERVICES	n.a.	n.a.	$73.45	$76.76	28	56
% increase over previous decade	n.a.	n.a.	n.a.	4.5%		

SOURCES: Computed from U.S. Department of Labor, Bureau of Labor Statistics, *Employment and Earnings, United States, 1909–78* (1979); W. V. Deutermann and S. C. Brown, "Voluntary Part-Time Workers: A Growing Part of the Labor Force," *Monthly Labor Review* 101 (June 1978), p. 9; U.S. Bureau of the Census, *Statistical Abstract of the United States: 1977* (Washington, D.C., 1977), p. 392.

[a] n.a. = not available.

[b] Wholesale trade, 24%; retail trade, 47%.

falling rate of affluence that was common to the workforce as a whole in the postwar period, made slight overall gains during the 1970s. On the other hand, construction workers did well until the mid-1960s but barely kept up with inflation in the 1970s, due undoubtedly to chronically high rates of underemployment and the increasing use of nonunion labor. In the last decade, in fact, the income of unionized construction workers has been seriously undercut by the soaring number of open-shop contractors. Contrary to the assumptions of convergence theorists, who argued that trade unions had become an accepted and permanent fixture of the American economic landscape, in little more than a decade, from 1968 to 1979, the open-shop share of the U.S. construction dollar increased from 20 percent to 60 percent, devastating the construction unions.[7]

WHITE-COLLAR STATUS PANIC

Although this overview of earnings by industry offers a more detailed picture of income trends than earnings for the economy as a whole, it still conceals large internal variations for individual occupations. In Table 9, therefore, I have presented trends in earnings for a large group of blue- and white-collar workers during the major period of overall income stagnation—1967 to 1978. Although I shall argue in a subsequent chapter that the poor have been the biggest losers in this period, there have also been both moderate winners and losers among blue- and white-collar workers.

Despite all the research that has been done in the last decade exploring the impact of inflation on American life, one central fact has been overlooked. This inflation, unprecedented both in duration and extent, has produced some unplanned, unanticipated, but dramatic shifts in the customary income differentials between white-collar and blue-collar workers.

In only eleven years, between 1967 and 1978, prices as reflected in the consumer price index virtually doubled. Thus, in order to stay even with inflation before taxes, a worker's pay had to double. In the context of this kind of inflation, the figures presented in Table 9 reveal that among a wide range of wage and salary workers in the U.S., only those in strong trade unions who have been able to win substantial cost-of-living allowances have been protected from the ravages of inflation and have actually continued to increase their real wages much as they had done in the earlier postwar period. The figures given here are all before taxes, however, and because recent inflation has driven all wage and salary earners into higher tax brackets the after-tax trends in income are far gloomier across the board. Nonetheless, the relatively small group of workers in steel, auto, mining, trucking, and the like, whose wages are indexed to the cost of living have still managed to ride the inflation escalator and make decent gains during this period. It can be stated, then, that the industrial worker's greatest hedge against inflation in the last decade has not been gold, silver, stamps, coins, antiques, or baseball cards, but a strong trade union behind him.

Blue-collar workers in weaker unions and/or in industries hit hard by imports (textiles, apparel, shoes) have either seen their living standards fall or are barely holding their own. The same is true of the great mass of white-collar workers, most of whom, of course, are nonunionized. A few high-level white-collar workers have made modest gains, but most nonunionized white-collar clerical, sales, and professional workers are slipping backwards or barely keeping up. White-collar workers who have relatively high incomes—in the form of salary rather than capital gains or other tax-favored forms enjoyed by the rich—have been especially damaged by salary increases that continually push them into sharply higher tax brackets. The clearest example of this situation are full professors, whose real salaries between 1967 and 1978 dropped 9.5 percent before taxes and approximately 17.5 percent after taxes. In fact, of some forty occupations examined here, full professors lost a greater share of their after-tax earnings than any other group.

Because the wages of blue-collar workers protected by strong cost-of-living allowances are rising so much more rapidly than the salaries of white-collar workers not so protected, these industrial

Table 9. TRENDS IN EARNINGS, SELECTED OCCUPATIONS, 1967–1978

Occupation (SIC code[a] where appropriate)	Average Gross Annual Income		% Change After Inflation
	1967	1978	
Consumer price index	100	195.4	
Steelworker (331)	$7,426	$19,573	+34.9%
Coal miner (11,12)	7,738	19,822	+31.1
Automobile worker (3711)	7,613	18,658	+25.4
Truck driver (421,423)	6,843	16,432	+22.9
Food-store worker (54)	4,638	10,899	+20.3
Registered nurse (industrial)	6,188	13,416[b]	+19.5
Laundry worker (721)	3,598	7,800	+10.9
Plumber	11,149	22,360[b]	+10.5
Restaurant worker (58)	3,120	6,677	+9.5
Federal civil servant, GS-16 (nonpolitical manager)	20,982	44,756	+9.2
Accountant, level V (top)	12,795	27,301	+9.2
Personnel director, level IV (top)	19,186	40,835	+8.9
Messenger (urban)	3,666	7,202[b]	+8.2
Electrical/electronics worker (36)	5,762	12,126	+7.7
Textile worker (22)	4,285	8,923	+6.6
Rubber (tire) worker (301)	7,862	16,266	+5.9
School teacher (urban)	7,464	15,450	+5.9
Accountant, level III (of V)	8,879	18,115	+4.4
Department store employee— nonsupervisory (513)	4,285	8,736	+4.3
Policeman (municipal)	6,482	13,190	+4.1
Buyer, level IV (top)	11,806	23,853	+3.4
Secretary (urban)	5,772	10,816[b]	+3.2
Federal civil servant, GS-12 (white-collar professional)	11,461	23,087	+3.1
Furniture worker (25)	4,846	9,734	+2.8
Chemist, level III (of VIII)	9,719	19,453	+2.4
Typist (urban)	3,874	7,176[b]	+2.1
Buyer, level II (of IV)	8,211	16,195	+.9

Occupation (*SIC code*[a] where appropriate)	*Average Gross* *Annual Income*		*% Change* *After* *Inflation*
	1967	*1978*	
Consumer price index	100	195.4	
Computer programmer	9,984	19,608	+.5
Engineer, level III (of VIII)	10,330	20,194	0
Engineering technician, level III (of V)	7,235	14,062	−.5
Apparel worker (23)	4,222	8,195	−.7
Chemist, level VIII (top)	24,676	47,156	−2.2
Engineer, level VIII (top)	22,235	42,106	−3.1
Federal civil servant, GS-5 (clerical)	5,565	10,507	−3.4
Insurance company employee— nonsupervisory (63)	5,782	10,878	−3.7
Shoe worker (314)	4,181	7,800	−4.5
College professor (average all ranks)	11,114	17,601[c]	−7.1
Bank employee—nonsupervisory (60)	4,864	8,757	−7.9
College professor (full)	17,158	30,353	−9.5
Librarian	7,305	11,894[b]	−10.3
Welfare recipient (per family)	1,894	3,089	−16.5

Sources: Compiled from Bureau of Labor Statistics, *Employment and Earnings, United States, 1909–78* (Washington, D.C., 1979); *Handbook of Labor Statistics 1977*, Bulletin 1966 (Washington, D.C., 1977); *Occupational Earnings in All Metropolitan Areas, July 1977* (September 1978); *Current Wage Developments* 31 (March 1979); *National Survey of Professional, Administrative, Technical, and Clerical Pay, March 1978*, Bulletin 2004 (Washington, D.C., 1978); *Time,* January 15, 1979; American Association of University Professors (AAUP), "No Progress this Year: Report on the Economic Status of the Profession," *AAUP Bulletin* (August 1977).

[a] SIC: Standard Industrial Classification.

[b] 1977. Income change calculated on basis of 1977 Consumer Price Index, which was 181.5.

[c] Comparison is 1967–68 academic year with 1976–77 academic year. Income change calculated on basis of 1976 Consumer Price Index, which was 170.5.

workers have made striking gains on most salaried employees in the last decade. Table 10 compares the earnings of automobile workers with the earnings of various white-collar employees to illustrate these crucial income shifts.

The wages of auto workers, which are tied to the cost of living, have dramatically outpaced the salaries of white-collar workers at all levels during this period of high inflation. With respect to low-level clerical and retail salesworkers, auto workers have widened their already commanding lead. With respect to middle-level white-collar workers, professionals, and technicians, auto workers have achieved parity and in some cases have pulled ahead. And even with respect to the highest paid white-collar employees, auto workers have narrowed the gap somewhat. It must be conceded, then, that within the larger overall framework of class stagnation, a mini-pattern of class convergence, in economic terms, has developed among a thin stratum of highly unionized workers.

Nonetheless, the arguments of the stability theorists should not be forgotten. However large their gains may seem, these blue-collar workers are still far behind substantial professional and managerial occupations. And, as we noted in Chapter 1, it is important to bear in mind the price—in terms of the content of blue-collar toil—that manual workers pay for their modest affluence, as well as the limitations of that affluence. Though their earnings may seem large, manual workers are still hourly employees, with all the vicissitudes and uncertainty which hourly work implies. Blue-collar workers still have far less job security, are far more vulnerable to chronic and unpredictable layoffs, and have considerably higher unemployment rates than salaried white-collar workers. Although steelworkers and auto workers made income gains in the 1960s and 1970s, massive plant closings by American steel companies (see Chapter 3) and the potentially devastating impact upon auto workers of the deepening problems at Chrysler and the crisis in the U.S. auto industry generally, were merely the most visible symbols in the late 1970s of the fragility of working-class affluence. It must also be remembered that the income ladder for blue-collar workers is highly compressed, especially compared to top-level white-collar jobs where the salary range is much wider. Although the average auto worker's wage may now seem comparatively high, he cannot go very far beyond the average.

Table 10. AVERAGE EARNINGS OF AUTOMOBILE WORKERS AS A PERCENTAGE OF AVERAGE EARNINGS OF SELECTED WHITE-COLLAR EMPLOYEES, 1967 AND 1978

Occupation	1967	1978
Typist	197%	253%[a]
Department store employee (nonsupervisory)	178	214
Bank employee (nonsupervisory)	157	213
Federal civil servant, GS-5 (clerical)	137	178
Insurance company employee (nonsupervisory)	132	172
Secretary	132	158[a]
Librarian	104	144[a]
Engineering technician	105	133
Registered nurse	123	127[a]
School teacher	102	121
Buyer, level II	93	115
Accountant, level III	86	103
Chemist, level III	78	96
Computer programmer	76	95
Engineer, level III	74	92
College professor (average all ranks)	68	88[b]
Federal civil servant, GS-12 (white-collar professional)	66	81
Buyer, level IV	64	78
Accountant, level V	59	68
College professor (full)	44	61
Personnel director, level IV	40	46
Engineer, level VIII	34	44
Federal civil servant, GS-16 (non-political manager)	36	42
Chemist, level VIII	31	40

SOURCE: Computed from sources in Table 9.

[a] 1977.

[b] 1976.

It is nonetheless true that in the 1960s and 1970s the mass of white-collar employees lost substantial ground to strongly unionized blue-collar workers. This will almost certainly have important social as well as economic consequences, particularly upon white-collar workers themselves, whose status has traditionally rested on income superior to the income of manual workers. The social position of white-collar work, based on its nonmanual characteristics, its setting in the office rather than the factory, and other features that distinguished it from manual toil, was both symbolized and enhanced by the higher income of the white-collar employee. Throughout the twentieth century, however, blue-collar income has been increasing somewhat faster than white-collar income, and, as noted in Chapter 1, the gap between highly-paid blue-collar workers and low-paid white-collar workers closed entirely some years ago. After a survey of historical trends in the comparative earnings of blue- and white-collar workers, economist Robert K. Burns, writing in the mid-1950s, concluded that "the earnings data for the period from 1890 . . . show a long-term trend of decline in white-collar earnings relative to those of the manual group. The situation of substantial superiority for salaried personnel which existed before World War I appears to have come to an end in recent years."[8]

What is new about the present period is not the somewhat faster growth of blue-collar earnings, but the *tremendous acceleration of this trend*. Table 11 illustrates this clearly. Between 1958 and 1968, auto workers, who already earned considerably more

Table 11. AVERAGE EARNINGS OF AUTOMOBILE WORKERS AS A PERCENTAGE OF AVERAGE EARNINGS OF BANK EMPLOYEES AND DEPARTMENT STORE EMPLOYEES, 1958, 1968, 1978

Occupation	*1958*	*1968*	*1978*
Bank employee (nonsupervisory)	155%	162%	213%
Department store employee (nonsupervisory)	185%	179%	214%

SOURCE: Computed from sources in Table 9.

than bank employees, gained only slightly on the latter. Between 1968 and 1978, however, auto workers stretched their lead enormously. In the decade 1958 to 1968, auto workers actually lost a bit of their large lead on retail department store clerks; in the following decade, 1968 to 1978, they made tremendous gains.

If relative deprivation is a fundamental cause of social discontent, then many white-collar employees now have a double reason for unrest: first, they are no longer making the economic gains they became accustomed to in the postwar era; and second, they are losing ground more rapidly than ever to a visible group of blue-collar workers. In a society where money is the measure of social worth, what happens when clerical workers and retail salespeople discover that factory workers are suddenly earning, not merely slightly more, but 2–2.5 times more than they; when school teachers and librarians are being left behind in the factory dust; when unionized blue-collar workers are quickly closing in even on college professors who have invested up to ten years in graduate school—not to mention their undergraduate years—to prepare for a career?

Today the middle-class struggle to maintain what have been for them appropriate income differentials is collapsing. Such salaried employees must inevitably develop the feeling that their income is no longer commensurate with their social worth and that people who are socially inferior to themselves are being allowed to pull outrageously ahead. When rank—or *imagined* rank—no longer gets its due, social order is in danger.

The stagnation of white-collar income, along with the rapid deterioration of their income relative to highly unionized manual workers, can be expected to intensify white-collar malaise, *Angst,* and *ressentiment,* and contribute to what C. Wright Mills called the white-collar status panic. In England, Sweden, and Israel, where superior white-collar earnings have collapsed or are in an advanced stage of disintegration, white-collar frustration is expressed in privatized anger and in furious trade-union or political struggle to recapture or retain what is left of traditional differentials.

Will the comparative decline of white-collar income in the U.S. lead finally to a much-delayed explosion in white-collar unionism?

Will the obvious success of strong industrial unions in protecting their members from inflation show the way for salaried workers? The consolidation of unionism among American public school-teachers, plus the rapid growth of public employee unionism, suggests the possibilities here. In the face of the unprecedented deterioration of their real income, the recent burst of support among college professors for faculty unionism, for the first time in the history of American higher education, also suggests the potential for unionizing heretofore unorganizable professionals. But for the mass of union-resistant clerical, sales, technical, and professional employees, the pressure on white-collar salaries could possibly dissipate into more lower-middle-class brooding, private anguish, and petty, individualistic grasping. It could create more class resentment against blue-collar workers and, from the white-collar perspective, against their socially disproportionate income. Finally, it could generate more, rather than less, white-collar antagonism toward trade unions and provide grist for journalistic tirades against blue-collar greed and inflation caused by excessive union wage settlements.

THE INTELLECTUAL RESERVE ARMY

> "A Long Island golf-course caddy with a master's degree in psychology, reportedly depressed at being unable to find work in his chosen field, tried to commit suicide yesterday by sawing off his left hand, Nassau County police reported."
>
> *New York Daily News,* May 23, 1979

The college-educated middle class, for years thought to be among the chief beneficiaries of postwar prosperity, is no longer immune to the stagnation of American capitalism. College-level jobs did not expand rapidly enough in the 1970s to absorb the millions of college graduates spilling into the job market. Many college graduates who had been assured by convergence theorists to expect the world are now selling shoes at the downtown department store, typing at the insurance company office, or waiting tables at the local restaurant. Throughout the 1970s, increasing numbers of graduates were forced to take jobs outside their fields

Table 12. MONTHLY STARTING SALARIES OF COLLEGE GRADUATES, 1967 AND 1976

Major	Salary Offered 1967	Salary Offered 1976	1976 Salary in 1967 Dollars	% Change in Purchasing Power, 1967–76
Business	$613	$872	$518	− 15.4%
Accounting	637	1,028	605	− 5.0
Humanities and social sciences	589	804	478	− 18.8
Chemical engineering	733	1,279	760	+ 3.6
Civil engineering	706	1,108	659	− 6.7
Biological sciences	543	810	482	− 11.3

SOURCES: College Placement Council, "Salary Survey: A Study of 1966–67 Beginning Offers, Final Report," and "Salary Survey: A Study of 1975–76 Beginning Offers, Final Report," reprinted in Neale Baxter, "Payoffs and Payments: The Economics of a College Education," *Occupational Outlook Quarterly* (Summer 1977).

of specialization and often, in fact, jobs that required little if any college education at all. The golden age of higher education, when graduating seniors could choose among a number of professional or managerial job offers, is over. Now, good professional and managerial jobs are scarce, and the competition for them has become maddening, almost macabre. Many bewildered graduates, especially in the humanities and social sciences, have begun to realize that on the job market they are, paradoxically, highly educated unskilled workers. Chronic underemployment, and even unemployment for many graduates, has created the beginnings of what I have called an intellectual reserve army of educated workers.[9] The figures in Table 12 provide a quantitative illustration of this new reserve army and of the real decline in starting salaries for college graduates in almost every field during this period.

"GIVEBACKS"

The stagnation of living standards has struck workers in the public as well as the private sector. The fiscal crisis of the cities and the deterioration of the public sector generally eroded the salaries of most municipal workers in the 1970s. Table 13 shows the changes in real income for municipal workers in various cities across the country from 1971 to 1976.

In most cities, the real income of municipal workers declined during the 1970s. In some cities—Buffalo, Pittsburgh, Atlanta, San Francisco, and New York—the decline was substantial, between 22 percent and 33 percent. By the late 1970s a new word, "give-backs," had entered the vocabulary of collective bargaining nego-tiations with local government workers, signifying the demand to

Table 13. CHANGES IN REAL GROSS INCOME FOR MUNICIPAL EMPLOYEES, 1971–1976

City	% Change in Average Monthly Wages Adjusted for Local Inflation Rate
Buffalo	−33%
Pittsburgh	−27
Atlanta	−26
San Francisco	−22
New York	−22
Chicago	−16
Philadelphia	−14
St. Louis	−13
St. Paul	−10
Baltimore	−10
San Diego	−5
Kansas City	−2
Detroit	−2
Los Angeles	−1
Houston	0
Boston	+2
Seattle	+8
Denver	+8
Dallas	+11
Indianapolis	+30

SOURCE: *New York Times,* June 7, 1978; data from Urban Insti-tute and U.S. Bureau of the Census.

relinquish previous gains in wages, salaries, or working conditions. In many cases things had come so far that a progressive contract was not so much one in which gains were made but one in which losses were minimized.

FAMILY INCOME: THE NEW FOUR-PASSENGER TREADMILL

Because the earnings of American men have not been increasing fast enough to satisfy the family's increasing material needs and desires, Americans have responded by sending more family members out to work. Unquestionably, the most dramatic change in the composition of the American labor force in recent decades has been the steady increase in the number and proportion of working wives (see Table 14). In 1940, only one in seven married women in the U.S. was gainfully employed. By 1960 the proportion grew to nearly one in three. Then in 1979, working wives

Table 14. LABOR FORCE PARTICIPATION OF WIVES, HUSBAND PRESENT, 1940–1979, SELECTED YEARS

Year	% of Wives in Labor Force[a]
1940	14%
1950	22
1960	31
1970	40
1979[b]	51

SOURCES: Juanita Kreps and Robert Clark, *Sex, Age, and Work* (Baltimore: Johns Hopkins University Press, 1975), p. 8; Bureau of Labor Statistics, Report #584, "Employment in Perspective: Working Women, Fourth Quarter 1979" (January 1980).

[a] From 1940 to 1960, women 14 years and older; in 1970 and 1979, women 16 years and older.

[b] December. Average of all of 1979 was 49.

passed the 50 percent milestone. At the end of that year, for the first time in American history, more wives were at work than were at home. If these trends continue, working wives will greatly outnumber non-working wives in the 1980s and become the dominant pattern in American society. Among the usual explanations for the rise of the working wife are declining birthrates, increasing educational levels and growing aspirations among women, egalitarian sex norms accompanying a revived feminism, and the great expansion of white-collar occupations (clerical, sales, and the semiprofessions) which have provided new economic opportunities for women. Undoubtedly, however, the central factor in the postwar rise of the working wife was the desire to boost family income and to offset whatever might have been perceived of the falling rate of affluence among individual workers.

Has the increasing number of breadwinners in the family been able to overcome the stagnation of income experienced by individual workers? Is it possible that although individual income has stagnated in the last decade and a half, family income has continued to grow as the number of gainfully employed workers in the family has risen? To explore this possibility we must examine a different set of data on total family income.

Income data collected by the Census Bureau's Current Population Survey (CPS) differs in several respects from the data collected by the Bureau of Labor Statistics. While the BLS gathers its income data on individual workers from the payroll records of business establishments, the Current Population Survey acquires its income figures on individuals and families through annual interviews in a national sample of some 56,000 households. While the BLS data cover only the earnings of production or nonsupervisory workers in private, nonfarm establishments, the CPS data includes earnings of all workers (sixteen years and over), self-employed as well as employees, farm as well as nonfarm, supervisory as well as nonsupervisory, public as well as private. While the BLS includes income only from wages and salaries, the CPS figures include, in addition, income from a wide variety of sources: 1) self-employment income; 2) interest; 3) dividends, net rental income, royalties, estates, and trusts; 4) alimony and child support; 5) unemployment compensation, workman's compensation, and veteran's payments; 6) public assistance; 7) Supplemental Security Income; 8) Social Security and Railroad Retirement income; and 9) pensions.

In at least two crucial respects, the CPS data treat inadequately the income of upper-income groups. First, the CPS figures exclude all income from capital gains, the vast majority of which accrue to a tiny fraction of upper-income families. A 1978 study by the U.S. Treasury Department, for example, found that families whose income exceeded $50,000 (only 2.5 percent of all families in 1977) accounted for over 67 percent of the nearly $7 billion in annual tax savings derived from the favorable tax treatment accorded capital gains income.[10] Second, in a curious practice, the CPS simply stops counting individual income from any single source listed above when that income reaches $99,999. Any person whose income from any one source exceeds this figure is recorded as earning $99,999. Thus, a top corporate executive whose salary is $800,000 is tabulated as receiving only $99,999. When asked to explain the reasons for this policy, officials from the CPS said that six-digit incomes caused "coding problems" on the questionnaire. And, indeed, the CPS questionnaire contains only five digits for recording income from each source.[11] Both this practice and the exclusion of capital gains income mean that the Current Population Survey's widely used figures underestimate the actual earnings of the rich and understate the inequality in the distribution of income in the U.S.[12] Nonetheless, the measure we are concerned with here—the median—is not affected.

The median income of American families since 1947 is presented in Table 15 below. The table reveals that the income of American families increased very rapidly in the postwar period, rising from $3,000 in 1947 to over $17,000 in 1978. Of course, the gains are less spectacular after inflation is taken into account. Even when adjusted for inflation, however, real family income doubled in just three decades, rising from $8,850 in 1947 (1978 dollars) to $17,640 in 1978 (see Table 15 and Figure 2).

Family income has risen substantially over the years, partly because of the increasing participation of wives in the labor force. In 1978, for example, the median income of families with a working wife was 37 percent higher than that of families without a work-

Table 15.   MEDIAN FAMILY INCOME, 1947–1978

Year	Current Dollars	Constant (1978) Dollars
1947	$3,031	$8,848
1948	3,187	8,634
1949	3,107	8,500
1950	3,319	8,991
1951	3,709	9,310
1952	3,890	9,557
1953	4,242	10,342
1954	4,167	10,110
1955	4,418	10,759
1956	4,780	11,468
1957	4,966	11,505
1958	5,087	11,472
1959	5,417	12,119
1960	5,620	12,374
1961	5,735	12,500
1962	5,956	12,838
1963	6,249	13,309
1964	6,569	13,810
1965	6,957	14,378
1966	7,532	15,134
1967	7,933	15,493
1968	8,632	16,179
1969	9,433	16,778
1970	9,867	16,569
1971	10,285	16,559
1972	11,116	17,326
1973	12,051	17,683
1974	12,836	16,973
1974[r]	12,902	17,060
1975	13,719	16,621
1976	14,958	17,134
1977	16,009	17,226
1978	17,640	17,640

SOURCE: U.S. Bureau of the Census, *Current Population Reports,* Series P-60, No. 123, "Money Income in 1978 of Families and Persons in the United States" (Washington, D.C., 1980).

[r] Based on revised methodology.

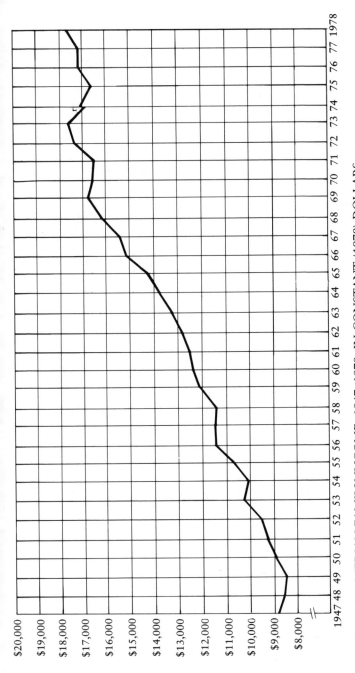

Figure 2. MEDIAN FAMILY INCOME, 1947–1978, IN CONSTANT (1978) DOLLARS

SOURCE: Figures in Table 15.

r: Based on revised methodology.

ing wife: $22,100 compared to $16,100. Thus, while part of the vaunted gains in postwar family income were due to the increased earnings of the primary breadwinner, a not insignificant share of the rising living standards of families stems from the growing number of wage earners in the family.

While family income rose steadily during most of the postwar period, the most recent period represents a decisive break with the past. Whether or not family income, like individual income, was subject to the falling rate of affluence over the entire postwar era depends on the base dates used, as the figures in Table 16 illustrate. But one fact is undeniable: there has been a dramatic decline in the rate of income growth in the last decade. Between 1968 and 1978, real gross family income rose only 9 percent, compared to more than 41 percent and 32 percent in the two preceding decades.

Since the figures shown here are all before taxes, the actual gains are even less favorable. Inflation has pushed families into higher tax brackets without raising their real incomes. Because prices doubled between 1967 and 1978, a family that earned $10,000 in 1967 had to earn $20,000 in 1978 just to stay even with inflation. But if a family had doubled its income in this period, it would have moved into a higher federal tax bracket, not to mention the effects of sharply higher Social Security taxes and

Table 16. INCREASE IN REAL GROSS FAMILY INCOME, 1948–1978, SELECTED DECADES

Decade	% Increase over Decade
1950–1960	39.9%
1960–1970	33.9
1970–1978	6.5
1948–1958	32.9
1958–1968	41.9
1968–1978	9.0

Source: Computed from figures in Table 15.

state and local income taxes in the latter period. This was partially offset by reductions in the federal income tax over the period for median-income taxpayers. In any case, Table 17 clearly reveals that under the impact of inflation and federal taxes alone, many families were worse off at the end of the 1970s than at the end of the 1960s.

Table 17. MEDIAN FAMILY INCOME, BEFORE AND AFTER FEDERAL TAXES AND INFLATION, 1969 AND 1979

| | | *Direct Federal Taxes* | | | *After-tax Income* | |
Year	*Median Income*[a]	*Income Tax*[b]	*Social Security*	*Total*	*Current Dollars*	*1969 Dollars*
1969	$ 9,277	$ 956	$ 374	$1,330	$ 7,947	$7,947
1979[c]	18,467	1,789	1,132	2,921	15,546	7,800

SOURCE: Tax Foundation, Inc., *Monthly Tax Features* 23 (October 1979).

[a] Median for all families with one earner employed full-time year-round.

[b] Married couple filing joint returns, two children.

[c] Estimated by Tax Foundation.

One might reasonably argue that even if living standards did cease to grow significantly in the 1970s, this stagnation came at the end of a generation of rising affluence, so that living standards now perch at their highest postwar level. This argument ignores the fact, however, that for many groups living standards are actually declining. And more important, for Americans as well as for theorists of the American class structure, what has always been crucial is not merely the absolute level of living, but the progress from year to year, decade to decade, generation to generation. The optimistic comparison of the present with the past and the present with the anticipated future has always been fundamental. As noted at the outset of this chapter, it is this expectation of continuous improvement that recent developments now threaten.

Some have blamed part of the stagnation of family income on the changing social composition of the family itself. As the divorce rate climbs, more families are headed by low-income females. But this cannot be considered a factor irrelevant to American society.

The rising rate of disintegration of the American family is itself an intrinsic part of the contemporary American scene, a crucial aspect of which is the downward economic mobility of the divorced—of ex-husbands as well as ex-wives.

"FOR YE HAVE THE POOR
ALWAYS WITH YOU"

The recent stagnation of income in America has had important implications for the poor. By any reasonable measure which takes current American living standards into account, the federal government's estimate of poverty seriously undercounts the actual number of low-income families. The government's poverty measure was devised in the mid-1960s by Mollie Orshansky, an economist with the Social Security Administration, and was adopted by the Office of Economic Opportunity in conjunction with President Johnson's War on Poverty. It has been widely adopted since that time and now constitutes the federal government's official estimate of the poverty population in the United States.[13]

From a 1955 study of family budgets, Orshansky observed that a low-income family generally spends about one third of its income on food. She argued, therefore, that one could establish a reasonable poverty line by taking the cost of an economy food budget and multiplying by a factor of three. As Orshansky wrote, the poverty threshold so devised was "based on the amount needed by families of different size and type to purchase a nutritionally adequate diet on the assumption that no more than a third of the family income is used on food."[14] Unfortunately, the U.S. Department of Agriculture diet selected as the poverty food budget was meant for "temporary and emergency use only," and Orshansky herself later wrote that among poor families who in fact spend no more than the allotted one third of their income on food, only about one in ten actually had a nutritionally adequate diet.[15]

Official poverty figures were projected backwards to 1959, and the poverty threshold for that year was set at $2,973 for a nonfarm family of four. The poverty threshold was readjusted annually on the basis of upward revisions of food costs until 1969; after 1969 it was linked to the overall increase in the consumer price index.* In 1978, the poverty threshold for a nonfarm family of four was $6,662. What this means is that the very richest of the poor, earning the top figure of $6,662 and using the customary one-third ratio for food expenditures, could spend $3,220 annually for food, which amounts to only $1.52 per day per person, or just 50¢ per meal. Moreover, a family that did manage to keep food expenses within this limit would have only $370 per month left for rent, utilities, transportation, clothing, medical care, entertainment, and all other expenses. Note that this is the budget for the aristocracy of the poor, at the top of the poverty pyramid; most poor families have considerably lower income than this. Although the official poverty line stood at under $6,700 in 1978, the Bureau of Labor Statistics also estimated in the same year that an urban family of four needed at least $11,500 to maintain what the bureau considered a low contemporary living standard. It is not surprising, therefore, that the government's poverty level is widely criticized and that it is most commonly proposed that the poverty cutoff be raised by one formula or another.[16]

Although the official poverty line is unrealistically low, it is consistently so from year to year, so an examination of trends in official poverty offers some indication of changes in the low-income population (see Table 18 and Figure 3). Poverty figures show basically the same trends as the other income data we have examined. Taking the entire period for which poverty figures are generally available, from 1959 to 1978, the trends in the number of poor are sharply downward, from nearly 40 million in 1959 to about 24.5 million in 1978 or from 22.4 percent to 11.4 percent of the

---

*Paradoxically, the way in which cost of living adjustments were made may not have reflected the actual increases in the cost of living for the poor. From 1959–69, annual revisions of the poverty line were based on the cost of the food budget; but in this period the cost of food increased considerably slower than did the consumer price index. After 1969, annual revisions in the poverty line were made using the overall consumer price index. But since 1969, the cost of food (on which the poor spend a greater proportion of their income than any other group) increased much faster than did the overall CPI (see Chapter 5).

Table 18. POPULATION BELOW THE OFFICIAL   U.S.   POVERTY   LEVEL, 1959–1978

Year	Number (In Thousands)	% of Total Population
1959	39,490	22.4%
1960	39,851	22.2
1961	39,628	21.9
1962	38,625	21.0
1963	36,436	19.5
1964	36,055	19.0
1965	33,185	17.3
1966	30,424	15.7
1966ʳ	28,510	14.7
1967	27,769	14.2
1968	25,389	12.8
1969	24,147	12.1
1970	25,420	12.6
1971	25,559	12.5
1972	24,460	11.9
1973	22,973	11.1
1974	24,260	11.6
1974ʳ	23,370	11.2
1975	25,877	12.3
1976	24,975	11.8
1977	24,720	11.6
1978	24,497	11.4

SOURCE: U.S. Bureau of the Census, *Current Population Reports,* Series P-60, No. 120, "Money Income and Poverty Status of Families and Persons in the United States: 1978" (Advance Report, 1979).

ʳBased on revised methodology.

population. Yet the stagnation we have noted after the mid-1960s is evident here also. Virtually all of the reduction in poverty came during the early and mid-1960s. After 1968 there was very little reduction in the total number of persons officially counted as

(Millions
of persons)

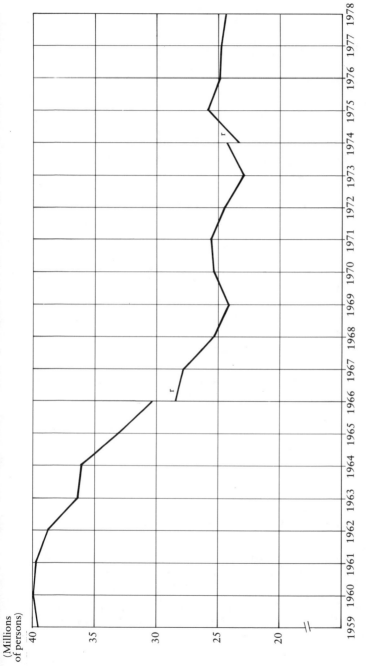

Figure 3. POPULATION BELOW THE OFFICIAL U.S. POVERTY LEVEL, 1959–1978

Source: Figures in Table 18.
r: Based on revised methodology.

poor. For a decade, therefore, America has been locked into an officially defined poverty population of some 25 million persons. As the income of the American people has become frozen, so too has the number of poor.

It is true that in the last decade the social composition of the poverty population has continued to change, as it had in previous years, in the general direction of what might be considered case poverty. Thus, the percentage of poor families headed by females rose from 34 percent in 1968 to 47 percent in 1977. Partly as a consequence of this, the percentage of the poor without a gainfully employed family member has increased.[17] But although the composition of the poor has changed, their enormous numbers have not. America has more officially defined poor people than the entire combined populations of Denmark, Sweden, Finland, Norway, and Israel. And Patricia Roberts Harris, President Carter's secretary of Health, Education, and Welfare, has observed that if the American poor formed a separate nation, its total population would exceed that of half the nations of the world.

Yet there are convergence theorists who believe that poverty in America has disappeared. The claim raised in the fifties was thus raised again in the seventies. Economist Martin Anderson of Stanford University's Hoover Institution, for example, declared that "the 'War on Poverty' that began in 1964 has been won. The growth of jobs and income in the private economy, combined with an explosive increase in government spending for welfare and income transfer programs, has virtually eliminated poverty in the United States."[18] Fundamental to the abolition of poverty in our time, according to such writers, has been the growth of income-in-kind going to the poor since the 1960s—food stamps, Medicaid, housing subsidies, and the like. Writing in 1976, economist Edgar K. Browning argued that if noncash benefits to the poor are counted as income, as he believes they should be, then "there is practically no poverty—statistically speaking—in the United States today, and, indeed, there has not been for several years."[19] The impulse arises to award such scholars, for whom poverty in America no longer exists, traveling fellowships to Appalachia, the barrios of the Southwest, the South Bronx, Bedford-Stuyvesant, and, indeed, to any of America's central city slums.

What about the argument that noncash government transfer payments have helped to eliminate poverty? It is true that income-in-kind going to the poor has increased sharply in recent years. If the total costs of these poverty programs were considered income to the poor, then the number of persons who fall below the official poverty level would have declined from 10 percent of the population in 1968 to only 6.5 percent in 1976.[20] Food stamps and other forms of income-in-kind have certainly mitigated the burden of poverty somewhat since the 1960s. But it is an error to consider the costs of these programs to the government as tantamount to income going to the poor themselves. First, unlike people with cash income, the poor have very little discretion over how most forms of income-in-kind can be spent. Moreover, Michael Harrington points out that "part of the increased 'income' of the . . . [poor] is that cost of unnecessary, and even harmful, medical care at inflated prices in Medicare mills; and the money which various real estate speculators rip off from housing subsidy programs."[21] Also, by counting income-in-kind as income, a poor person can enter the ranks of the rich simply "by suffering a catastrophic illness at government expense."[22] This is not merely an academic point, for much medical aid-in-kind for the poor provides for the treatment of serious or terminal illnesses. But this sort of rages-to-riches sequence is not quite what the American dream is all about.

The promise of American capitalism has always been that people could lift themselves by their own bootstraps without assistance from the government. And yet it is remarkable how many Americans cannot, in fact, earn their way out of poverty in the marketplace without income from government programs (see Table 19). At least since the 1960s, the richest economy in the world has been unable to provide sufficient market income to lift 18–20 percent of its population (36–45 million persons) above the government's meager poverty threshold.

In a generally unrecognized development, the poor have actually been slipping behind the rest of the nation. The official poverty line is *fixed,* adjusted only for annual changes in the cost of living to stay abreast of inflation. The median income of American fami-

Inequality in an Age of Decline

Table 19.   POVERTY IN AMERICA

Year	Official Measure (% of Population)	Pretransfer Measure[a]	
		(% of population)	(Total Number in Millions)
1965	17.3%	21.3%	41.4
1968	12.8	18.2	36.5
1976	11.8	21.0	45.2

Sources: Sheldon Danziger, "The War on Poverty Revisited," *Wharton Magazine* (Fall 1979), p. 63; U.S. Bureau of the Census, *Statistical Abstract of the United States: 1978* (Washington, D.C., 1978), p. 6.

[a] The pretransfer measure excludes all income from government programs.

lies increased during most of the postwar era, however, reflecting rising living standards. As a consequence, the gap between the poverty line and the median income has widened during most of the postwar period (see Table 20). In 1959 the poverty line was nearly half the median, but by 1978 it had slipped to under a third of the median. The poor have been defined in terms of a constant level of living while—except for the recent period—living standards for the rest of the population have risen.

But isn't poverty an absolute condition whose definition should

Table 20.   THE POOR LOSE GROUND AGAINST THE NON-POOR

Year	Poverty Line for 4-Person Family (nonfarm)	Median Income for 4-Person Family (U.S.)	Poverty Line as % of Median Income
1959	$2,973	$6,070	49.0%
1965	3,223	7,800	41.3%
1978	6,662	20,428	32.6%

Sources: U.S. Department of Health, Education, and Welfare, *The Measure of Poverty* (Washington, D.C., 1976), p. 72; U.S. Bureau of the Census, *Current Population Reports*, Series P-60, No. 120, "Money Income and Poverty Status of Families and Persons in the United States: 1978" (Advance Report, 1979).

remain constant? Not at all; poverty is as much a matter of relative as of absolute deprivation. Most of the American poor have indoor plumbing, electricity, heat, a radio or two, a television set, and perhaps an old automobile. In Asia, Africa, and Latin America the American poor would be considered rich. And the American poor living in the 1970s would have been considered affluent in the America of the early twentieth century. Yet the American poor feel poor simply because they have much less than most other people living around them today. Their reference group consists of other Americans living now, and in relation to this group they are poor. Poverty must thus be constantly redefined in the light of society's changing living standards. As society becomes more prosperous, the definition of what constitutes poverty should be revised upwards.

Two centuries ago Adam Smith recognized the comparative nature of poverty:

By necessaries I understand not only the commodities which are indispensably necessary for the support of life, but whatever the custom of the century renders it indecent for creditable people, even of the lowest order, to be without.[23]

Economist Victor R. Fuchs has argued that a relative definition of poverty would take into account changing social and economic standards.[24] Taking an arbitrary but reasonable figure, Fuchs suggested that people who earn less than half the median income in a society—whatever the median is—probably feel poor. A family living in a $40,000 home in a neighborhood of $85,000 homes may well feel poor; a family with an income of $8,000 in a country where the median income is $17,000 probably defines itself as poor. And, as W. I. Thomas observed in his well-known aphorism, things that are defined as real *are real* in their consequences. Fuchs has argued accordingly that to allow for changing standards a relative definition of poverty should replace the current absolute definition and that those earning less than half the median should be considered poor.

Applying Fuchs's definition, between 17–20 percent of the U.S. population would be defined as poor, rather than the official 11½ percent.[25] Moreover, if this relative definition were employed, the proportion of the population defined as poor would have declined hardly at all in the postwar period. According to this relative measure, the reduction of poverty would pivot on a redistribution of income, because only redistribution could reduce the population earning less than half the median. Because the distribution of income has changed little if at all in the postwar period, today roughly the same proportion of the population earns less than half the median income as a generation ago.

PUT UP THE TOP, THE SKY IS FALLING

The chronic stagnation of living standards in the U.S. has created a somber mood across the land, tempering traditional American optimism. The unexamined faith that Americans are somehow destined to achieve continuously higher levels of prosperity is eroding, and troublesome doubts are seeping quickly into the center of American life and consciousness. The future no longer looks so unambiguously bright; decline now seems as likely as advance; the word "austerity" has crept into the national vocabulary. The psychology of scarcity, limits, and retrenchment has replaced the optimistic vision of limitless growth and the arrogant assumption of increasing abundance in a world permanently dominated by American power and American ideology. Uncertainty, confusion, and an unaccustomed modesty in the face of Soviet, European, and Japanese competition have invaded the American spirit. "Made in USA" is no longer the selling point it has always been; disconcerting notions of European craftsmanship and Japanese ingenuity have eroded faith in the American product. Technology is no longer the unmixed blessing it was thought to be. The environment can no longer be wantonly manipulated; the ecological chickens—strangely mutated from their chemical diet—are finally limping home to roost.

By the late 1970s it had become apparent that the era of cheap food, cheap energy, cheap resources, cheap land, and cheap money was over. The prolonged postwar binge suddenly ended in a dreadful hangover. Americans, bewildered by the sudden turn of events, alarmed by an inflation that is threatening to become a way of life and to destroy what has been so carefully built, whose pockets have never been so full of cash and credit cards, continually wonder how so much money can buy so little. Public malaise surfaces daily in newspapers and television about belt tightening and the financial crunch which has hit not only the poor, the aged, and the working class, but the middle class as well. Amid the postwar affluence of the 1950s and 1960s, most Americans felt they were continuously gaining ground; in the 1970s, this gave way to a climate in which a great many felt they were losing ground, falling behind, or just barely hanging on.

Americans watched as unprecedented inflation assaulted their pensions and savings, threatening their retirement hopes and plans. Although Social Security payments managed to keep pace with inflation, it was virtually impossible to live on Social Security alone. In 1977, for example, the average Social Security benefit was only about $2,900; in that same year the federal poverty line for a man over 65 was $2,936. How curious that a person who received the federal government's average Social Security benefit was guaranteed poverty by that government's own definition.*

The 1970s turned growth into stagnation, optimism into gloom, and hubris into humility. At the end of the decade, gasoline had hit triple digits, confounding gas-pump gauges that had been manufactured for a simpler time, and gasoline lines appeared for the second time in little more than five years. The first gasoline lines of 1973–74 had a paradoxical quality. The events surrounding the energy crisis of 1973–74 signaled nothing less than a major and permanent transformation in world power. Yet Americans had little patience, aptitude, or inclination at the time for theories of history and thus saw the crisis as a temporary inconvenience, a passing episode, a brief tremor.[26] Americans were so used to living in a world of inexhaustible resources and perpetual abundance, a world where science had so often seemed to step in to save them,

---

* The same was true of the government's minimum wage. In 1979 the federal minimum wage was $2.90 an hour. On the basis of a 40-hour week and a 52-week year, the government guaranteed full-time workers an income of $6,032. But the poverty level for an urban family of four in that year was over $7,000. Ironically again, the federal government guaranteed poverty to those who earned what federal law required.

that they could not believe the gasoline lines were more than a momentary quirk of international politics.

But in 1979 the lines appeared again. And as anxious drivers lined up their hungry chariots, the image seemed to emerge of America strangling on its own profligate past. The nation was reaping the consequences of its failure—orchestrated over the years by the automobile companies with the complicity of a public hooked on private solutions to public problems—to provide an economical and civilized mass transit system as an alternative (or even a supplement) to the gluttonous private automobile. The gasoline lines of 1979 were more than déjà vu, more than a rerun of the 1973–74 experience. Despite the confusion and conflicting barrage of accusations and blame, Americans were gradually beginning to realize that this was not just another passing event but a sign that the nation was quickly losing control over both the supply and price of its oil. In the gas lines of 1979, Americans began to see the future, and it didn't work. By the late 1970s it had become evident that we were at an historical turning point in the use of energy and were undergoing a transition from oil to other energy forms which, with all its painful dislocations, might require 25 to 50 years to complete. There is some solace in the knowledge that this is but a short time in the history of a society; unfortunately, however, this transition happens to coincide with the adult lifetime of an entire generation or more. One's historical patience is necessarily limited by the parameters of the human life span.

Momentous events have signaled the end of the postwar era. But small events may have significant meaning, too. One might say, for example, that the end of the convertible as an American production car in 1976 in its own way signaled the end of the postwar era. The convertible, after all, was not merely an automobile but a state of mind and a way of life. For the generation of postwar Americans, a convertible meant a life of carefree adventure, intentional impracticality, top-down fun, and easy affluence. The postwar environment was friendly, safe, and healthy, and the convertible opened riders up to that environment and put them in direct contact with it. The convertible was Detroit's version of Thoreau's man in the open air; parked openly, unmolested, on city streets, that convertible signified an era of trust and infrequent crime. But that innocent era hospitable to the convertible ended as Americans became less carefree and more worried. The world became a much more practical and dangerous place. Convertibles were not practical: they were heavy and got poor gas mileage; they were more expensive than sedans; they were unsafe in accidents.

The old environment was wholesome and inviting. The new environment was sick, poisonous, and hostile. The top-down convertible now opened one to the wretched fumes, noise, and pollution of the city, and to the thieving, vandalizing lumpenproletariat that would not go away, but grew. The car for this new human and environmental onslaught was not the convertible but the tight sedan—a tank, a fortress—that insulated passengers from this threatening milieu, a sealed-in, closed-up, air-conditioned car where one needn't ever risk contamination from the outside world by even opening a window, much less lowering the top.

By the mid-seventies the convertible was gone, and by the late seventies the other foremost automotive symbols of conspicuous consumption, conspicuous waste, and conspicuous fun—the Detroit road locomotive and the huge V-8 engine—were about to follow the convertible to the junkyard, victims of gas lines, triple-digit gas prices, the 55-mph speed limit, and the federal government's fuel economy standards. The great American drag race was becoming part of the fond remembrance of things past, and a pleasure drive was becoming a contradiction in terms.

As America entered the 1980s, it was not only the mood at the gas station that had changed but at the food store and real estate office as well. Old people wander the aisles of supermarkets, eyes aglaze with disturbed disbelief at the prices, clutching piddling discount coupons, comparing costs of item after item, spending hours to save pennies. The food industry, trying to contain the soaring cost of food, markets generic brands with stark black-and-white labels that read simply "apple sauce," "ketchup," "green peas," committing what amounts to a heresy on one of the system's most sacred beliefs, that packaging is everything. Meanwhile, the price of housing is climbing beyond the ability of most people to pay; and builders try to cut costs and enlarge the market with "no-frills," "price-buster" houses made with cheaper and shoddier materials throughout—as concrete a testimony to declining living standards as may be imagined.

In the 1950s, the Editors of *Fortune* declared that in affluent America things that had once been luxuries for the few were quickly becoming necessities for the many. What an ironic reversal that just twenty years later some of the basic necessities were in fact becoming luxuries. During most of the postwar era the cost of gas, heating oil, and electricity was for most families an inexpensive afterthought to the household budget. By the late 1970s, however, the climbing cost of energy made such an elemental necessity as keeping warm in the winter a luxury that not every family could afford.

The world had changed. But was that change permanent?

There are, it seems, two alternate possibilities. One can reasonably argue, first, that America's problems are merely *cyclical,* that in the last decade the economy has been hit particularly hard by inflation and recession, conditions aggravated by such unique circumstances as the energy crisis; but as economic cycles are indigenous to capitalism, one expects periodic downturns to be followed by renewed prosperity and growth.

While one certainly cannot discount this possibility, one must also consider the possibility that the recent stagnation of income is a consequence of *permanent* and *structural* weakness in the economy, that the best of times for the American economy have run out and that America in the late twentieth century, like Britain in the late nineteenth century, is entering a long period of economic decline.

Although the U.S. economy is still the largest and most productive in the world, ominous trends suggest an unmistakable decline, compared both to America's economic performance earlier in the twentieth century and to the performance of dynamic economies around the world. In some areas, the American economy has improved its performance, but not as quickly as have other countries, thus reducing the American lead. In other areas, the performance of the American economy has declined absolutely. Some economists, in fact, now speak of this decline as an "American climacteric"—a kind of economic menopause through which an aging America is now passing.[27] It is to this decline that we turn in the following chapters.

CHAPTER THREE

Decline: I

The transformation of the American economy from a position of apparent invincibility to one of growing weakness has occurred so quickly and dramatically that economic irony is piled on irony in a continuing and almost unbelievable economic melodrama. Along the American economic highway in the late 1970s there were so many signs of the times they seemed to violate all the anti-billboard statutes. Some of these were minor, others serious, some front-page news, others obscure, but most pointed in the same ominous direction.

INNOCENTS ABROAD AND THE FALL OF THE DOLLAR

> "That Europe is nothin' on earth but a great big auction, that's all it is, that bunch of old worn-out places, it's just a big fire-sale. . . ."
>
> Big Daddy in Tennessee Williams's
> *Cat on a Hot Tin Roof,* 1955

For decades, the United States enjoyed the highest per capita income of any industrialized nation; many people in fact came to consider it part of the natural order of things. How disconcerting, then, that in 1975 the Organization for Economic Cooperation and Development (OECD), composed of the 24 leading non-Communist industrial countries in Europe, North America, and Asia, announced that in national income per capita Switzerland had for the first time bumped the U.S. into second place. In 1976, the U.S. fell to third place behind Sweden. In the 1978 OECD yearbook, the United States, with per capita GNP of $7,910, dropped to fourth place behind Sweden with $9,030; Switzerland with $8,870; and Canada with $8,410.[1]

This fall from grace did not necessarily mean that the United States had been replaced as the world's most affluent nation; indeed, in terms of real living standards, the U.S. was managing to hold on to a shaky lead. Because international per capita income figures are based on prevailing exchange rates against the dollar, what the relative decline of American income per capita revealed most clearly was the precipitous decline in the value of the dollar in the 1970s.[2]

By the end of the 1970s, it was clear that the hoary phrase, the "almighty dollar," had become of historical relevance only, and in a few years its use in textbooks may require an explanatory footnote for the benefit of confused young readers. Although the value of the dollar held up against most of the world's currencies during the 1970s (primarily those of developing nations), its performance was poor against the leading industrial democracies as a whole, and against the world's three strongest currencies a disaster. From mid-1971 through mid-1979, hit by two devaluations and a relentless downward drift, the dollar lost about 25 percent of its value against the currencies of ten major industrial countries. Between 1970 and 1980, the dollar lost one third of its value against the Japanese yen (its value fell to nearly half from 1970 to 1978, but then rebounded), over 50 percent against the West German mark, and nearly two thirds against the Swiss franc. In 1978 alone the dollar was in such disarray—falling nearly 30 percent against the Swiss franc and 22 percent against the Japanese yen in the first ten months of the year—that it began to destabilize international trade relations and weaken U.S. credibility abroad, creating for the first time in decades the spectre of international financial panic, and, by raising prices of imported goods, contributing substantially to domestic inflation. Only drastic monetary action by the Carter administration late in 1978 managed to stabilize the situation, however precariously.[3]

While the living standards of Americans at home stagnated in the 1970s, the living standards of Americans abroad fell dramatically. For a generation after World War II, students and other Americans of even the most modest means and class position roamed across Europe exhilarated by the magic of the American dollar and the freedom and power it granted its possessors. It was possible, indeed, to see Europe on $5 a day. For Americans, as Tennessee Williams wrote in 1955, Europe was just an auction, a firesale, a big bazaar. By the late 1970s, however, the world had turned upside down, and even affluent Americans came home from abroad sobered by inflation and the dramatic transformation in the once-potent but now puny currency they carried.

After World War II, free-spending and prosperous American GIs in Germany gave away cigarettes and chocolates to grateful and impoverished natives. Today the situation is reversed, as American soldiers stationed in Germany are themselves impoverished by the cost of food, rent, travel, and entertainment, paid for with sinking dollars. Enlisted men who have brought their families overseas at their own expense are hit especially hard and find it impossible to make ends meet with the macabre arithmetic of recent exchange rates. Officers' wives collect food and old clothes for GIs who are down and out in Frankfurt and Heidelberg, and one black GI wife has said that living in Germany now is "like living in the ghetto, only worse."[4]

Half way around the world, in Japan, a U.S. sailor compares things today with the good old days—a decade ago: "I was here in 1965–67 with the 7th Fleet. You could travel, stay in hotels, buy watches and gifts, and never even think about it. Then I was making a third of what I am now, but it went three times as far."[5] In this topsy-turvy world of the plummeting dollar against the yen, a lowly Japanese guard at an American army base in Japan in the late 1970s earned more—in terms of the prevailing rate of exchange—than a lieutenant colonel in the U.S. army.[6]

TRADE

The decline of the dollar reflects the weakening of the American economy, especially the enormous balance-of-payments problem and unprecedented trade deficits. Before the 1970s, the United States registered a trade surplus in every year of the twentieth century; in fact, the U.S. had not had a trade deficit since 1893. Between 1960 and 1965, a robust postwar American economy ran large trade surpluses, averaging $6.3 billion annually. After the mid-1960s, however, trade surpluses began to decline, averaging only $2.3 billion annually between 1966–70. And in 1971 the U.S. ran its first trade deficit of the century, $2.3 billion. Then, in six of the following eight years of the decade, the U.S. had a negative trade balance, capped by deficits in each of the last three years of the decade ranging from roughly $25 billion to $28.5 billion, the largest by far in U.S. history. By the mid-1970s, imports had become a more significant share of U.S. gross national product than at any time in the postwar era. For most of that period, imports comprised only about 4.5 percent of GNP; by the mid-1970s, that figure doubled, to 9 percent or more, falling only slightly to 8.7 percent by the end of the decade.[7]

The deteriorating U.S. trade position is often blamed on expensive oil imports, yet American trade deficits began in 1971 and 1972, before the jump in world oil prices. As late as 1977, even if U.S. trade with all OPEC nations had been eliminated, the U.S. would still have had a trade deficit of nearly $8 billion. Moreover, West Germany and Japan, far more dependent upon imported oil than the U.S., have managed to run trade surpluses despite the cost of imported oil: in West Germany every year since the initial boost in oil prices; and in Japan, huge surpluses in 1977 and 1978, and a modest surplus in 1979.

Although expensive oil imports were not at the root of American trade deficits, they obviously aggravate the problem and pose a potentially devastating threat to the U.S. economy. In 1973, the U.S. paid $7.5 billion for imported oil; by 1979, despite plans, programs, and hopes for energy independence, the U.S. bill for imported oil rose to nearly $60 billion. In 1978, shortly before the Iranian Revolution, Daniel Yergin, of Harvard Business School's

Energy Project, warned that unless the U.S. adopted a radical energy conservation program, the scenario of the mid-1980s would be ever-increasing U.S. dependence on imported oil; much higher oil prices; even more massive trade deficits; further erosion of the dollar; and hyperinflation—all leading to a repeat and intensification of the energy anarchy of 1973–74.[8] The chain of events following the Iranian Revolution began to confirm virtually all of Yergin's predictions even sooner than he predicted. The question at the beginning of the 1980s was whether any other scenario was even possible.

While a steadily devalued currency and persistent trade deficits often signify a weakening economy, government economists remained undaunted through the late 1970s. In addition to the cost of imported oil, U.S. trade deficits were attributed to the fact that America's trading partners recovered more slowly from the recession of the mid-1970s, slowing their imports from the U.S. and driving their own goods into export. While this may have been a limited contributing factor, what was often overlooked was the growing noncompetitiveness of much of American industry. The American steel industry is an excellent case in point.

THE DECLINE OF AMERICAN STEEL [9]

> "The distinguishing characteristic of the American steel industry is its tremendous productiveness, a quality which other countries have been unable to emulate so far."
>
> John S. Tennant, General Counsel for U.S. Steel, 1958

> "We're seen as Big Business. Really, we're a sick industry and neither the public nor the government wants to recognize that."
>
> Roger Brown, Republic Steel Corporation, 1978

> "What are you gonna do? Foreign steel killed us."
>
> Tony DeCarlo, steelworker at bankrupt
> Alan Wood Steel Company, 1978 [10]

Steel remains the foundation and central symbol of an advanced industrial economy, and for generations the American steel industry was the perfect embodiment of American industrial might. Until the early 1950s, the United States produced more steel than all other nations of the world *combined,* produced it more efficiently, and was a net exporter of steel. The golden age of American steel ended in the late 1950s, however, and the industry has been fading fast ever since. What is crucial is not only that the Soviet Union now produces 30 percent more steel than the U.S., nor that the U.S. share of total world steel production fell from 55 percent in 1950 to only 16 percent in the late 1970s. It was natural that the U.S. share of world steel production should fall with the postwar rebuilding of Europe and Japan. Despite it, the U.S. is still the largest producer of steel in the non-Communist world. More important than the decline in the U.S. share in world output is the fact that the American industry is losing its technological lead in steel production. That technological edge was vital, for it helped to offset the higher wages paid to American workers and thus kept American steel competitive. As the U.S. lead in steel technology and productivity dwindled in the 1960s and 1970s, American steel has been steadily losing its international advantage, and foreign imports have made increasingly serious inroads into the U.S. steel market. By the end of 1977, before the trigger-price system restricted sales of inexpensive foreign steel, import penetration had reached an unprecedented 21 percent of the domestic market. Although imports declined somewhat after 1977, industry specialists predicted that despite the trigger-price mechanism, foreign steel could account for as much as 50 percent of the domestic market by the end of the 1980s. Thus, the American steel industry, which had dominated the huge American market for generations, now finds itself besieged from all sides—by steel from Japan (which accounted for over half of U.S. steel imports in the 1970s), from Europe, and from growing steel industries in the developing countries.

The decline of American steel is largely traceable to two related factors: complacency arising from its long-term oligopolistic position; and growing technological obsolescence. The American steel industry is highly concentrated and has been since the creation of the U.S. Steel giant in 1901. In the late 1970s, only eight companies accounted for 95 percent of domestic steel production, and two firms—U.S. Steel and Bethlehem—alone produced about 40 percent. In industries where few firms dominate the market, price competition usually disappears, and this has been the case in steel. In fact, price competition in the American steel industry came to an end in the early days of the twentieth century. Ironically, only when foreign steel penetrated the American market in the 1960s did price competition reappear in the industry. The American steel industry was so accustomed to a sheltered market and administered prices that it forgot what free enterprise was all about. Price competition was so new that when it appeared the American industry called it unfair. According to domestic producers, foreign manufacturers are dumping steel into the American market (selling below their costs of production) to conquer new markets or are receiving subsidies from their own governments that are unavailable to American producers. Meanwhile, the U.S. government allegedly penalizes domestic producers by imposing severe pollution control regulations and not allowing adequate capital depreciation.

Most observers outside the industry have found that charges of unfair foreign competition and of adverse government treatment of the American industry have been vastly exaggerated and are not at the root of the declining competitiveness of the American steel industry.[11] With respect to America's leading domestic competitor, Japan, the issue is very simple: the Japanese steel industry is able to sell steel more cheaply because its efficiency is greater.

Large, oligopolistic firms generally do not compete by price; yet Schumpeter suggested that such firms have sufficient size, resources, and incentive to compete through innovation and technological advance. The history of the American steel industry, however, casts considerable doubt upon what has become the conventional wisdom and suggests that the complacent oligopolistic position of domestic steel allowed American firms to cease competing by innovation as well as by price. In his respected work on economic concentration, John M. Blair argued that the American steel industry has traditionally been indifferent to innovation due to its comfortable domination of the domestic market. Of this "entrenched backwardness," Blair wrote, "For over fifty years, the major steel companies of the U.S. have been noted for their unresponsiveness, if not hostility, to new technologies."[12]

Many consider the basic oxygen furnace (BOF) the most important advance in steelmaking in the twentieth century, and both the BOF and continuous casting yield great increases in steelmaking productivity. Nonetheless, after World War II, the major American steel companies were among the last in the industrialized world to adopt these two most important postwar steelmaking innovations.[13] These delays in harnessing major innovations produced serious and perhaps irreversible erosion in the competitive position of American steel. In the mid-1960s, the American industry attempted to make up for its late start, but it was almost impossible to overcome the lead it had forfeited so early.

During the 1950s and early 1960s, while the American steel industry delayed, the Japanese built up the new technology at astonishing speed. As early as 1969, 77 percent of Japanese steel was produced in BOF converters compared to only 43 percent of American steel. In the 1970s the U.S. narrowed the gap, but the Japanese lead was still substantial. By 1976, the proportion of crude-steel output produced in basic oxygen furnaces was 81 percent in Japan and 63 percent in the U.S. And in 1979, 50 percent of Japanese steel was continuously cast compared to only 11 percent of American steel.

While the oligopolistic American steel industry tended to compete neither by price nor by innovation, there is the additional problem that the bulk of American steelmaking facilities are, by contemporary standards, quite old. After the 1950s, the American industry found itself with aging, obsolescent, and, by current measures, small facilities, most of which had been built before World War II. With such an enormous investment in older plant and equipment, the American steel industry found it difficult and expensive to adapt to new technologies, even where there was an incentive to do so. Piecemeal modernization involved great equipment retirement costs and often led to distorted materials flow in many companies. Meanwhile, U.S. steelmaking technology was leapfrogged by modern facilities built from the ground up in Europe, Japan, and more recently, the developing countries.[14]

Table 21. MAN-HOURS REQUIRED
PER TON OF STEEL

	1956	1964	1976
Japan	60.7	25.5	10.0
USA	16.7	13.1	11.8

SOURCES: *Wall Street Journal,* August 3, 1977;
Helen Shapiro and Steven Volk, "Steelyard
Blues: New Structures in Steel," *NACLA (North
American Congress on Latin America) Report
on the Americas* 12 (January/February 1979),
p. 9.

The Japanese steel industry has made extraordinary gains on its
American counterpart, as Table 21 reveals. In 1956, productivity
in the American steel industry was 3.5 times greater than in the
Japanese steel industry. As a consequence of enormous productivity gains since then, the Japanese steel industry had become the
most productive in the world by the mid-1970s.

Paradox piles upon paradox. The *Wall Street Journal* reported
in 1977 that American visitors expressed "wonder" at Japanese
steel facilities. Inland Steel, when building its first new blast furnace since World War II, called on Nippon Kokan K. K. of Japan
for "technical assistance." [15] In a 1977 report on the world steel
industry, the CIA wrote that Japanese mills were "the best in the
world, and the highly efficient oxygen furnace operations are the
envy of the world's steelmakers." [16]

By the end of the 1970s, West Germany and France were rapidly closing the productivity gap on American steel. Between 1964
and 1974, productivity in the German and French steel industries
increased about three times faster than that of the American steel
industry, and German steel, which started the decade only slightly
over half as productive as American steel, ended the decade with
productivity levels up to 90 percent of their American counterparts. [17]

Steel is no longer a very profitable enterprise for American producers. In fact, of 41 manufacturing industries in the U.S., steel

ranked last in return on net worth during most of the 1970s. For this reason, and because steel is a highly capital intensive industry which requires an investment of about $6 billion annually just to maintain production levels, the once-supreme American steel industry is, ironically, getting out of the steel business. While national interest would seem to be served by having a modern domestic steel industry, corporate interest requires forsaking steel for more lucrative endeavors. The chairman of the board of U.S. Steel said in 1979 that, "Return on investment will dictate where our money goes." Accordingly, between 1976 and 1979 Big Steel's *nonsteel* assets grew 80 percent, while its steel assets grew only 13 percent. U.S. Steel has been moving into chemicals, coal and uranium mining, transportation (barges, railroads, shipping facilities), and countless other fields.[18]

While American steel companies require billions of dollars to modernize, many companies have "borrowed up to their limit" and others have been nearly red-lined by U.S. banks. Meanwhile, American banks are making massive loans to foreign steel companies, both in developed and developing countries. Between 1975 and 1977, for example, U.S. banks increased their loans to the six largest Japanese iron and steel companies from $280 million to over $1 billion.

American banks are thus helping foreign steel undermine the American steel industry. Why? Because capital inevitably flows to where the profits are. Modern multinational enterprises (banks included) have now transcended national loyalties as well as national boundaries, and American banks lend to Japanese steel simply because it has a better long-term profit outlook than American steel. American banks are also providing substantial working capital for the new steel industries in Brazil, South Korea, Taiwan, and elsewhere in the developing world. As we shall see, this is part of a global transfer of capital, industry, and technology from the developed countries, especially the U.S. where wages are high and unions are strong, to developing countries where wages are low and unions are weak or absent.

After World War II there were only 32 countries producing steel; by the late 1970s there were nearly 70. Steel industries in developing countries like Brazil have the advantage of abundant natural resources, cheap labor, and a fresh start which allows the use of the most modern technologies. Thus, the American steel industry is threatened not only by steel industries in the advanced countries of Europe and Japan, but by steel industries in the developing world as well.

In the American steel industry, as in other aging industries or those pressed hard by foreign competition, plants close and jobs disappear. The most dramatic steel shutdowns of the decade occurred in the Mahoning Valley around Youngstown, Ohio, an area that has been called the "American Ruhr" and that was one of the earliest steelmaking regions in the country. Because of aging facilities, competition from cheaper imported steel, and declining world demand for steel in the late 1970s, Youngstown Sheet & Tube permanently closed its Campbell works in 1977 and fired 5,000 workers, creating economic chaos in the region. After the shutdown, an old-time steelworker who had spent his working life in the mills talked about his co-workers and the jobs they had lost:

This is their livelihood . . . this is their bread and butter. They raise their families, pay their homes out, and they know that this is their life. And now it's just like somebody cut your legs out from underneath you and down you go.[19]

The Youngstown closing was the most dramatic of the year, but it was just the tip of the iceberg, for in 1977 some 20,000 steelworkers nationwide lost their jobs due to plant closings and cutbacks at U.S. Steel, Bethlehem, Kaiser, Republic, and National Steel. Virtually every steel town in the country was hit. At that time industry observers estimated that by the early 1980s, in a drive to eliminate unprofitable facilities, U.S. mills would close down 10 percent of American steel-making capacity, or about 15 million tons a year, and displace tens of thousands of steelworkers.[20]

Then, in 1979 U.S. Steel announced the largest shutdown of steelmaking facilities in the history of the industry: 16 plants will be closed, eliminating the jobs of about 13,000 steelworkers or 8 percent of U.S. Steel's work force. The Youngstown area was hit again, with the scheduled closing of two facilities. Shortly after the announcement, union members occupied the Youngstown offices of U.S. Steel, demanding either jobs or negotiations with the union to buy the plants. In what might be taken as a symbol of the potential destiny of contemporary steelworkers across the country, workers removed two paintings of steel mills from the lobby and hoisted them to the roof, as one steelworker said, "to show the world what our ancestors built and what we are going to have taken from us."[21] The United States, virtually alone among industrial nations, allows large companies to close plants at their own whim and in their own interests with no advance notice and no public review of the impact these decisions may have on the communities and workers involved. In an ironic twist on the meaning of the term, in "postindustrial" America one of the major issues of the 1980s will undoubtedly be the economic and political struggle over plant closings, in steel and other industries.

In industries pressed by foreign competition, production jobs are eliminated, hastening the larger industrial shift from unionized jobs in manufacturing to nonunionized jobs in the tertiary sector. Because of this trend, trade unions represent a steadily shrinking share of the American labor force. Unions lose not only numerical strength but bargaining power as well. Also, weakened industry is unable or unwilling to make the kind of wage settlements it made in the past. Earlier we saw that steelworkers' wages rose rapidly in the 1970s, yet an assault on wages is probable in the future. At the end of the 1970s, for example, U.S. Steel gave workers at several of its facilities a choice between a three-year wage freeze or a permanent plant shutdown.

Unions in industries threatened by foreign competition begin to relinquish their traditional adversary position vis-à-vis management when they perceive foreign imports as the main enemy. Labor is co-opted to the management position, becomes increasingly protectionist, and collaborates with management in raising productivity. Thus, the steelworkers union has developed a quasi-formal "community of interest" with the steel companies, institutionalized in joint labor-management productivity committees in the mills. There has not been a national steel strike since 1959, and, in fact, the Experimental Negotiating Agreement of 1973 prohibits nationwide strikes and requires arbitration when national contract negotiations fail to reach agreement. In return for the no-strike agreement of 1973, steelworkers receive automatic wage and benefit gains, but, as noted, how long this will continue is uncertain. Steelworkers are already on the defensive on working conditions related to productivity, shop discipline, and safety.

In industries disrupted by foreign imports, as in steel, plant conditions often deteriorate. To meet the foreign threat, management may attempt to speed up production, challenge union work rules, and neglect safety regulations. Attempting to boost the sagging profitability of their domestic steel operations in the late 1970s, U.S. Steel embarked on a policy of "cracking down on labor," as *Business Week* described it. In 1979 the president of United Steelworkers Local 1013 at U.S. Steel's aging Fairfield, Alabama, plant reported that, "There have been more discharges, suspensions, and discipline slips in the last two months than in all of the last several years. Morale is real low." [22] On-the-job injury rates in the steel industry have been rising steadily since the 1960s, reaching a high point in the mid-1970s. In the late 1970s, with the spectre of foreign steel in the background, one steelworker described the atmosphere of frenzied speedup in his company as management attempted to push antiquated equipment to its limit:

Foremen [are] urged to operate furnaces in a reckless fashion to get the highest ton-per-hour rate possible and all maintenance is of the patch-and-go variety so that down time is minimized. The furnaces are in a sad mechanical state and suffer an increasing number of small delays. Recently, the foremen took some bad risks and two major breakdowns resulted. These repairs, along with the chronic short delays, made for several months of substandard production.[23]

Is this the shape of things to come?

NOT MADE IN USA

How extraordinary that the world's greatest industrial power has become a massive *importer* of manufactured goods. Since 1960 U.S. imports of chemicals, machinery, and transport equipment have grown enormously (see Table 22), and, except for chemicals,

Table 22. U.S. IMPORTS OF CHEMICALS, MACHINERY, AND TRANSPORT EQUIPMENT, 1960 AND 1977
(In Millions of Dollars)

	1960	1977	% Increase
Chemicals	$ 807	$ 5,737	711%
Nonelectrical machinery	438	9,742	2224
Electrical apparatus	286	8,786	3072
Transport equipment	742	19,353	2608
TOTAL IMPORTS	15,073	153,695	1040%

SOURCES: Seymour Melman, *The Permanent War Economy: American Capitalism in Decline* (New York: Simon and Schuster, 1974), p. 92; U.S. Bureau of the Census, *U.S. General Imports: Schedule A, Commodity by Country* (December 1977).

have increased 2–3 times more rapidly than total imports (even when total imports include the soaring value of imported oil).

But perhaps the export of American manufactures has more than kept pace with imports. In an advanced industrial society one naturally expects that the export of manufactured goods will greatly exceed the import of such goods. Indeed, in the first half of the twentieth century, the U.S. did export far more manufactures than it imported (see Table 23).

Table 23. MANUFACTURED IMPORTS AS A PERCENTAGE OF MANUFACTURED EXPORTS, 1900–1950[a]

1900	69.5%
1910	85.1
1920	40.3
1930	56.6
1940	30.0
1950	56.7

SOURCE: Computed from U.S. Bureau of the Census, *Historical Statistics of the U.S., Colonial Times to 1970, Bicentennial Edition, Part 2* (Washington, D.C., 1975), pp. 889–90.
[a] Includes semifinished and finished manufactured goods.

In the early postwar period, despite considerable annual variation, manufactured imports as a proportion of exports rose gradually. Then, in the late 1960s, with the economic recovery of Europe and Japan, U.S. industry became less competitive internationally and manufactured imports began closing quickly on exports (see Table 24). Finally, in the 1970s the gap closed completely, and during several years of the decade (1971–73 and 1977–78), the U.S. was importing more manufactured goods than it was exporting. If these trends continue, the U.S. will soon become a regular net importer of manufactured goods, a truly astonishing landmark in the postwar decline of American industrial supremacy.* In this respect there is a disconcerting parallel between the United States today and Britain a century ago. After the mid-nineteenth century the mix of British imports changed, as she began importing more manufactured goods. From 1850 to 1913 manufactures rose from 7 percent to 20 percent of Britain's total imports and "reflected Britain's relative deterioration as an industrial power."[24]

In many fields, moreover, massive imports of manufactured goods have become a formidable threat to domestic production, employment, and wages (see Table 25). Although American semiconductor technology still leads the world, the U.S. consumer electronics industry, especially TV, radio, and high fidelity components, has simply been routed by foreign competition. As late as 1965, the U.S. ran a $300 million trade surplus in electronics and communications equipment. By 1968 that surplus had disappeared, and by 1976, the U.S. suffered an electronics trade deficit of $3.1 billion—a remarkable transformation in little more than a decade.[25]

From 1967 to 1976, the value of imported television sets alone rose from $126 million to $837 million ($586 million of which

* It is true, however, that the U.S. still maintains a large trade surplus in such high-technology, R&D-intensive sectors as electrical and nonelectrical machinery, chemicals, aircraft and parts, and professional and scientific instruments. The only country with which the U.S. has a trade deficit in high-technology manufactures is Japan. See U.S. National Science Board, *Science Indicators—1976* (Washington, D.C., 1977), pp. 35–41.)

Table 24. MANUFACTURED IM-
PORTS AS A PERCENTAGE OF MAN-
UFACTURED EXPORTS, 1957–1978[a]

1957	45.8%
1958	52.2
1959	74.0
1960	54.2
1961	59.5
1962	67.3
1963	60.0
1964	59.3
1965	69.7
1966	87.4
1967	82.0
1968	95.0
1969	93.1
1970	95.8
1971	108.2
1972	120.8
1973	109.1
1974	95.4
1975	77.7
1976	89.2
1977	103.1
1978	114.6

SOURCES: Computed from U.S. Bureau of the
Census, *Statistical Abstract of the United States*
(Washington, D.C., various years).

[a] Includes machinery, transportation equipment,
and all other manufactured goods.

was from Japan), a nearly sevenfold increase in less than nine
years, extraordinary even allowing for inflation. In 1950 more
than 140 companies in the United States manufactured television
sets. By 1977 when imports captured about 40 percent of the U.S.
color-television market, only seven U.S. manufacturers remained,

Table 25. U.S. IMPORTS OF SELECTED COMMODITIES, 1966 AND 1977

(In Millions of Dollars)

	1966	1977	% Increase
TV, radio, telecommunications	$ 481	$3,719	773%
Phonographs, recording equipment	200	1,538	769
Shoes	189	1,847	977
Clothing, textiles	1,516	5,926	391
Iron and steel	1,305	5,804	445

Sources: *U.S. News & World Report,* February 14, 1977; U.S. Bureau of the Census, *U.S. General Imports: Schedule A, Commodity by Country* (December 1977).

all of which had extensive foreign assembly operations. Among U.S. producers, Zenith was the last to move substantial component manufacturing and assembly abroad. In 1977, unable to compete with cheaper labor costs abroad, Zenith announced layoffs of 25 percent of its domestic work force, or 5,600 of its 21,000 workers, and the transfer of considerable portions of its TV module, chassis, and high-fidelity assembly operations to its plants in Mexico and Taiwan. In a letter to his employees, the president of Zenith said:

As a result of the flood of imports, all of our major American competitors—companies like RCA, General Electric, Sylvania and Admiral—have found it necessary to move thousands of jobs out of the United States to lower labor cost areas.

We think Zenith has tried longer, has tried harder and has tried more successfully than any other U.S. company to protect the jobs of its American employees.[26]

However. . . .

Foreign penetration of the U.S. television industry has taken other forms as well. In 1974 Matsushita of Japan bought the Quasar TV division from Motorola; some time later a subsidiary of the Dutch giant, Philips, purchased Magnavox; and in 1977,

Sanyo bought out Warwick Electronics, the TV manufacturer for Sears.[27]

The latest development in consumer electronics, video cassette recorders—expected to be a $1 billion industry in 1980—has been a complete victory for Japanese electronics technology. The U.S. has produced nothing that can compete with the two dominant video tape formats developed by the Japanese: Beta, devised by Sony, and VHS (Video Home Systems), developed by Matsushita. U.S. firms have been relegated to marketing these products under license from Japan.

Triumphant in its achievements in radio, television, and high-fidelity audio, the Japanese electronics industry's next target is the massive U.S. lead in semiconductor technology. *Fortune* reported in 1978, for example, that the Japanese had established a $250-million joint government-industry Very Large Scale Integration (VLSI) program to develop the requisite advanced techniques to enable them within a short time "to leapfrog the United States in semiconductor technology and thus gain dominance of the world's computer and electronics market."[28]

Japanese exports of sophisticated integrated circuits to the U.S. increased enormously in the late 1970s. In 1974 Japanese shipments of integrated circuits to the U.S. amounted to less than $10 million. By the end of the decade, Japanese firms, led by Hitachi, Fujitsu, and Nippon Electric, exported integrated circuits valued at $170 million to the U.S. and captured fully 40 percent of the American market. And industry spokesmen claimed that the quality control of the Japanese product was exceptional.

Foreign imports have also struck the American shoe industry a devastating blow. In 1968 imports took a little over 20 percent of the domestic market, but in 1979 the American shoe industry passed a dreary milestone. In that year, for the first time, more shoes were imported into the U.S.—over 400 million pairs—than were produced here. Accordingly, from the early 1960s to the late 1970s the number of shoe factories in the U.S. declined from 1,000 to 350, many closing in one-factory towns. In the 1970s alone, nearly two out of five shoe workers lost their jobs, as employment in the industry fell from 230,000 in 1970 to less than

150,000 in 1979. Import quotas imposed on Taiwan and South Korea in 1977 revived the domestic shoe industry for a while, but then many of the other 68 countries exporting shoes to the U.S. increased their share of the market. Whether artificial protectionist measures can provide a genuine long-term rescue of the American shoe industry is doubtful.

Two contradictory trends are occurring simultaneously in the American apparel industry. French designers, of course, have traditionally dominated the world of fashion. Now, however, such American designers as Bill Blass, Calvin Klein, and Ralph Lauren are offering Paris its first competition in decades. But while more apparel is being designed in America, less is being manufactured here, as a shopper in almost any clothing store in America can readily testify. Imports are rapidly decimating the American apparel industry. In 1979 imports took 22 percent of the domestic market, compared to only 6 percent in 1967. During the 1970s the number of apparel firms in the U.S. fell from 18,000 to 15,000. Some industry observers estimate that in the 1980s, import penetration could rise to 50 percent and slice the remaining number of American firms in half.[29]

Figures gathered by the International Ladies' Garment Workers Union (ILGWU) reveal the explosion of import penetration in women's and children's clothing (see Table 26). In some fields, coats and jackets, knit sport shirts, sweaters, and rainwear, for example, the gain in import penetration has been phenomenal in its speed and extent. As a consequence of rapidly rising imports, domestic employment has fallen sharply. Senator Daniel Patrick Moynihan estimated that between 1970 and 1977, one job in three was lost in the New York City apparel industry, contributing heavily to the devastating loss of manufacturing jobs in the city since the late 1960s. And the ILGWU concluded that between 1961 and 1976, imports cost over 151,000 jobs in the garment industry nationwide.

The reason for this avalanche of apparel imports is not difficult to discern. In a labor-intensive industry, where labor costs constitute 24–39 percent of the price of the product, domestic manufacturers employing American workers cannot hope to produce as

Table 26. IMPORT PENETRATION AS A PER-
CENTAGE OF DOMESTIC PRODUCTION OF
WOMEN'S AND CHILDREN'S CLOTHING

	1961	*1976*
Coats and jackets	1.1%	49.5%
Dresses and suits	.8	7.2
Knit sport shirts	5.9	107.6
Sweaters	5.1	119.1
Skirts	.4	10.5
Slacks and shirts	25.8	40.6
Rainwear	5.5	62.9
Dressing gowns and robes	1.5	7.8
Nightwear and pajamas	2.4	2.5
Underwear	.2	2.6
Brassieres	15.2	50.3

SOURCE: Lazare Tepper, *Women's and Children's Apparel and
the Multifiber Textile Arrangement* (New York: International
Ladies' Garment Workers Union, 1977), p. 6.

cheaply as firms operating in less-developed countries abroad
which pay wages that are a fraction of what American workers
earn. Thus, in the late 1970s, U.S. garment workers earned about
$4.00 an hour, far less than the average for all U.S. manufacturing
workers. Nevertheless, that wage was far higher than the garment
worker's wage of $1.00 an hour in Hong Kong, 50¢ an hour in
Taiwan and South Korea, 25¢ an hour in Sri Lanka, and under
20¢ an hour in China (the latest source of imported clothing).
Moreover, superior American productivity can no longer overcome these wage differentials, for as the ILGWU's research director writes, "Technology and managerial know-how in the industry
is relatively simple and it is internationalized—the same machine
producers and management consultants frequently operate
throughout the world and provide firms everywhere with similar
equipment and advice."[30] The rapid international diffusion of
technology, which we shall see characterizes other industries as
well as apparel, thus undermines the traditional American edge in
efficiency.

The implicit motto of many U.S. companies has consequently become, "If you can't beat 'em, join 'em." Many U.S. companies have simply moved part or all of their production offshore or increased their own imports from abroad. As late as the 1960s, U.S. firms were reluctant to put their brand names on what were considered cheap and shoddy goods imported from the Far East. But in apparel as in other fields, that negative image disappeared with the arrival of quality products, and American firms have climbed aboard the import bandwagon. For example, more than 30 percent of Manhattan and Van Heusen shirts are now imported from abroad, compared to less than 10 percent a decade ago. Retailers, too, find imported apparel profitable, for imports cost them up to 20 percent less than domestically produced goods, even after duties have been paid. The attraction is the possibility of higher markups for the retailer, not necessarily lower costs for the customers.

In another development that is ironic in its symbolism, the very "nuts and bolts" of American industry are increasingly foreign made and imported from abroad. These "metal fasteners," as they are called, are the glue of modern industry—3,500 are used in the average automobile, and 500,000 in one Boeing 747. From 1968 to 1976, the value of imported nuts and bolts increased nearly fivefold to over $300 million. Imports in 1978 accounted for 45 percent of the market, up from 36 percent just four years earlier; and 7,000 American workers, or more than a third of the industry's labor force, has been laid off since 1973.[31] In a related field, miniature ball bearings, another key component of modern industry, more than 50 percent of domestic consumption was imported from abroad by the early 1970s.[32]

Recent figures compiled by the AFL-CIO show that from 1973 to 1977, four crucial years during which total employment in the U.S. economy grew by over five million workers, hundreds of thousands of jobs in various manufacturing sectors disappeared while manufactured imports in these sectors soared (see Table 27).

The loss of some manufacturing jobs over time is natural in an advanced industrial society which, with increasing productivity, moves steadily from secondary to tertiary employment. Nonethe-

Table 27. CHANGE IN EMPLOYMENT AND IMPORTS, U.S. MANUFACTURING INDUSTRIES, 1973–1977

SIC Code		Change in Employment[a]	Dollar Change in Imports (in %)[b]
	DURABLE GOODS		
25	Furniture and fixtures	−8,000	+87%
32	Stone, clay, and glass products	−39,000	+50
33	Primary metal industries	−149,000	+98
34	Fabricated metal products	−40,000	+91
35	Nonelectrical machinery	+76,000	+78
36	Electrical machinery	−90,000	+87
37	Transportation equipment	−79,000	+72
38	Instruments and related products	+23,000	+23
	NON-DURABLE GOODS		
20	Food and kindred products	−28,000	+29%
21	Tobacco products	−14,000	+130
22	Textile mill products	−34,000	+14
23	Apparel and other textile products	−99,000	+106
26	Paper and allied products	+3,000	+85
27	Printing and publishing	+14,000	+46
28	Chemicals and allied products	+20,000	+131
29	Petroleum and coal products	+15,000	+150
30	Rubber and plastic products	+3,000	+87
31	Leather and leather products	−23,000	+80

SOURCE: Testimony of Rudolph Oswald, director of AFL-CIO Research Department, before the Subcommittee on Trade, House Committee on Ways and Means, January 25, 1978.

[a] From December 1973 to December 1977.

[b] From third quarter 1973 to third quarter 1977.

less, much of the recent heavy loss of manufacturing jobs in electrical equipment, textiles, apparel, transportation equipment, leather goods, and primary metals must be attributed to the growing noncompetitiveness of U.S. industry and the growing volume of manufactured imports. These trends are inexorably cutting into the strength of American industrial unionism. In just the ten years from 1969 to 1979, for example, the AFL-CIO lost more than 12 percent of their members in manufacturing, as union rolls in industry declined from 4.8 million to 4.2 million.

Of course, many of these manufactured goods are imported from Japan. Even the most casual American consumer is by now well aware of Japanese imports of radios, television sets, bicycles, motorcycles, automobiles, cameras, optical equipment, and watches. In 1978 the U.S. ran a $12 billion trade deficit with Japan, which amounted to over 40 percent of this country's trade imbalance that year. In fact, the U.S. trade deficit with Japan has risen every year since 1973. What is particularly ironic is the nature of the U.S. trading pattern with Japan: increasingly Japan imports agricultural and raw materials from the U.S.—soybeans, lumber coal, corn, wheat, wood pulp—and exports sophisticated finished goods to the United States. This is the typical trading pattern of an industrialized nation with a less developed nation.[33]

This pattern of economic relations with Japan is creating its own peculiar sociological reverberations. In 1977 a group of American executives working for Japanese companies in the United States brought suit against these firms, charging discrimination against American employees. Complaining that they were being treated like second-class citizens in their own country, the Americans alleged that the Japanese companies maintained dual systems of employment and promotion which favored Japanese nationals. They charged that Americans at the same corporate rank as their Japanese counterparts received lower pay and fewer fringe benefits and that there was an invisible plateau above which American employees could not rise; hence all top-level executives were Japanese. They pointed out that whenever a crucial corporate issue was under discussion, the language of discourse would suddenly change from English to Japanese.[34]

Such discriminatory patterns have, of course, long been the practice of imperial nations, favoring their own nationals in the companies they established in the "colonies." The natives of these less developed lands had to learn their place. In this strange, new world, Americans must now apparently learn *their* place.

THE UNITED STATES AS AN
UNDERDEVELOPED COUNTRY

> "That light at the end of the tunnel is the South Bronx burning."
>
> Anonymous

In the 1950s, C. Wright Mills disparagingly called America "overdeveloped," in contrast to what were usually called "underdeveloped" countries. One signal characteristic of underdevelopment is the lack of a sound industrial infrastructure, that combination of electrical power, communications facilities, roads, and railroads that are the necessary underpinnings of any industrial society. Yet with the disintegration of urban centers in America, many inner cities are beginning to lose hold of their industrial infrastructure and are consequently beginning to assume the contours of underdevelopment. Seymour Melman observed the ironic juxtaposition of underdevelopment in New York City on the day the U.S. landed a man on the moon:

While President Nixon was hailing the manned lunar landing in August 1969 as "the greatest week since the Creation," a rather different technological drama was enacted in America's largest city. Millions of New Yorkers were suffering the effects of breakdowns in basic industrial services. Firms that could no longer be reached by phone placed ads in the newspapers to announce that they were still in business. The telephone service, normally taken for granted, seemed to be falling apart as ordinary local and long-distance calling became annoyingly difficult. At the same time the gradually deteriorating commuter railroads into New York City reached a new low in unacceptable performance, with collisions, casualties, train cancellations and delays.

Even more disastrous for normal functioning in modern urban life were the successive breakdowns in electric-power-generating plants of Consolidated Edison during the August heat waves, leaving buildings without air conditioning, elevator service or proper illumination.[35]

Since this was written, New York City's physical plant, along with its social services, have deteriorated further, following the near-bankruptcy of the city and continuing fiscal woes. "How does a city die?" ask Jack Newfield and Paul DuBrul in their recent book on New York City:

> More than a million citizens on welfare. A $13 billion paper debt. A decline in population of more than three hundred thousand in four years. The loss of 450,000 manufacturing jobs in six years. Thirty thousand apartment units abandoned every year . . . Ten percent unemployment— 40 percent among black teenagers . . . An upsurge in drug use, pornography, alcoholism, and gambling—all escapes from an unbearable reality.[36]

On the Upper West Side of Manhattan, thousands of released mental patients, unemployed and helpless, dumped into shabby welfare hotels, wander the streets in bizarre costumes, lost in their own strange world, mixing with the aimless lumpenproletariat and street criminals who prey on them, lending a macabre, circus quality to the decaying urban landscape.

In 1978 two reporters for New York City's *Village Voice* investigated the condition of the city's infrastructure,

> . . . its subways and streets, its water mains, bridges and sewers, in an attempt to discover if conditions can possibly be as bad as they seem. We encountered an endless stream of personal and horror stories, dire predictions and gloomy prognoses . . . [V]irtually everything . . . has been allowed to deteriorate to states ranging from dilapidated to dangerous. The repair bill is conservatively estimated at more than $20 billion over the next decade.[37]

When an empire collapses, do its roads and bridges not fall into disrepair? The disintegration of the roads and highways in New York City can be taken simply as the most visible symbol of the underdevelopment afflicting America's flagship city—and other central cities across the land. Of New York City's 6,200 miles of roads, 2,300 need to be replaced, not merely repaired. There are about one million potholes to fill every year. Some streets resemble minefields which motorists must negotiate with extreme care. In some areas, when potholes become unusually deep residents place garbage cans or stanchions into them to prevent passing cars from smashing into the craters. As organized society ceases to function, individual citizens must step in to save themselves. Despite the effort, defective roads and overgrown potholes cost city motorists more than $50 million a year in repair bills. The F.D.R. Drive on Manhattan's East Side, its drainage problems almost beyond repair, begins to resemble the West Side Highway, large parts of which simply collapsed several years ago. A section of the Brooklyn-Queens Expressway slowly disintegrates where "the waste from a crumbling sewer has been eating away the soil beneath the highway."

A recent study by the U.S. Department of Transportation found thirteen of New York City's 130 waterway bridges and 120 other bridge structures in "poor" condition, requiring "major reconstruction or replacement."[38] The investigative reporters for the *Village Voice* found that the city's waterway bridges and raised highways "all suffer to greater or lesser degrees from structural rust, salt corrosion, useless drains and bearings, broken expansion joints, crumbling breakwaters and piers, cracked walls—and neglect." According to the Department of Transportation, the Willis Avenue Bridge, a major link between Manhattan and the Bronx, which carries 53,000 cars daily, "has potholes, slabs of concrete roadway that have begun to crumble, bearings that have rusted from steady winter saltings and some weak structural steel that dates back to 1890."[39]

The city's fleet of garbage trucks and mechanical brooms is so old and the shortage of mechanics so serious that at any one time 40–50 percent of the trucks are out of commission, making efficient collection of New York's daily load of 22,000 tons of garbage impossible.[40] Through attrition, layoffs, and budget cuts, the Sanitation Department had 2,600 fewer men to collect garbage and sweep the streets in 1978 than it had in 1974. Not surprisingly, objective studies by the Fund for the City of New York concluded that the streets of the city were far dirtier in 1978 than they were four years earlier.

The 75-year-old subway system daily reaches new depths of human and physical degradation. Sea walls crumble at Coney Island and Battery Park. The West 11th Street pier collapses. Each year the city pays out nearly $9 million to persons injured by broken and hazardous sidewalks.

Even more ominous, beneath the streets of American cities there is an invisible but dangerous deterioration of the urban infrastructure on which an advanced industrial society depends:

America's large, old cities are facing a hidden and largely ignored problem under their streets—an uncharted maze of aging water mains, sewer lines and other subterranean facilities that have deteriorated to the point where they threaten public health and safety.[41]

Built in the late nineteenth or early twentieth centuries, with a life expectancy of no more than 50–75 years and not replaced or even adequately maintained through the years, thousands of miles of wires, pipes, cables, tunnels, and conduits lie in advanced states of decay and obsolescence. Boston is losing half its water supply and Houston 20–30 percent through leaky pipes; San Francisco's inadequate sewage system has polluted the Bay; ground water seeping into Baltimore's sanitary sewers is overloading treatment facilities; New York's streets are flooded by spectacular water main breaks. The Twentieth Century Fund has said that the situation in New York City has reached the critical stage, and the Joint Economic Committee of Congress has stated that neglect of this part of the urban infrastructure is probably the "greatest problem facing our nation's cities," requiring billions of dollars to modernize facilities. The Urban Institute, conducting a study of the decay of underground networks of water mains, sewage systems, cables, and the like, believes that many American cities are "sitting on a time bomb." Because of urban fiscal crisis and federal inaction, however, the deterioration continues.

Thus, America takes on qualities of underdevelopment. Some years ago, Mayor Kevin White of Boston, surveying the rubble of the Bedford-Stuyvesant slum in Brooklyn, observed that what lay about him seemed to be the first tangible signs of the decline of a great civilization. But these signs lie not only in the aging cities of the Northeast. A short automobile drive across the border from the urban problems of Detroit to the urban triumph of Toronto is likely to shake the smug chauvinism of even the most patriotic Legionnaire.

America's decline deepens.

CHAPTER FOUR

Decline: II

THE PERMANENT WAR ECONOMY

How did all this happen? How has the apparently invincible American economy been so quickly weakened? It does no good to argue that American goods are being priced out of the market by the high wages paid to American workers. Since the United States became an industrial power, wages here have always been higher than wages abroad. As mentioned in Chapter 1, at the turn of the century Sombart observed that American workers lived as well as the German middle class; but American industry stayed competitive by offsetting high wages with superior mechanization, capital investment, research and development, management, and work organization. In short, the superior efficiency and productivity of American industry more than compensated for the relatively high earnings of American workers. Not only was U.S. industry the most productive in the world, U.S. productivity growth far exceeded that of other industrial countries. Between 1870 and 1950, for example, productivity of the American economy grew 60 percent faster than that of Europe and 70 percent faster than that of Japan.[1]

After 1950, however, productivity growth of the American economy declined steadily and was soon overtaken by most other industrialized nations. Productivity in the U.S. private sector grew at an annual rate of 3.4 percent from 1948 to 1955, but then fell to 3.1 percent from 1955 to 1965, to 2.3 percent from 1965 to 1973, and to just 1 percent from 1973 to 1977.[2] From 1978 through 1979—in a fitting conclusion to the decade—productivity actually declined.

The rate of productivity growth generally reflects the health and dynamism of an economy, because rapid productivity gains are linked to so many other aspects of overall economic improvement: technological innovation; increased capital intensity; upgrading of the labor force; improved management and organization of production. Moreover, central to our concern, there is a crucial link between productivity growth and increasing living standards. In 1978 the President's Council of Economic Advisers called the productivity crisis "one of the most significant economic problems in recent years," and stated that "Gains in real living standards must come primarily from improved productivity. Without gains in productivity, improvement in real income for some Americans can come only at the expense of others."[3] By the end of the 1970s the Carter administration and government economists recognized that deteriorating productivity was a chronic and central problem of the American economy and predicted slow rates of productivity growth into the 1980s. They argued that the drag in productivity gains was not only paralyzing the growth of living standards but contributing significantly to inflation, limiting the rate of economic growth, and hampering efforts to reduce unemployment.[4]

Labor and the left are understandably uneasy about the "collapsing productivity" thesis, especially when it comes from business, for although it need not be, " 'increased productivity' is all too often a catch phrase and excuse for a variety of attacks on unions, laws protecting worker health, safety and the environment, the tax structure and essential public facilities and services."[5] AFL-CIO economists argue that productivity data outside of manufacturing, especially in tertiary fields—private schools, hospitals, night clubs, bowling alleys, movie theaters, etc.—are very unreliable and that the so-called productivity problem may actually be a measurement problem in the growing tertiary sector of the economy. It could also be argued that even if measurements are accurate, a decline in productivity growth is to be expected in a mature, "postindustrial" society. As employment in such societies shifts from goods-producing sectors to service-producing sectors, and as productivity gains are harder to make in service-producing than in goods-producing sectors, one naturally anticipates overall productivity gains to decline, both absolutely and relative to other less advanced industrial societies.

This does not explain, however, why U.S. productivity growth in *manufacturing* has fallen so far behind other industrialized countries. For example, from 1950 to 1967, U.S. productivity in manufacturing grew at an annual rate of only 2.7 percent, compared to 8.6 percent in Japan, 6.2 percent in West Germany, 4.9 percent in France, and 3.0 percent in Britain.[6] Some argue that the high postwar productivity growth in Europe and Japan is a temporary consequence of normal recovery from wartime devastation, the borrowing or buying of advanced U.S. technology, the rapid urbanization and industrialization of a heretofore low-productivity agricultural labor force, and the expansion of international trade which benefited Europe and Japan more than the U.S. because of the latter's already huge internal market.[7] Nonetheless, manufacturing productivity gains in Europe and Japan continued to outdistance the U.S. by a wide margin throughout the late 1960s and 1970s (see Table 28). Although the American economy is still probably the most productive in the world, the gap between the U.S. and other advanced nations is rapidly closing. According to projections made by a top OECD economist, the output per man-hour in West Germany, Sweden, Norway, and Belgium should exceed that of the United States by the end of the 1980s. The National Science Board could not have concluded otherwise when it wrote in 1976 that, "A continued slowdown in U.S. productivity growth rates coupled with accelerated growth abroad may have serious long-term implications for the nation's economic position in the world."[8] Indeed, it already had.

Clearly, things are not what they once were. But why have things changed?

Seymour Melman has been for many years the most prophetic voice and theoretician of the decline of American capitalism.[9] Since World War II, Melman observed, a national consensus developed around the belief that war bestows prosperity on capitalism. That, after all, seemed to be the lesson of the Second World War.

Table 28. MANUFACTURING OUT-
PUT PER HOUR, U.S. AND SELECTED
INDUSTRIAL COUNTRIES

	1977 (1967 = 100)
Japan	206.6
Belgium	204.0[a]
Netherlands	198.9[a]
Denmark	185.1
France	171.6
West Germany	169.6
Italy	162.3
Sweden	156.6
Canada	143.3
United States	126.9
United Kingdom	126.6

SOURCE: U.S. Department of Labor, Bureau of
Labor Statistics, News Release, May 12, 1978,
pp. 6–9.
[a] 1976.

Military spending associated with the war accomplished what
years of the New Deal had not: it lifted the United States out of
the Depression, eliminated enormous unemployment overnight,
and brought prosperity to the nation. In our time the belief that
war is good for the economy has become a part of the mythology
of the entire political spectrum. Radicals embraced the belief as a
general indictment of capitalism; liberals saw it as a confirmation
of a kind of military Keynesianism; and conservatives took it up in
order to buttress their argument for Cold War policies.

According to Melman, however, what is true of a *temporary*
war economy is not necessarily true of a *permanent* war economy.
Temporary war production may invigorate an economy, as it did
during World War II; permanent war production debilitates it.
For nearly four decades, Melman argues, the United States has
diverted gargantuan amounts of money, manpower, and resources
into military production, the inevitable by-products of which have
been the neglect, depletion, deterioration, and exhaustion of vast

areas of the civilian economy, its industrial base, and the underlying infrastructure. Since 1946 the United States has spent nearly $2,000 billion on defense, and in recent years the annual U.S. defense budget has alone exceeded the GNP of all but a handful of other nations. During the postwar period, the U.S. spent a greater share of its GNP on the military than did any other advanced capitalist nation. In the late 1960s, for example, the U.S. spent about 9 percent of GNP on defense, compared to 4 percent in France, 3 percent in West Germany, 2 percent in Italy and less than 1 percent in Japan.[10] Throughout this period the U.S. also devoted a far larger share of federal expenditures to the military than did other nations. In the late 1960s, over 40 percent of all U.S. federal outlays were for military purposes, compared to only 10–11 percent in France and West Germany, 7 percent in Italy and under 6 percent in Japan.

It is true that as a percentage of GNP, U.S. military expenditures have been falling slowly over the years, from a high of about 13 percent at the peak of the Cold War in 1953 to about 5 percent in the late 1970s. Yet even at 5 percent of GNP, the absolute amount of military spending is so huge and so concentrated in crucial industrial and geographical areas that its overall impact on the economy is enormous.

While there have been undeniable spinoffs from the defense program to civilian industries (commercial aircraft, computers, and semiconductor technology), the benefit to the civilian sector has been exaggerated. How else can we explain the fact that the U.S., which leads the world in weapons technology, has lost its lead in civilian productivity growth and is losing its lead in innovation? According to Melman, military spending has one uniquely debilitating feature:

From the economic standpoint the main characteristic of war economy is that its products do not yield ordinary economic use-value: usefulness for the level of living (consumer goods and services); or usefulness for further production (as in machinery or tools being used to make other articles).[11]

A tank can neither be used to increase production nor be purchased and used by consumers to enhance their standard of living.

Melman argues that the United States has spent a hundred kings' treasure over the decades on essentially nonproductive investment. Meanwhile, the hundreds of billions of dollars spent on weapons have meant lost opportunities for the vital building and rebuilding of the American economy.

In Chapter 3 we touched upon the decline of U.S. consumer electronics. Melman believes that defense and aerospace priorities have essentially dried up the U.S. consumer electronics industry. While military spending spawned the civilian computer industry, ". . . a host of consumer electronics industries like radio and television manufacture, left to their own devices, have suffered massive depletion, closing of factories, transfer of work abroad, and loss of employment opportunities in the United States." [12]

The decline of the most exotic U.S. consumer electronics industry—high-fidelity audio—provides an instructive example in microcosm of how military and aerospace priorities can drain capital, manpower, and research funds from civilian industry which then succumbs to foreign competition. High fidelity was an American invention—both the word and the industry—created by hobbyists, engineers, and old-fashioned entrepreneurs after World War II. Until the mid-1960s the consumer audio industry was dominated by such pioneering American companies as Bogen, Scott, Fisher, Bell, Webster-Chicago, Pilot, and others who produced here for a domestic market. In the last decade and a half, however, the Japanese have totally overwhelmed the U.S. high-fidelity industry, especially in electronics—amplifiers, receivers, tuners, and tape recorders—with an amazing array of products of infinite variety in price, innovation, and styling. While solid-state electronics equipment was developed here, it was perfected by the Japanese who have dominated the market ever since. Many U.S. firms have been driven down or out completely, some (like Fisher) were purchased by foreign companies, and others (like H. H. Scott, Sherwood, and Harman Kardon) transferred some or all of their electronics manufacturing to the Far East. As a result of the foreign, mainly Japanese, onslaught, the remaining U.S. firms have been left with a radically diminished share of the market. Ironically, American companies now languish in the backwash of an industry they created, and audio stores across the country provide glittering testimony to the triumph of foreign technology and merchandising. Only in pickup cartridges and assembled loudspeakers do U.S. manufacturers still prevail. Cartridges, however, amount to a very small share of high-fidelity sales (perhaps $30 million in a $2–3 billion-a-year industry). And the Japanese, who heretofore could not design a loudspeaker pleasing to American ears, are now succeeding, often with the aid of computers. Such Japanese companies as Kenwood, Pioneer, Technics, and Yamaha are moving steadily into the loudspeaker market, the last significant U.S. stronghold. How ironic that the U.S., which can hit a kopek in the Kremlin with a missile launched from Omaha, cannot seem to produce a tape recorder for the consumer market to compete with the Japanese. In these peculiar priorities, however, lie part of the explanation for the decline of American capitalism and the stagnation of American living standards.

What happened to the American high-fidelity industry in the 1960s and 1970s? Why was sophisticated American technological leadership so quickly and utterly swamped by Japanese competitors? A writer on the audio industry explains.

. . .[T]he best [American engineers] just weren't interested in making better phonographs when there was pie in the sky. President Kennedy's promised journey to the moon was drawing the brightest young engineers into the space program, where challenges were greater, the pay higher and the stars seemingly within reach.

Later, Vietnam not only drained the technical talent pool but also preempted production. Profitably engrossed in "smart bombs," people sniffers, and other warlike wizardry for what came to be known as the automated battlefield, American electronics manufacturers lost the taste for home entertainment. Hi-fi manufacturers were eagerly hopping along in the arms race on lucrative contracts for subassemblies. By the time Lyndon Johnson got the Great Society in full swing, nearly the whole electronics business was tied up in outer space or southeast Asia. Where once had been a healthy, consumer-serving radio industry—with hi-fi as an exquisite adjunct—there now was a vacuum.

Swiftly, as if to act out a textbook case in classical market theory, the Japanese rushed into this vacuum. . . . Unburdened by military obligations and just having completed the rebuilding of their war-devastated cities, the Japanese were free to turn all their productive energies and formidable technical acumen toward consumer goods. Cadres of fresh-minted engineers, unbeholden to traditional technologies, poured from their universities and concentrated on the nascent yet enormously promising field of solid-state electronics. Unlike their tradition-minded counterparts in the American radio industry, the industrially newborn Japanese felt at home in the brave new world of transistor electronics. In a veritable burst of creative engineering, they produced a new generation of audio equipment with unprecedented cost-performance factors.[13]

In sum, a permanent war economy, with its voracious appetite for money and manpower, can have devastating effects upon civilian industry and cripple its international competitiveness.

Aside from its effects on consumer electronics, Melman traces other costs of the permanent war economy. Even the richest country in the world cannot have both guns and butter forever. While sophisticated military hardware rolls off the production line, the U.S. infrastructure decays. Missile stocks are built up while railroad rolling stock and roadbeds deteriorate. Railroad track and roadbeds have been allowed to deteriorate to such an extent, in fact, that their sorry condition accounts for a large and growing proportion of U.S. railroad accidents. In 1976, 55 percent of the 7,700 train derailments in this country were caused by poor track conditions, up from 48 percent in 1973.[14] Despite the nation's need for fuel-efficient transit systems, the U.S. long ago lost the lead in railroad technology to France, Japan and other nations.

To upgrade urban bus service in this country to provide an attractive and significant gas-saving alternative to the private automobile would require building about 10,000 buses a year, according to the U.S. Department of Transportation. But even if the U.S. wished to do that, the two remaining American bus manufacturers would be unable to provide such buses in either the quantity or quality needed, and the U.S. transportation industry, paradoxically, would have to turn to European firms for technical assistance. Meanwhile, in 1979 the Carter Administration announced a $33–$100 billion mobile MX missile system, the largest public works project in American history, involving huge transport vehicles to pull missiles around on thousands of miles of circular tracks to confuse the Russians. Mass transit for missiles but not for people.

In still another area, Melman asserts that the crucial and once-supreme American machine-tool industry has been suddenly by-passed by German and Soviet production, with the Japanese not far behind. In 1978 America in fact passed another milestone—for the first time in history the U.S. ran a trade deficit in machine tools; and that deficit, $50 million, was expected to grow.

It is perhaps significant in examining the deleterious effects of military spending on economic growth that in the mid-1970s for every dollar of gross domestic fixed investment, the sluggish U.S. economy spent 33¢ on the military, compared to only 13¢ and 2¢ respectively in the fast-growing economies of West Germany and Japan.[15] During the same time, the amount of fixed capital investment as a percentage of GNP—crucial both for economic growth and productivity gains—has been far lower in the U.S. than in West Germany or Japan. Thus, between 1973 and 1977 capital outlays as a percentage of GNP were 35 percent in Japan, about 22 percent in West Germany, but only approximately 15 percent in the U.S. This U.S. investment gap of the mid-1970s was not merely a function of recessionary times, but was a continuation of a roughly similar investment gap in the 1960s.

An additional contribution to America's economic decline, according to Melman, is the colossal inefficiency of the defense industry, stemming from cost-plus or similar arrangements with the Pentagon. Such arrangements do not reward cost minimization, the usual motive in private capitalism; on the contrary, they encourage cost maximization. As a consequence, enormous cost overruns are not unanticipated exceptions but the expected norm generated by the "approved, built-in operating characteristics" of the system itself. Melman writes:

Big [defense] contracts . . . are arranged by negotiation with one selected supplier, so there is no competitor selling to the single buyer, the Pentagon. And the Pentagon, having ordered a product, usually wants it. Thus even if the price turns out to be as much as three to four times the originally negotiated amount, the Pentagon finds the money to pay for it. Under such conditions the managers of military-industry firms are under no external pressures to do all of the demanding work of problem-solving that is involved in trying to minimize costs through internal efficiencies. Why bother? If costs go up, so too can prices, and thereby profits. This, in a nutshell, is the logic of *cost-maximization*. . . .

One of the consistent themes among product developers inside military firms is "Who cares about the cost?" If the product is more complex, it costs more and justifies a higher price; all this is called "gold plating" in the trade. In one major enterprise the product-development staffs engaged in contests for designing the most complex Rube Goldberg types of devices. Why bother putting brakes on such professional games as long as they can be labeled "research," charged to "cost growth" and billed to the Pentagon? [16]

Analyzing the pricing practices of defense firms, Melman found that a TV set that cost $100 to make in the civilian sector would cost, depending on the firm, between $250 and $2,393 to make for the Defense Department. Such habits of gross inefficiency do not promote international competitiveness.

A dynamic economy obviously requires massive research and development funds to design new products and increase the productivity of labor and capital. Economists estimate, for example, that 45 percent of U.S. economic growth between 1929 and 1969 was due to technological innovation.[17] From the end of World War II to 1972 the United States has spent a prodigious $200 billion on R&D; yet 80 percent of this went for defense, space, and atomic energy. Melman argues that much of this military-related R&D has been economically nonproductive: research that raises the firepower of weapons does not raise living standards or increase productivity; designing ships for the navy does not improve the proficiency of the U.S. merchant marine; scientists researching military rocket engines are unavailable for research into urban mass transit or for designing the kind of high speed trains developed in Europe and Japan. In short, "One of the major casualties of this military emphasis has been the potential effort forgone in the design of new productive equipment, and the innovation of technologies for fabricating the means of production themselves." [18]

In *The Affluent Society,* John Kenneth Galbraith set forth his theory of social balance, suggesting that in any society there should be a rough balance between the supply of private goods and services and the provision of public goods and services. Galbraith observed that American society suffered a terrible imbalance, that private affluence coexisted with public squalor. In a sense, Melman's analysis of the military vs. the civilian sector suggests the reverse, that the military (public) sector basks in state-of-the-art exotic technological opulence at the expense of the civilian (private) sector which has now become impoverished.

While the United States has been spending up to 80 percent of its research and development dollars in the essentially nonproductive areas of defense and space, the Japanese have been spending less than 5 percent of R&D funds in these areas. And since the 1960s the U.S. has been spending only 3–9 percent of R&D funds on economic development compared to 25–30 percent in Japan.[19] Moreover, the total R&D spending in the U.S., both civilian and military, declined from about 3 percent of GNP in 1964 to 2.2 percent in 1978.

Once again the chickens are coming home to roost. The American position in the research and design of sophisticated light machinery, for example, is weakening, and the U.S. has been running an annual trade deficit in light machinery of $6–9 billion. Writing in *Science,* professor of mechanical engineering Delbert Tesar offers two unsettling recent examples of America's growing vulnerability in this field.

The weakness of U.S. mechanical technology may be partially illustrated by the sale of the industrial sewing machine Consew (owned by Toyota of Japan), which runs faster, is more reliable, has four times less downtime for bobbin interchange, and costs 25 percent less than a similar U.S. machine. (Note that the trade deficit for sewing machines was $141 million in 1977.) Another example involves a new tobacco manufacturing plant in Georgia that is the third largest in the United States. All of the machines are of Italian, German, or English origin and are maintained by foreign craftsmen. The plant manager confirms that appropriate technology did not exist in the United States in 1976 to fulfill the specifications for competitive machines.[20]

In 1967 the French writer J. J. Servan-Schreiber published his influential volume, *The American Challenge,* expressing a fear then common on the continent that the technology gap between the United States and Europe was widening and that Europe would either be left behind or dominated by superior American technique. Ironically, however, by the time the book appeared,

American economic power had already begun to ebb.[21] Only a decade later, anxiety had crossed the Atlantic. Gone were the halcyon days of the 1950s when the Editors of *Fortune* could write as if it were an eternal verity that American technology was "of course" the best in the world. By the late 1970s apprehension was widespread that the U.S. had lost its technological dynamism. According to the disturbing conclusions of a 1978 poll of American industrial R&D managers, "A grim mood prevails today among industrial research managers. America's vaunted technological superiority of the 1950s and 1960s is vanishing, they fear. . . ."[22]

THE FUTURE FOR SALE

Aside from the hemorrhaging effect of military spending on the civilian economy, U.S. technical superiority is breaking down for a number of additional reasons. Technological monopolies have become increasingly difficult to maintain in the postwar world, as transportation and communication improvements spread knowledge and technique quickly across international frontiers. We observed with respect to foreign competition in the garment industry, for example, that rapid international diffusion of technology and managerial know-how are undercutting American technical superiority. Also, as technology and industrial organization rely increasingly on scientific knowledge that is basically accessible to all, the traditional American advantage dissipates.[23]

It is not the natural process of technological diffusion alone that has eroded America's lead, however. By their massive sale of advanced technology abroad, via licensing agreements, patent sales, and other forms of technology transfer, American corporations are exporting America's future and undermining its industrial base. The United Electrical, Radio and Machine Workers of America (UE) reported that of some 11,600 foreign technical aid agreements concluded by Japanese firms from the end of World War II to 1970, approximately 6,000 were with American companies. Developing these patents in the U.S. originally cost over $120 billion, but Japanese industry bought the patent rights for these technological developments for only $2.7 billion, or at what the AFL-CIO calls "firesale prices." [24]

The sale by U.S. corporations of advanced technology has reached enormous proportions. By the early 1970s some 1,700 American firms had foreign licensing agreements, and by 1977 U.S. companies earned $2.95 billion in fees and royalties on transfers of technology, compared to $666 million in 1965—a 4.5-fold increase in only a dozen years. [25] For international economic development, the transfer of American technology abroad could of course be beneficial. But most U.S. technology transfers are between U.S.-based multinationals and their foreign subsidiaries. And of the great number of technology transfers to noncontrolled foreign enterprises, the vast majority are to firms in Western Europe, Japan, the Communist bloc, or resource-rich developing countries.

Not only have U.S. companies continued to transfer technology abroad at a tremendous rate but there has lately been a radical change in the *kind* of technology U.S. firms are selling. Until the late 1960s U.S. companies would never release the most advanced, so-called "front-end" technology, realizing that it would be tantamount to trading away the U.S. competitive advantage. Traditionally, American firms released only aging or "mature" technology to noncontrolled foreign companies. Only when a particular technology had been thoroughly exploited, when the products based upon it had saturated the domestic market and much of the foreign market as well, was that technology released. In the postwar years, for example, U.S. firms sold established techniques for building television sets, which were then used by foreign firms to satisfy local markets. In the early 1970s, however, by corporate choice and corporate necessity, U.S. companies began to release the latest generation of advanced technology to sophisticated foreign firms which are able to take this technology, develop it, and eventually outflank the U.S. in international trade. The Amdahl Corporation, for example, a computer firm founded by ex-IBM computer designer Gene Amdahl, licensed its electronics know-how to Fujitsu, a Japanese computer manufacturer, in return for an investment of about $23 million. While Amdahl thus acquired the venture capital which it needed and was unable to obtain in the U.S., Fujitsu acquired "fourth generation computer technology" which tremendously enhanced its international competitive position in the computer industry. Jack Baranson, one of America's leading specialists on U.S. technology transfers, observed in 1978 that "the infusion of Amdahl's technology has allowed Fujitsu to close approximately a three-to-five year gap between it and the U.S. industry. By 1980, the Amdahl-Fujitsu joint venture may sell a sufficiently large number of its advanced systems in North America, Western Europe and Japan to displace more than $500 million in revenue to IBM."[26] Meanwhile, by the late 1970s Fujitsu had moved the technology it had acquired from Amdahl to Spain and had begun negotiations for sharing Amdahl technology with Siemens of West Germany.

Why have U.S. corporations begun to transfer the latest generation of American technology abroad? As the Amdahl case demonstrates, a company that exports its technology generally doesn't lose in the transaction, at least in the short run, but its competition may. Thus, as U.S. firms sell their technology abroad and damage each other's position, the invisible hand works to everyone's disadvantage—another illustration of the peculiar genius of a competitive market economy. By the late 1970s even writers for *Fortune* and the *Wall Street Journal* were becoming a bit uneasy as they observed U.S. corporations releasing technology which would ultimately be used to defeat American products at home and abroad.[27] But U.S. technology transfers continued apace.

In general, the decision by U.S. firms to release front-end technology abroad reflects rapid global political and economic changes, especially the relative decline in the strength and international leverage of American companies. First, selling advanced technology to foreign firms is a quick and safe means of acquiring funds from abroad without the dangers of direct foreign investment in an increasingly uncertain and hostile world. Second, the bargaining power of U.S. corporations in the sale of technology has diminished, while the bargaining power of technology purchasers has increased. As advanced technology spreads throughout the world, the U.S. is no longer the sole potential supplier. If American companies refuse to release their technology, purchasers can go elsewhere. Thus, buyers of advanced technology can now, as never before, play one country (or firm) off against another. Third, foreign governments increasingly want to acquire high-technology productive capabilities and thus wish to obtain American technology itself, not just American products made from it. These governments also possess enhanced leverage now to obtain this technology. Countries that desire advanced technology in computers and in aircraft, for example, are able to deny entry by means of various nontariff barriers to U.S. firms which are unwilling to release their technology. On the other hand, for those U.S. firms willing to share front-end technology via such arrangements as joint ventures with a consortium of foreign firms, the host government may make irresistible offers to subsidize some of the tremendous R&D and production-tooling costs.

Finally, as America loses its comparative advantage in many areas of manufacturing, some U.S. companies are gradually shifting their corporate efforts from manufacturing domestically to developing and marketing technology abroad. "There is mounting evidence," Baranson writes, "that U.S. firms are faltering in their will and determination to continue to design and engineer for the high-wage U.S. economy."[28] Instead of directing their energies toward producing competitively in the U.S., some firms now find it easier and more profitable simply to transfer manufacturing operations—and the advanced technology underlying it—abroad. The Cummins Engine Company, for example, is the largest producer of diesel engines in the world. In the early 1970s, after seven years of research on its state-of-the-art K engine, Cummins decided to assign the bulk of K-engine production to a longtime licensing partner, Komatsu, Ltd. of Japan, an advanced equipment manufacturer rather than produce the engine in the U.S. Assessing the impact of this decision on the U.S. economy, Baranson concludes:

. . . the fact that the bulk of the production is sourced from Japan translates into a loss of jobs and income for the U.S. Equally important, it means that the know-how for the newest generation of a highly sophisticated U.S. product has been released to a foreign, non-controlled affiliate. And, in this case, the affiliate has already demonstrated itself to be fully capable of absorbing advanced technology as well as astute and successful in entering new markets. . . . It is clear . . . that the agreement has resulted in a further erosion of the U.S. production and technological base.[29]

Where U.S. corporations have exported advanced technology abroad, it is apparent that corporate interest is not necessarily national interest. After a meticulous examination of 25 cases of technology transfer by U.S. firms to noncontrolled foreign enterprises, Baranson argued that his findings "firmly challenge the viewpoint that decisions made by U.S. corporations in their own self-interest regarding the sale of industrial technology coincide with and protect the interests of the U.S. economy."[30] By exporting the latest generation of American technology abroad to highly competent foreign firms which are able to harness these new techniques, U.S. corporations are undermining the international position of the American economy, eroding the U.S. manufacturing base, and contributing to a further loss of production jobs at home.

MEASURES OF DECLINE

Every two years the National Science Board of the National Science Foundation issues *Science Indicators,* a report of the state of science and technology in America and an assessment of U.S. performance compared to other industrial nations.[31] Although the Board makes no overall evaluation of America's international standing, the 1974 and 1976 editions of *Science Indicators* provide considerable evidence that the once-commanding U.S. lead in science and technology is dwindling. In some fields, the U.S. still maintains a formidable lead, as for example in the proportion of Nobel prizewinners who are American or working in the United States. In other areas, however, the U.S. lead is disappearing quickly, and in still others the U.S. has already fallen behind other nations.

Of 500 major technological innovations brought into commercial use between 1953 and 1973 in six advanced industrial countries—electronic beam welding, weather satellites, cryosurgery, oral contraceptives, etc.—the United States, although still far ahead of any other single nation, has accounted for a declining share of all innovations in recent years. At the same time, the U.S. patent balance with ten industrial countries—the number of foreign patents granted to American inventors compared to the number of U.S. patents granted to foreign nationals—has dropped sharply. Between 1966 and 1975 the U.S. patent balance declined 47 percent, as an increasing number of foreign nationals obtained U.S. patents and a decreasing number of Americans received foreign patents. Although still maintaining a positive patent balance with most industrial countries, the U.S. has had a negative patent balance with West Germany since 1969 and with Japan since 1974. The number of U.S. patents obtained by Japanese inventors has increased more than fivefold between 1966 and 1975.

Science Indicators has also noted the falling rate of productivity growth of the U.S. economy, both absolutely and relative to other industrial nations, and the steadily declining proportion of GNP spent on U.S. research and development since the mid-1960s. In research and development as a proportion of GNP, the Soviet Union passed the U.S. in 1970 and greatly exceeds it today. In a related area, the number of scientists and engineers engaged in research and development per 10,000 population declined in the U.S. after 1969 but increased in the European countries studied and in Japan. Again, the Soviet figure passed the U.S. figure in 1969 and now exceeds it by a great margin. Ironically, in terms of our previous discussion, one of the very few "positive" developments noted by *Science Indicators* was a striking increase in the U.S. balance of payments from the sale of patents, licensing agreements, and other large-scale transfers of technology abroad.

NOT ALL FOREIGN COMPETITION IS FOREIGN

Electronic Assembly

"Reduce your electronic and electromechanical assembly costs by 60 percent. Competitive rates from financially sound company with competent technical management. Assistance with U.S. customs problems."

P.O. Box 33
Port-Au-Prince, Haiti

Advertisement in *Electronic News,* March 13, 1978

We have seen in Chapter 3 that foreign competition is creating problems for the American economy. But not all foreign competition is foreign; much of it is now American. Contributing to the stagnation of the American economy is the migration of U.S. multinationals to offshore facilities around the world. Before the 1960s U.S. investment abroad was concentrated in extractive industries such as mining and petroleum. Since the 1960s, U.S. multinationals have invested billions of dollars in offshore manufacturing facilities, closing down factories in the U.S., removing them either to Europe in order to get access to markets there or, more recently, to developing countries where wages are low, trade unions are weak or absent, and, with tax, duty, and foreign subsidy arrangements, costs are a fraction of what they are in the United States. The Bureau of Labor Statistics estimates that New England, the Middle Atlantic, and the Great Lakes states have lost 1.4 million manufacturing jobs since 1966—in apparel, textiles, rubber, auto parts, and electronics.[32] Some of these jobs disappeared, some went South, but many went abroad.

Direct foreign investment of U.S. corporations is massive:

1. By 1976 the book value of U.S. direct foreign investment was $137 billion, up from $75 billion in 1970, $31 billion in 1960, and only $11.6 billion in 1950.[33] By some measures, overseas U.S. investment in the 1970s constituted the third largest economy in the world, after the U.S. itself and the Soviet Union and was undoubtedly one of the fastest growing.

2. In 1974 foreign investment of U.S. manufacturing corporations was 31 percent of their domestic investment, up from 21 percent in the late 1960s. In all fields, investment of U.S. companies in foreign operations was 23 percent of domestic investment in 1974, compared to 16 percent in the 1967–70 period.[34]

3. Because of the scale of these investments, many major U.S. corporations now have an enormous share of their assets outside the country. The U.S. chemical and pharmaceutical industries have about one third of their assets abroad; consumer goods industries, 40 percent; and the U.S. electrical industry, fully 74 percent.[35]

4. In the early 1970s, between 25–30 percent of corporate profits derived from foreign investment. A 1972 study by the U.S. Commerce Department of 300 of the largest multinationals

found that they earned 40 percent of their combined net profits abroad. In 1973 the seven largest U.S. banks earned 40 percent of their profits abroad, up from 23 percent only two years earlier. And in the same year, Sperry Rand, Pfizer, IBM, Hoover, National Cash Register, Gillette, and many others earned 50 percent or more of their profits abroad.[36]

5. Foreign sales reported by U.S. foreign affiliates in 1973 totaled some $300 billion, about three times greater than all U.S. exports. In the same year, the United States imported $9.5 billion worth of manufactured goods produced by U.S.-based multinationals abroad, which amounted to over 20 percent of U.S. manufactured imports.[37]

6. By 1970 employment by U.S. offshore manufacturing subsidiaries reached 17 percent of domestic manufacturing employment, and in the early 1970s, U.S. firms operating overseas employed over five million workers.[38]

Conservative supporters and radical critics of multinational corporations have always disagreed over whether foreign investment helps or harms the host country; but both conservatives and radicals have always believed that foreign investment benefits the investing country. Within the last few years, however, mounting evidence suggests that massive foreign investment abroad may seriously damage the economy of the investing nation by: reducing domestic investment; altering the distribution of income in favor of capital and to the disadvantage of labor; causing a loss of domestic employment and of government tax revenue, especially where tax laws provide incentives for overseas investment (as in the U.S.); speeding the diffusion of economic power and technological know-how abroad; and increasing the domestic market concentration of large firms. Robert Gilpin has argued persuasively that of the two ways of earning foreign exchange, foreign *trade* and foreign *investment,* the former is by far more beneficial to the economic and political interests of the nation. Yet corporate America has clearly moved toward the latter, despite the domestic distortions it has engendered.[39]

In a formidable study done for the Senate Foreign Relations Committee in 1975, economist Peggy Musgrave contended that the major domestic effect of massive U.S. foreign investment has been to increase the inequality of income distribution. She found that much foreign investment does in fact replace domestic investment; it thus reduces domestic capital stock and consequently lowers labor productivity and labor income. On the other hand, foreign investment increases the flow of income to investors because it yields higher returns than does domestic investment. Musgrave concluded:

Our analysis suggests that if the capital accumulated abroad as of 1968 had been invested domestically, labor income after tax would be 4 percent [or $10 billion] larger, while after tax capital income would have been 17 percent [or $8 billion] smaller. This is not an insignificant shift, and a factor which should be allowed for in determining public policy toward foreign investment.[40]

American labor has long been familiar with the domestic runaway shop—the textile firm that flees New England for the antiunion, low-wage South. Since the 1960s this phenomenon has developed on a far vaster scale as we have witnessed the *internationalization* of the runaway shop. In electronics, textiles, apparel, footwear, sporting goods, toys, sheet glass, and myriad other industries, American companies have shut down U.S. plants and reopened them overseas, to manufacture or assemble goods there which are then reexported to the United States. With American labor threatened by these developments, the AFL-CIO declared in a 1975 resolution on multinational corporations:

U.S.-based multinational firms have destroyed and exported the jobs of millions of American workers and have left behind communities devastated by the closing of plants upon which their economies have depended. As far as the multinationals are concerned, U.S. technology, capital, services and even construction are for export to those nations where they can make the greatest profit. . . .

The U.S.-based multinationals and their foreign-based counterparts have brought a new look to the economic, political and industrial scene. They have institutionalized the runaway shop, the runaway ship, the runaway film and have converted them into international facts of life. . . .

The American economy is damaged by this new development. The industrial base that is the heart of our national economy is already seriously eroded. Massive export of U.S. jobs and technology adds to unemployment and economic instability and weakens the nation's ability to cope with the massive domestic problems that now confront us.[41]

Electronics is America's quintessential runaway industry. In 1973 *Fortune* observed that "in no other industry have U.S. corporations moved so much of their manufacturing overseas for the purpose of export back to the American market." As early as 1971 a high proportion of consumer electronics products turned out by American firms were manufactured or assembled abroad: 54 percent of American black and white television sets, 32 percent of phonographs, 91 percent of radios, and 18 percent of color TVs. Today there are virtually no "American" radios or black and white television sets assembled in the United States.

The economics, technology, and politics of the American electronics industry has made the flight of jobs and capital from the U.S. almost irresistible, especially in consumer electronics and component production.[42] The industry is highly competitive, both internationally, where foreign competition is pressing much of the American electronics industry very hard, and domestically as well. The relative ease of entry in many fields and the constant technological innovation, which diffuses quickly and is almost impossible to monopolize, regularly churns up the industry, providing opportunity for new firms and danger for established ones. Electronics is one of the few industries in which capitalism works as theory says it should: competition and technological innovation have driven prices down. A hand-held calculator that sold for $150 in the early 1970s sold for 10 percent of that in the late 1970s; a semiconductor that cost $25 in the mid-1960s cost 15¢ in the late 1970s.

Some of the industry is highly concentrated, as, for example, mainframe computers, where in 1975 the top six firms accounted for 92 percent of all sales (IBM alone accounted for 66 percent of the market). On the other hand, there are thousands of small firms employing less than 100 workers each and with yearly sales of under $5 million, many of which supply component parts for the rest of the industry. Much of the electronics industry, especially component production, is highly labor intensive, and in this regard (measured in assets per employee) electronics is second only to textiles and apparel. Because so much of the industry is both extraordinarily competitive and labor intensive, U.S. firms have been driven to close dozens of factories in the United States, lay off tens of thousands of high-wage American workers, and move plants offshore in a relentless worldwide search for cheaper labor. The runaways include virtually all American producers of radios and television as well as the giants of the semiconductor industry: Texas Instruments, Fairchild, Hewlett-Packard, National Semiconductor, Intel.

U.S. electronics firms established a beachhead in Asia in the 1960s. Fairchild built the first Asian assembly plant in Hong Kong in 1962. Later, other U.S., Japanese, and European firms moved into Hong Kong, Taiwan, and South Korea. Searching for even lower-wage areas, U.S. electronics companies subsequently established offshore operations in Singapore (1969), Malaysia (1972), Thailand (1973), Indonesia, and the Philippines (1974).[43] In the same period, U.S. firms set up assembly operations in Mexico, the Caribbean, and Central and South America.

Technologically, electronics lends itself perfectly to a global division of labor, an international split between head work and hand work; it is a model of the Tayloristic separation of conception from execution writ large. In electronics the assembly line is now not just a few hundred feet long but extends halfway around the world—from "Silicon Valley" in California to Southeast Asia and back again. Sophisticated operations such as design, development, engineering, and testing are done in the U.S., while components are shipped abroad for assembly and then shipped back to the U.S. (or other markets abroad) for sale. Because electronics parts have a high value-to-weight ratio, it is relatively inexpensive, especially considering the savings in labor costs, to ship components between offshore plants and the United States. And it is the savings in labor costs that make it all worthwhile: in the mid-1970s when U.S. electrical workers earned an average of about $4.10 an hour, the average wage in U.S. offshore electronics firms was 17¢ an hour in Indonesia, 26¢ an hour in Thailand, 32¢ an hour in the Philippines, and 62¢ an hour in Singapore.

The paradox of labor in the electronics industry is that while the products themselves are highly sophisticated—computers, calculators, television sets, digital watches—and require highly skilled labor to design and engineer them, the labor to assemble them involves unskilled, repetitive, conveyor-belt operations. Where U.S. electronics firms have penetrated Third World countries, an almost entirely female labor force performs close, tedious, eye-straining labor assembling television receivers, miniature silicon circuit chips, and tiny printed circuit boards. Not only are wages low, but in most of the countries where U.S.-controlled firms operate, unions are either prohibited, feeble, or government-controlled, strikes are illegal, and few if any of the basic International Labor Organization labor standards are observed. As one U.S. businessman in Singapore wrote, "If I had been assigned to write the Singapore labor ordinances, I couldn't have done a better job for my company or any other."[44]

Because of their insatiable quest for cheap labor, most runaway companies "sleep with their shoes on," ready to move at a moment's notice. On the Mexican border where U.S. firms have established dozens of runaways since the 1960s, when militant labor action in 1974–75 began to improve wages and conditions many runaways simply shut down almost literally overnight and moved operations to quieter and lower-wage areas elsewhere. Ironically, labor productivity in U.S. offshore electronics plants in Asia and Latin America often exceeds labor productivity in the United States, as supervision is double and triple that in domestic plants, and factory discipline is reminiscent of the early days of the industrial revolution.[45] Besides the usual discipline, U.S. offshore firms in Asia now employ sophisticated personnel policies among the young Asian female workers which both exploits the attributes of passivity and submissiveness central to women's role in these traditional societies and tempts them with the prospect that their wages can buy the clothes, makeup, style, and glamour associated with Western women.[46]

The U.S. government has encouraged runaways, not only by providing tax loopholes (see below) but by providing customs loopholes, especially the Items 806.30 and 807.00 of the U.S. Tariff Code, which stipulate that intermediate manufactured components shipped abroad for further processing and later returned to the U.S. need pay duty only on the value added. Since the value added consists only of the low wages paid for overseas assembly, customs duty is minimal. In 1973, 1,200 U.S. runaway companies in electronics, apparel, and other fields made use of Items 806/807, and as early as 1969, 8 percent of the value of all U.S. imports consisted of products imported under these provisions of the Tariff Code.[47] Between 1965 and 1975, the value of electronics goods imported from U.S. runaways under Items 806/807 increased from $122 million to $1.2 billion, a tenfold increase in a period in which factory sales of electronics in the U.S. did not quite double.

U.S. runaways have decimated domestic employment in the electronics industry, especially in radio and television manufacturing. Domestic employment in these industries alone declined by some 250,000 between the mid-1960s and the mid-1970s. Meanwhile, although international employment fluctuates considerably depending upon demand, the North American Congress on Latin America (NACLA) estimates that U.S.-based runaways in electronics employ about 500,000 workers in prosperous years in offshore plants around the world.[48]

American workers are further disadvantaged by a pair of ironies associated with U.S. runaways. First, electronics firms have established foreign operations in countries with authoritarian regimes: Indonesia, Malaysia, the Philippines, South Korea, Taiwan, and Thailand. Despite their differences, these countries generally share repressive and anti-union policies which have played a crucial role in keeping wages low. Between 1946 and 1975 the United States granted over $16 billion in military aid to these nations. This military aid, derived in part from taxes on American workers, has been used to strengthen regimes whose anti-labor climate attracts U.S. runaway corporations. These runaway plants lead to the displacement of American workers. The taxes of American workers are thus used to help destroy their own jobs—surely an element of alienated labor worthy of a postscript to Marx's *Economic and Philosophical Manuscripts*. Second, to acquire American capital and technology, some Communist governments now offer the same anti-labor appeal as right-wing authoritarian regimes. Thus, a Polish official lauding the establishment of a Singer plant in Poland boasted that his country offers both cheap labor and "a reliable source of supplies not threatened by industrial conflicts."[49]

U.S. companies operating offshore might turn their lower costs into lower prices for their goods at home. But runaways often prefer to turn low overseas wages into higher earnings for the company rather than into lower prices for the American public. The President of Admiral International said some years ago that assembling color television sets in Taiwan "won't affect prices stateside, but it should improve the company's profit structure. Otherwise we wouldn't be making the move."[50] The markup is simply higher.* Paul Jennings of the International Union of Electrical, Radio, and Machine Workers (IUE) has said that American companies operating overseas have "the best of both worlds. . . . They can hire employees in the lowest labor market of the world at the same time as they are able to sell products of that labor in the highest price market, the USA."[51] A 16-inch black-and-white television set assembled abroad in the 1970s had an import price of $48, Jennings observed, but retailed in American stores for $142.50.

THE DE-INDUSTRIALIZATION OF AMERICA?

We have seen that the loss of domestic production jobs in electronics is occurring in innumerable industries. American industrial dominance in the twentieth century was based fundamentally upon its superior technology. That technological lead, translated into high economic productivity, offset the comparatively high wages paid to American workers. Until recently, the relatively slow international diffusion of technology assured that the American lead would be maintained. But we no longer inhabit a planet whose continents are remote and isolated from one another, a condition which in its time served to retard the spread of technol-

---

* Even that move didn't save this company's television operations from furious "domestic" and foreign competition; in 1979 Admiral went out of the television business.

ogy. The world has indeed assumed the proportions of Marshall McLuhan's "global village," and as our world is now a small, accessible community, there is a vast increase in the pace at which technology diffuses. This is happening for a number of reasons, many of which we have discussed: the speed and ease of global transportation and communication, permitting tremendous mobility of capital and industry; the spread of multinational corporations which can effortlessly transfer technology from one end of the earth to the other; the creation of world markets on a scale never before achieved; the dependence of technology upon universally known scientific principles; the decision of advanced U.S. firms to sell front-end technology abroad. Whatever the cause, the effects are the same—the neutralization of U.S. technological leadership.

As technology spreads and manufacturing is transferred offshore, economist Raymond Vernon's well-known theory of the international product cycle takes on an entirely new meaning. Vernon observed that because of the traditionally high wages of American workers and the huge domestic market, consumer goods as well as advanced labor-saving machinery have typically been produced here first. U.S. manufacturers satisfy the domestic market and generally export to other developed countries and to some developing countries as well. As technology slowly diffuses and products become standardized, manufacture of these products gradually shifts to other developed countries and then to developing countries which produce for their own consumption and for export to the U.S. and elsewhere.[52]

What seems to be happening now is not merely the acceleration of the international product cycle, but the omission of whole stages, as front-end technology and manufacturing are transferred abroad. The gradual diffusion of technology is now being replaced by its almost instantaneous transfer and implantation. A 1978 study for the Joint Economic Committee of Congress, examining the future threat to American industry by foreign imports, found that the United States is rapidly moving into the waters between Scylla and Charybdis. Concretely, the study concluded that the U.S. is "being squeezed between the advanced industrial nations, which have largely eliminated the technological lead that the

United States enjoyed for some 20 years after World War II, and developing nations that are becoming exporters of progressively more sophisticated standardized products." [53]

Having closed the technology gap in most areas, the advanced industrial countries are now beginning to trespass on such heretofore exclusively American preserves as civilian aircraft and computers. The Concorde may have been a commercial failure, but it was a technological symbol, followed by the more practical and competitive European-made Airbus. Meanwhile, younger industrial countries in Asia and Latin America are building their own steel, chemical, and auto industries and are beginning to export advanced manufactured goods to other developing nations and to the industrialized world. The congressional study predicts that the U.S. will be able to retain an unassailable position only in a diminishing number of exotic fields which are either on the outermost technological frontier or which require a huge integrated market for their development—satellite communications and photography, deep-sea mining, and very large-scale electrical generating systems. Aside from these few specialized fields, the prospects are that "the United States will confront intense foreign competition across the full range of manufactured products." [54]

In this industrial competition, America, the industrial giant, finds itself suddenly at a disadvantage. As advanced technology diffuses and becomes internationally more equalized, capital and industry will naturally move to those countries where labor costs are lower. We have seen that in a growing number of industries the U.S. has become a singularly unfavorable place in which to manufacture, because a similar technology is often available elsewhere with a cheaper labor supply. What we are witnessing, therefore, is nothing less than a global redistribution of industry, as manufacturing moves out of high-wage developed nations such as the United States and some European countries, and into lower-wage developing nations. In their analysis of the decline of American steel, economists Helen Shapiro and Steven Volk observed:

The internationalization of capital—the spread of the multinational corporation, the remarkable upsurge in foreign lending by banks, the creation of unregulated, "offshore" money markets—reflects and bolsters a shift in manufacturing in general from the advanced to the underdeveloped capitalist countries; from countries where unions are relatively well developed and wages and conditions relatively high to countries where unions are outlawed, weak or co-opted and wages are abysmally low.[55]

This global shift in manufacturing has enormous consequences for the class structure of advanced countries, particularly the United States. Those on the political left have long contended that "economic imperialism" in the form of foreign investment in underdeveloped countries benefited not only the capitalist class of the investing nations but indirectly the working class as well. Now, as jobs, factories, and technology flow out of the U.S., the new global restructuring of industry is striking a blow at American workers, eliminating countless manufacturing jobs, weakening the labor movement, and intensifying patterns of class stagnation.

Some observers have raised the spectre of an eventual de-industrialization of the United States, as manufactured imports increase and domestic plants flee to offshore facilities. As America's industrial foundation weakens, the country begins to acquire characteristics of a rentier economy—an economy which attempts to live off its investments—with corporate "rentiers" at the top and a nation of service-sector workers—*luftmenschen*—below, unsupported by a wealth-producing manufacturing base. Such a scenario is attractive to many economists at the Harvard Business School and the Brookings Institution, as well as to sectors of American business and some public officials who argue that America must now become, in George Lodge's words, a "service-oriented island in a labor-intensive archipelago." To prosper, they believe, postindustrial America should specialize not in the export of manufactured goods, but in the export of knowledge, technique, capital, and managerial services.

There are enormous perils in overinvestment abroad, however, and both Robert Gilpin and Peggy Musgrave see ominous similarities between America's drift toward the rentier economy and the rentier economy Britain created a century ago. After 1870 British portfolio investment abroad accelerated dramatically. Between 1900 and 1914 British foreign investment rose eightfold, from £25 million to £200 million annually. By the beginning of World War I British investors were sending more than 75 percent of the country's national savings overseas, seeking higher profits than could be earned from the weakening domestic economy. Instead of revitalizing domestic manufactures, British investors chose to pour enormous sums into foreign industries—jute, cotton, iron, steel, paper, tobacco, and engineering. Musgrave writes:

It was during this period that the British terms of trade turned down, domestic capital per head of the population grew at a slow pace and real wages declined slightly. This brought out the underlying conflict between the interests of capital-owners and labor, and much of the pamphlet literature of this period attributed British industrial stagnation and loss of labor productivity to the heavy foreign investment of the period.[56]

Economic historian A. K. Cairncross summarized Britain's experiment as a rentier economy thus: "Foreign investment, it was apparent, might lower the standard of living instead of raising it."[57]

Robert Gilpin has perceptively observed that while massive foreign investment can signify the dynamism of an expanding economy, under other circumstances it reveals the growing weakness of a declining economy. Undoubtedly, the tremendous increase in British portfolio investment toward the end of the nineteenth century signified a lack of profitable investment opportunities at home and the growing noncompetitiveness of British industry. Similarly, it is clear that much U.S. foreign investment today, especially American manufacturing runaways, reveals the growing defensiveness and vulnerability of U.S. industry vis-à-vis European and Japanese competition.[58]

Foreign direct investment by U.S. corporations has distorted both the U.S. economy and American foreign policy in many ways. By exporting its capital, technology, and know-how, the United States has reduced domestic growth in productive capacity and hastened the international shift of economic and political power. In her study of direct investment abroad, Peggy Musgrave concludes that while the *corporate* net rate of return on foreign investment is positive, because of the tax loss to the U.S. Treasury, the *national* net rate of return from foreign investment is negative.

Or, as Robert Gilpin has written, the benefits of foreign investment are private, but the costs are public. Insofar as foreign investment displaces domestic investment, domestic needs are neglected. Resources sent abroad are unavailable for housing, mass transit, energy research, and environmental restoration, as well as for renewing the economic infrastructure and revitalizing industry's aging capital stock. Supporters of multinationals argue that the alternative to foreign investment is not domestic investment but no investment at all, because profitable investment cannot always be made at home. While from their perspective multinationals might not be able to find attractive and profitable investment here, it is certain that democratic planning and control of investment decisions would yield abundant uses for domestic investment. The economic needs of America have not yet been met.

Foreign investment may also increase the domestic concentration of economic power, for only the largest firms are able to invest widely abroad. In the early 1970s, for example, about 60 percent of U.S. overseas assets were owned by just 45 large corporations. Equally important, as Britain discovered decades ago, investor nations are highly dependent on unpredictable political events in the host country and vulnerable to political blackmail. In this regard, John Maynard Keynes himself wrote over a half century ago of the advantage of domestic over foreign investment:

Consider two investments, the one at home and the other abroad, with equal risks of repudiation or confiscation or legislation restricting profit. It is a matter of indifference to the individual investor which he selects. But the nation as a whole retains in the one case the object of the investment and the fruits of it; whilst in the other case both are lost. If a loan to improve South American capital is repudiated, we have nothing. If a Poplar housing loan is repudiated, we as a nation still have the house. If the Grand Trunk Railway of Canada fails its shareholders by reason of legal restriction or rates chargeable or for any other cause, we have nothing. If the Underground System of London fails its shareholders, Londoners still have the Underground System.[59]

Overseas investment also undermines a democratic American foreign policy insofar as it creates vested interests supporting such repressive regimes as South Africa, post-Allende Chile, Taiwan, South Korea, Thailand, and other countries where U.S. multinationals are comfortably ensconced.

As suggested above, Congress has contributed to the depletion of the U.S. economy by providing tax laws which offer economic incentives for U.S. firms to close factories here and move them abroad:

1. In shutting down a domestic plant, a company can write off the old plant against profits elsewhere, deduct the relocation cost as a business expense, include new equipment under the federal investment tax credit, and claim accelerated depreciation for the new equipment.[60]

2. Foreign subsidiaries of U.S. multinationals can *defer* paying U.S. taxes until they return profits to the United States. This amounts to an interest-free loan from the government, encouraging multinationals to retain foreign earnings abroad and reinvest there rather than returning them to the United States.

3. Once profits are returned to the U.S., the foreign tax *credit* allows multinationals to subtract the taxes paid to foreign governments from their U.S. taxes. This is not a "deduction" from taxable income, as when a company deducts state and local taxes from its federal tax liability, but a full dollar-for-dollar tax credit against U.S. taxes. A dollar paid in tax to a foreign government is a dollar less paid to the U.S. government. For energy companies, royalties count as foreign income taxes and can also be credited. By the mid-1970s the tax deferral and tax credit provisions represented a $9 billion loss to the federal government annually.

4. The Domestic International Sales Corporation (DISC) was created in 1971. By its provisions, multinationals can set up dummy companies to transact their export business. Substantial amounts of the profits from these companies are exempt from tax until they are turned over to the parent company—if ever. To qualify for this exemption a corporation need not increase exports; multinationals are allowed to count goods they would have shipped out anyway. DISC also provides incentives to export new technology, machines, and equipment for offshore facilities. By the mid-1970s DISC was costing the U.S. treasury $1.5 billion annually.[61]

These subsidies explain the phenomenally low domestic taxes paid by U.S.-based multinationals. In 1974 U.S.-based corporations paid $1.7 billion in taxes on foreign-source income of $53.6 billion—an effective tax rate of only 3.2 percent. And offshore U.S. manufacturing corporations had an effective tax rate of only 5.6 percent of their new foreign-source income in 1972.[62]

No one questions that U.S. runaways have drastically eliminated jobs in particular industries (electronics, apparel, etc.). The major argument centers around whether foreign investment has caused a *net* loss of jobs, or whether jobs lost in some sectors have been more than made up elsewhere. As on many other foreign investment issues, there is no consensus here, mainly because conclusions depend largely on the assumptions made—whether, for example, capital invested abroad decreases investment at home or supplements it. On the one hand, Seymour Melman estimated that three to four million jobs could have been added to the U.S. economy between 1960 and 1970 if all U.S. foreign investment in manufacturing and other substitutable fields had been invested domestically.[63]

On the other hand, some economists argue that because profits returned to the U.S. from overseas investment currently exceed the capital invested abroad, there is a net return of capital to the country, which generates more employment. But this, too, is controversial. Even if it could be proved that there is a net gain of jobs when an electronics firm moves assembly operations to Mexico and that the loss of electronics jobs in Massachusetts is made up, say, in service jobs in Arizona, the entire burden of dislocation and the costs of readjustment are thrust on the shoulders of the displaced workers and the abandoned communities. In periods of high unemployment, plant closings often mean long periods without work for dismissed employees, especially as plant shutdowns frequently occur in already declining communities. Recent U.S. Labor Department studies, for example, have found that about 40 percent of workers idled by plant closings remain unemployed for two years or more.[64]

The international mobility of capital has given corporations enormous leverage over workers and unions. The threat of closing down and relocating abroad is a formidable weapon, inhibiting organizing drives, undercutting the fight for improved health and safety regulations, and keeping labor generally docile, thankful, and obedient. Also, a company with offshore facilities can ease the effects of a strike by domestic workers by simply increasing production overseas. Finally, insofar as companies that move abroad are those which are unionized and pay high wages, the trade union movement is weakened and U.S. wage rates and living standards are undercut.

THE PENALTY OF TAKING THE LEAD

Amid the chorus of explanations for America's growing economic woes, perhaps we ought to resurrect Thorstein Veblen's ingenious theory of the "penalty of taking the lead," formulated in 1915 to explain the growing weakness of the British economy.[65] Veblen observed that Britain had built the world's first national railway system, which in its time contributed to that country's industrial supremacy. By the turn of the century, however, much of Britain's railway network was obsolete; the tracks were far too narrow-gauge for contemporary needs and the "silly little bobtailed carriages" used for freight which had worked "well enough in their time, before American or German railway traffic was good for anything much, . . . have at the best a playful air when brought up against the requirements of today."[66] Yet the British railway system was not easy to modernize. Piecemeal improvements were difficult because terminals, tracks, roadbed, shunting facilities, engines, and rolling stock were all part of an interdependent system; on the other hand, total replacement of the system was far too costly.

Later in the century when Germany, the United States, Russia, and other nations built their railroad networks, they were able to learn from the leader's—Britain's—mistakes, by adopting a wider gauge, and in general utilizing more modern railroad technology than had been available earlier in the century. Thus Britain, while gaining an initial advantage from taking the lead in railroad construction, ultimately had to pay the penalty of taking the lead in terms of obsolescent facilities that were difficult to bring up to modern standards.*

Veblen argued that what was true of Britain's railway system was becoming true of its entire industrial apparatus. Having been the world's industrial pioneer, Britain found itself saddled with industrial facilities which, though advanced for the period in which they were built, were becoming obsolescent:

Towns, roadways, factories, harbors, habitations, were placed and constructed to meet the exigencies of what is now in a degree an obsolete state of the industrial arts, and they are, all and several, "irrelevant, incompetent and impertinent" in the same degree in which the technological scheme has shifted from what it was when these appliances were installed.[67]

In Veblen's lovely phrase, the British were penalized for the "restraining dead hand of their past achievement." In 1900 British capitalism was still based on the products of the first Industrial Revolution—iron, textiles, and coal—while the U.S. and Germany were moving into the second Industrial Revolution, based on steel,

---

* For a contemporary illustration of the penalty of taking the lead in transportation, compare the rapid transit systems of New York City and San Francisco. The New York subway system is now three quarters of a century old. New Yorkers have thus had the use of a subway system for decades while San Franciscans have not. But New Yorkers have also had to pay a penalty for being the national leader in subway construction, for the city is now saddled with a system that is ancient, decrepit, and obsolete. Meanwhile, the Bay Area Rapid Transit system (BART), built in the late 1960s and 1970s, had all the advantages of a late developer and utilized the latest technology to create a computerized, high-speed, whisper-quiet system out of the twenty-first century that is so pleasant the natives take tourists on it for fun. Few people ride the New York subway for fun. The New York system surely ought to be discarded—junked—and replaced, but it is part of the penalty of taking the lead that the pioneer is stuck with an enormous obsolete investment that is too costly, too cumbersome, too "impractical," and too inconvenient to replace. On the other hand, because BART itself is a late twentieth-century pioneer in urban mass transit, that system has been paying its own penalty of taking the lead—in terms of stubborn bugs, frequent breakdowns, and occasional accidents.

chemicals, and electricity. Britain had ceased to be innovative and was losing ground. In 1870 Britain accounted for nearly one third (32 percent) of the world's manufacturing. By the 1880s Britain's share of manufacturing had fallen to 26 percent and had been outstripped by the United States. Between 1900 and 1910 the British share dropped to under 15 percent and was bypassed by Germany. By 1936–38 Britain accounted for a mere 9 percent of the world's manufacturing output.[68]

Ironically, Veblen's remarks on the British iron industry in 1915, with a few modifications, could apply to the American steel industry in 1980:

Even in such an all-underlying and specifically British line of work as the iron industry, observers from other countries—e.g., German, Swedish or American—have latterly had occasion to find serious and sarcastic fault with the incompetently diminutive blast-furnaces, and antiquated appliances for moving materials, and the out-of-date contrivances for wasting labor and fuel.[69]

A comparison with the current problems of the American steel industry is instructive:

Most of the United States steel facilities were built well before World War II. Given the wide geographical dispersion of customers and the location of iron ore and coal deposits, these plants were built over a wide area extending, for the most part, from Eastern Pennsylvania to Illinois. In addition, the plants tended to be relatively small by today's standards, often crammed into river valleys.

When the new technology of the 1950s and 1960s was introduced, the Japanese and other emerging steel producers could accommodate it in a manner which allowed for balanced materials flow and large-scale operation. Moreover, they were able to build at deepwater ports, thus taking advantage of the sharp decline in shipping costs. The U.S. firms could not easily adapt to the changing technology nor to the sharp decline in ocean-borne shipping costs. Their plants had been designed to accommodate the small blast furnaces and the open-hearth steelmaking of pre-World War II years. For them to replace their iron- and steelmaking facilities and maintain a balanced set of plants was difficult if not impossible. Eventually, open hearths were modernized or replaced by basic oxygen furnaces, but only at some penalty in terms of retirement costs and contorted materials flow. Clearly, the river valleys in the east and midwest would not have their current problems if anyone could have foreseen the developments in modern technology.[70]

Almost all the problems mentioned here—of plant, equipment, size of facilities, and location—stem from America's early lead in steelmaking. Nations the bulk of whose steel industries are of more recent construction have easily avoided the problems the aging American steel industry is heir to. It is clear that latecomers have one crucial advantage: they can stand on the shoulders of the pioneers.

In a period of rapid social change, America has become an aging industrial power overnight; the "new world" is becoming old. By 1968 nearly two thirds (64 percent) of the metalworking machinery in American factories was ten years old or older, in sharp contrast with the much newer factory equipment in West Germany, Japan, and the USSR.[71] Newer industrial countries, those which are building from the ground up or those which have built upon the ashes of World War II, without the great investment in the technological status quo, have been able freely to take advantage of the most recent techniques, as in steel, and can learn from the past mistakes of the leader.

Is it not possible that the deepening problems of the American economy—the decline of productivity gains, the growing noncompetitiveness of American products in world trade, the dissipation of American scientific and technological superiority—are due in part to the fact that America is a "mature" industrial power, burdened with an enormous investment in aging plant, equipment, processes, and technology not easily replaced, and is now being passed by other nations whose industrial facilities are of more recent, and thus more modern, vintage? Is America itself now feeling the "restraining dead hand of its past achievement"?

Veblen's theory of the penalty of taking the lead suggests a continuous rise and fall of nations to positions of world economic leadership, a dynamic of succession in which one nation takes the lead and then decades later, burdened with aging facilities, is leapfrogged by other, newer economies. The passage of world economic leadership in the last century from older to newer industrial powers, from England to Germany to the United States, and now the problems of an aging America suggest that this Veblenian dynamic is operating.*

There are contemporary variations of Veblen's theory which differ in detail but have in common the idea that "new" economic powers are advantaged and "old" economic powers are penalized: Raymond Vernon's product cycle theory; notions of an economic climacteric, whether of the British or American variety; and Robert Gilpin's modern restatement of the hypothesis that there is an

. . . historic tendency of advanced economies to decline industrially relative to their foreign competition. Through the spread of technology and know-how, the industrial leader, over a period of time, loses more and more of its initial comparative advantages relative to its rising competitors. . . . The consequences of this tendency is a gradual redistribution of wealth and poverty within the international system.[72]

FAILURE OF NERVE AT THE TOP

The Conference Board, a business research group, sponsored a series of meetings in 1974–75 with 360 top-level corporate executives from more than 250 of America's largest companies. Over the course of a year these executives held off-the-record conversations and exchanged views on American business frankly, candidly, and privately. Leonard Silk, business writer for the *New York Times,* and David Vogel, professor of business administration at the University of California at Berkeley, attended these sessions and wrote a revealing account of the conference.[73]

A pervasive feeling of gloom about the prospects for capitalism ran through these meetings. It is true that 1974–75 was a period of unusual economic difficulty for the United States. Yet missing

---

* Veblen's theory of the penalty of taking the lead obviously also applies to regional developments within a nation. We witness, for example, the decline of the aging American Northeast, America's first industrial region, now unattractive to capital for a number of reasons associated with its age and obsolescence, and the rise of the new industrial Sun Belt.

from the meetings was the traditional American optimism under adversity, courage before a challenge, and the familiar American can-do philosophy.* There was a sense, as one executive phrased it, that "America is capitalism's last chance," and there was widespread anxiety about the fragility of American capitalism itself.

In the words of high-level executives of some of America's leading corporations:

The American capitalist system is confronting its darkest hour.

At this rate business can soon expect support from the environmentalists. We can get them to put the corporation on the endangered species list.

There is a hole in the ship of free enterprise, and I see torpedoes ahead.

We should not be misled by the appearance of a light at the end of the tunnel. It is probably an oncoming train.

Americans are learning for the first time in the postwar period that a high standard of living is not guaranteed.[74]

Some saw in the decline of Britain the imminent scenario for the United States:

We are following England to disaster, trying to beat them where they are going.

We are heading to the basement to join Great Britain.

England is our future over the next decade.[75]

---

* Despite traditional American business optimism, Robert Heilbroner writes that throughout the history of world capitalism, its most fervent ideological supporters have exhibited manic-depressive symptoms. Heady exuberance alternates with gloom and despair because supporters of the system have never been able to repress completely the knowledge that capitalism's perennial problems—boom and bust, unemployment, inflation, depression—have never been and probably never can be solved, and they have historically been unable to quell that queasy feeling that, however well it seems to be working, the system may, at any unpredictable moment, collapse. (See Robert L. Heilbroner, "Boom and Crash," *The New Yorker,* August 28, 1978.)

These attitudes were perhaps best symbolized at the end of the 1970s when America's two foremost business publications, *Fortune* and *Business Week*, ran cover stories on the decline of American power: *Fortune*'s story, an assessment of U.S. and Soviet military strength with the remarkable title "What It's Like to Be Number Two" and *Business Week*'s on "The Decline of U.S. Power," with its cover showing the Statue of Liberty in tears.[76] The objective signs of American decline are being paralleled by a subjective loss of confidence and failure of nerve at high levels. When a dominant class begins to lose confidence in its own system, surely that system is in trouble.

CHAPTER FIVE

Divergence

INFLATION

Dominant postwar opinion held that a growing egalitarianism in American society was narrowing the gap between classes, creating a pattern of class convergence. Other postwar writers disputed this claim and contended that while all classes were moving up that inclined plane, the distance between classes was not narrowing, producing what I have termed class stability. Contrary to the assumptions of both models of the postwar American class structure, however, in the recent period the living standards of the American people considered as a whole have stagnated or even declined. In this chapter I shall argue that there is now a growing body of evidence not merely that living standards have ceased to rise but that within the stagnation there has been an actual widening of the gap between strata, producing what I have called *class divergence*. This pattern might be illustrated roughly as follows, and suggests that the upper strata are generally holding their own while the lower strata decline, thus increasing actual inequality.

Patterns of class divergence, to the extent that they are now in fact developing, are based fundamentally on the high rates of inflation in the U.S. in the last decade and the differential effect which this inflation has upon the living standards of the various classes. Although unanticipated by postwar American economists, inflation has become central to the current crisis of American capitalism. Unexpectedly and without precedent, the rate of inflation has increased dramatically in recent years compared to the earlier postwar period. From 1950 to 1965, the consumer price index (CPI) rose at an average annual rate of only 1.9 percent. During the late 1960s, the inflation rate more than doubled, rising an average of 4.3 percent annually. Then in the decade of the 1970s prices leaped upwards again, rising an average of 7.5 percent a year. Of course, price increases in some years greatly exceeded these averages. Inflation in the 1960s peaked at 6 percent in the final year of the decade, but by the standards prevailing since the late 1970s that rate now seems refreshingly low. After a brief decline in the early 1970s, the inflation rate hit double digits, over 12 percent, in 1974. Although price increases began to moderate subsequently, they began moving upward again in the late 1970s, rising 9 percent in 1978. This rate was soon eclipsed by the events of 1979 when, paced by the extraordinary increase in energy costs, prices rose over 13 percent, the highest increase since 1946, when wartime price controls were removed.

To halt this inflation, three administrations in the 1970s—Republican and Democratic—pulled out their entire bag of economic tricks, but except for short periods, they all failed: "wage/price controls (1971–74), wage/price guidelines (1978–79), recessions (1969–70, 1973–75), budget cuts (1973, 1979), high interest rates (1973–74, 1978–79), and attacks on health and safety regulations (1975–79)."[1] By the late 1970s inflation had clearly become the nation's most serious problem, both for the public, as reflected in periodic opinion polls, and for the Carter Administration. And virtually all economists agreed that the chronic inflation of the 1970s would not soon abate but would be a continuing and intractable characteristic of the American economy for years to come.

Contemporary inflation in the U.S. is both quantitatively and qualitatively different from inflation in most previous eras of American history. The period ending in the late 1970s produced one of the highest sustained rates of inflation the country had ever experienced, as the consumer price index doubled in only eleven years from 1967 to 1978. Before 1967, by contrast, prices had not doubled for 45 years. The consumer price index, which stood at about 50 in 1922, did not reach 100 until 1967, but hit 200 in 1978. Throughout most of American history, moreover, periods of rising prices have been followed by periods of falling prices. In our time, however, prices have moved in only one direction. Because we live in a world in which inflation seems to be a fact of daily life, it is difficult to comprehend that the general drift of prices in the U.S. during the nineteenth century was downward. Although prices increased sharply during the War of 1812 and during the Civil War, there was a secular decline of prices throughout the nineteenth century; and, testifying to the effectiveness of an unconcentrated and more competitive economy, wholesale price levels were actually lower in 1900 than they were in 1800.[2]

Many economists argue that contemporary inflation is also qualitatively different from the inflation of the past, that it is no longer merely a matter of excess demand that can be easily dampened by holding wages down, increasing unemployment, and cutting the budget or the money supply, but is a function of structural changes in the U.S. and world capitalist economies. In an important work, Leslie Ellen Nulty was among the first to argue that the 1970s ushered in a "new inflation" caused by global demographic, structural, and resource problems related to scarcities of energy, food, land, and other vital materials.[3] Contemporary inflation is fueled by the cartelization of the earth's shrinking energy supplies, the rising demand for U.S. grain in a more populous and affluent world, and housing shortages generated in part by the increasing demand of a growing population in the context of shortages of desirable land. Such inflation can no longer be remedied by the typical fiscal and monetary measures employed by governments in the Western capitalist world.

The concentration of economic power in America has also

played a role in the underlying inflationary trends of the twentieth century. According to the economic gospel of capitalism, the impersonal forces of the market ably serve to control inflation. Textbooks explain that in the marketplace of competitive capitalism, many sellers confront many buyers, and as each seller accounts for only a small share of the market, no one firm can control or manipulate prices. Sellers compete by price in order to gain additional customers, and buyers are protected against arbitrary price increases, for if one seller raises prices, buyers can turn elsewhere.

The most important reality about the American economy, however, has little or nothing to do with this "rhetoric of competition," as C. Wright Mills called it. The overriding reality is that the American economy is dominated by a few hundred corporate giants which represent a tiny fraction of all firms and yet occupy the center of the economic stage. The "commanding heights" of American capitalism—in manufacturing, energy, transportation, communication, banking, and insurance—do not operate in markets where many sellers confront many buyers but where few sellers confront many buyers. In an economy where the largest 200 manufacturing corporations (.001 percent of the total) control about 60 percent of all manufacturing assets and employ nearly two thirds of all manufacturing workers, where the big three, four, six, or eight account for the majority of sales of a particular product or service, the competitive system is transformed, the impersonal market is destroyed, and price competition virtually disappears.[4] Without any formal collusion, the few firms in an oligopolistic industry confront an enormous number of unorganized buyers and gain control over prices. As Galbraith observed, each firm realizes in pursuing profit that price competition is both senseless and unnecessary. Competition then shifts away from price to product design, marginal product differentiation, and advertising image.

Having gained control over prices, oligopolistic firms need not reduce prices in the face of declining demand, as should normally occur in a competitive market. A major reason why fiscal and monetary policies designed to reduce demand and thus moderate prices failed to control inflation in the 1970s is that declining demand leads to lower prices only in competitive markets. In markets where oligopolies prevail, declining demand is likely to produce not lower prices but lower sales, then reduced production, then ultimately higher unemployment. The coincidence of high unemployment and high inflation during the 1970s—stagflation— is testimony that the market no longer works according to theory.

During the Great Depression, economist Gardiner C. Means conducted his now-classic studies of the pricing behavior of oligopolistic firms. He discovered that, compared to unconcentrated industries, prices in concentrated industries are far more inflexible and decrease far more slowly (if at all) when demand declines. In concentrated industries, Means argued, what we get are not market prices but "administered" prices. Despite vigorous attempts by many economists over the years to disprove Means's findings, the noted economist John M. Blair concluded after an examination of the literature that, "Neither the theoretical criticism nor the attempts at empirical refutation have cast any serious doubt on Means's original observations." [5]

In a recent study reminiscent of those conducted by Means, economists Howard M. Wachtel and Peter D. Adelsheim examined the pricing behavior of firms in industries with high, medium, and low concentration ratios during five postwar U.S. recessions. [6] They found that in four of the five recessions a majority of firms in highly concentrated industries were able to stonewall declining demand and *raise* prices, presumably in order to maintain a targeted rate of profit in the face of declining sales. Thus, recession and inflation ironically coexist; in fact, in a highly concentrated economy recession generates inflation as oligopolistic firms raise prices in order to offset declining sales. Wachtel and Adelsheim also found that although firms in industries with medium and low concentration ratios were less likely than firms in highly concentrated industries to raise prices during recessionary periods, the trends over the years showed that an increasing proportion of these firms raised prices also.*

---

* If economic concentration is a fundamental cause of inflation, then how can we explain the low rates of inflation during the 1950s when the economy was only slightly less concentrated? Galbraith speculates in part that corporations had not yet learned how easily they could pass the costs of wage settlements on to the public. Also, wage increases won by work-

If in the postwar period America needed a social psychology of affluence, in the current period America needs a social psychology of inflation, tools to aid in understanding the psychic distress arising from continuously increasing prices. Although the economics of contemporary inflation has been laboriously studied, its social psychology has been inadequately treated. Among the components of a social psychology of inflation is, first, the weakening of traditional economic values. In an inflationary economy, where debtors win and creditors lose, the traditional Protestant Ethic virtues—saving money, building a bank account, avoiding debt, deferring material gratification—no longer make sense and are, in fact, economically unwise. Confusion and disillusion with conventional values inevitably develop. This normative disintegration is compounded by what might be termed the Las Vegas syndrome. Citizens observe that success and economic security no longer depend on the usual virtues of hard work and saving, but on inflationary currents over which they have no control, as well as on personal luck, chance, and caprice—the accidental windfalls of home ownership, for example. The anomie characteristic of a gambling casino develops throughout the society.

Long-term inflation also creates a mood of economic injustice. Workers see their wage increases as the just rewards for hard work, talent, and ingenuity. Rising prices are not only outside their control but are perceived as something which cheats them of the rewards they have earned and rightfully deserve. Aggravating this, the perception of inflation is apt to be even worse than its reality. Inflation is continuous and constant. Prices go up all around and all the time. Wages, on the other hand, may go up once a year, perhaps even less. The daily assault of inflation seems to be inadequately met by an annual increase in pay. One is always behind and trying to catch up.[7]

Inflation also generates a sense of economic rootlessness, a feeling that one is living in a constantly changing, hostile, and unpredictable world. Well-ordered lives with futures planned through

ers in the 1950s were offset by substantial gains in productivity. With productivity growth currently low, corporations must either absorb the cost of wage settlements or pass these costs on to the public. They much prefer to do the latter.

retirement now become endangered as the value of the dollar diminishes and savings steadily shrink. Fear begins to filter into previously well-planned lives. Aside from the obvious economic benefits of stable prices, there is something psychologically reassuring about prices that are constant from year to year, a feeling of security when one can always count on knowing the price of a loaf of bread, a gallon of gasoline, a ticket to the movies. Such stability contributes to one's sense of familiarity, comfort, and *Gemeinschaft* in the marketplace. Constantly rising prices, on the other hand, undermine that community and create a sense that one is a continual stranger in a marketplace where everyone is grabbing for more in a milieu of permanently inflationary greed. The social fabric begins to unravel on the exhausting treadmill to keep up.

Lurking just beneath the surface at the beginning of the 1980s was the dread of runaway inflation, the plague that has swept across nations and not only brought down governments but destroyed political systems and created social chaos. Hyperinflation—a phenomenon best described not by economists but by specialists in collective behavior. As the new decade began and price increases mounted, inflation was beginning to pass from the realm of a serious economic problem to a potential social crisis.

We noted that the theory of class divergence is based on the differential effects of contemporary inflation upon various income strata. These effects are played out somewhat differently in the consumption of necessities and in the consumption of non-necessities.

CLASS DIVERGENCE IN NECESSITIES

To understand the differential impact of inflation upon various classes in the realm of necessities, one must first understand what is known as Engel's Law. This celebrated proposition derives not from Marx's colleague, Frederich Engels, but from the nineteenth-century German statistician Ernst Engel, who studied the family budgets of Belgian workers in the 1850s. From these studies Engel observed that lower-income groups spend a high proportion of their income on food. Specifically, Engel stated that there is an inverse relation between income and the fraction of that income a family spends on food: as income falls, the proportion of income a family spends on food rises. A contemporary illustration of Engel's Law can be seen in Table 29, taken from a study of 5,000 families conducted by the University of Michigan's Institute for Social Research. In 1972, families in the lowest income decile spent over 40 percent of their income on food. As income rose, the proportion spent on food declined consistently; at the highest decile, families spent less than 11 percent of their income on food.

Table 29. FOOD EXPENDITURE AS A PROPORTION OF INCOME, BY INCOME DECILE, 1972

Income Decile	*% of Income Spent on Food*[a]
Lowest	40.1%
Second	31.1
Third	25.1
Fourth	21.2
Fifth	19.1
Sixth	17.5
Seventh	15.8
Eighth	14.0
Ninth	13.1
Highest	10.8
Average	22.8%

SOURCE: Greg J. Duncan, "Food Expenditure Changes between 1972 and 1974," in Greg J. Duncan and James N. Morgan, eds., *Five Thousand American Families—Patterns of Economic Progress,* Vol. IV (Ann Arbor, Mich.: Institute for Social Research, University of Michigan, 1976), Table 7.4, p. 208.

[a] Includes expenditures on food at home and in restaurants. For food stamp users, the money spent for stamps is included in the expenditure figures but not the bonus value of the stamps.

Engel's Law applies not merely to food but in fact to most of the basic necessities. In her monograph on the new inflation, Leslie Ellen Nulty chose four items from the consumer price index that she considered the fundamental necessities: food, shelter, energy, and medical care.* Table 30 shows clearly that the proportion of income spent on each of these necessities, and on all necessities together, generally rises as income falls. As a rule, families in the lower strata spend a substantially greater share of their income on basic necessities than do others. In fact, the lowest income groups spend virtually all, or even more than all (incurring debts), of their income on the basic necessities. Most important, because the forces of the new inflation have struck with great severity at food, fuel, housing, and medical care, the cost of the basic necessities has been rising much faster than the cost of everything else. In 1976, for example, the consumer price index for all necessities was 182 (1967 = 100), compared to 154 for non-necessities. On an annual basis between 1970–76 the cost of necessities rose 44 percent faster than the cost of non-necessities—7.5 percent compared to 5.2 percent respectively. As Nulty observed, inflation has not primarily struck such luxury items as "air fares, electric toothbrushes and yachts," but food, housing, and energy, goods on which the lower strata spend the bulk of their income.

The trends that Nulty traced to 1976 continued into the late 1970s. In fact, the inflation gap between necessities and other goods has been widening. Between 1973 and 1977 the cost of necessities rose more than 40 percent faster than the cost of non-necessities. In 1978 the price of necessities increased about two thirds faster than non-necessities. But in the last year of the decade, inflation in the necessities (17.6 percent) was nearly three times the inflation in everything else (6.8 percent). The crucial fact, therefore, is that inflation has become most severe precisely in those areas that affect the lower strata disproportionately. This can readily be seen by examining the effects of inflated food prices

* Although Nulty's 1977 monograph was prepared for and published by the fairly obscure National Center for Economic Alternatives in Washington, D.C., her dichotomy between inflation in the necessities and the non-necessities was picked up by the daily press and has since become part of the national vocabulary in discussions of contemporary inflation.

Table 30. EXPENDITURES ON BASIC NECESSITIES AS A PERCENTAGE OF NET FAMILY INCOME, BY INCOME TENTHS, 1973–1974[a]

Expenditure as % of Net Income	Bottom 10%	Second 10%	Third 10%	Fourth 10%	Fifth 10%	Sixth 10%	Seventh 10%	Eighth 10%	Ninth 10%	Highest 10%
Food	107.6%	44.2%	32.8%	28.2%	26.1%	24.7%	22.2%	19.1%	17.6%	15.5%
Energy	41.7	17.7	14.1	12.2	10.6	10.5	9.6	8.2	7.4	6.1
Shelter	105.2	37.0	23.1	19.0	18.4	16.6	14.6	11.4	10.9	12.2
Medical Care	29.4	12.7	9.8	7.9	7.0	6.2	5.6	4.3	4.0	4.6
ALL NECESSITIES	284%	111.6%	79.8%	67.3%	62.2%	58.0%	52.1%	42.9%	39.9%	38.4%

SOURCE: Leslie Ellen Nulty, *Understanding the New Inflation: The Importance of the Basic Necessities* (Washington, D.C.: Exploratory Project for Economic Alternatives, 1977), pp. 55–56. The original data was taken from Bureau of Labor Statistics, *Consumer Expenditure Survey*, especially the Diary Survey, 1973–74.

[a] Net family income was computed by deducting from gross income all taxes, personal insurance and pension payments, gifts, and other contributions.

[b] On the enormous excess of expenditures over income in the poorest income tenth, Nulty comments that the original data probably understate gross family income and overestimate expenses for personal insurance, pensions, gifts, and contributions.

during the early 1970s upon different income groups (see Table 31).

Between 1972 and 1974 food prices increased very sharply. The consumer price index for food (1967 = 100) jumped from 124 in 1972 to 162 in 1974, probably the largest two-year increase in U.S. history. The differential effect of this kind of inflation is most apparent when comparing the experience of the lowest with the highest income deciles. In this period the lowest decile increased the proportion of its expenditures on food by over 16 percent, the highest by only 5.6 percent. Expressed another way, the lowest decile increased the fraction of its income spent on food by 6.5 percentage points, the highest by only .6 percentage points. Al-

Table 31.   FOOD EXPENDITURE AS A PROPORTION OF INCOME, BY INCOME DECILE, 1972 AND 1974

Income Decile	% of Income Spent on Food[a] 1972	1974	% Increase 1972–1974	Percentage Point Increase 1972–1974
Lowest	40.1%	46.6%	16.2%	6.5%
Second	31.1	32.7	5.1	1.6
Third	25.1	28.0	11.5	2.9
Fourth	21.2	22.4	5.6	1.2
Fifth	19.1	20.8	8.9	1.7
Sixth	17.5	18.9	8.0	1.4
Seventh	15.8	17.6	11.4	1.8
Eighth	14.0	14.9	6.4	.9
Ninth	13.1	14.3	9.1	1.2
Highest	10.8	11.4	5.5	.6
Average	20.7%	22.8%	10.1%	2.1%

SOURCE: Computed from Greg J. Duncan, "Food Expenditure Changes between 1972 and 1974," in Greg J. Duncan and James N. Morgan, eds., *Five Thousand American Families—Patterns of Economic Progress,* Vol. IV (Ann Arbor, Mich.: Institute for Social Research, University of Michigan, 1976), Table 7.4, p. 208.

[a] Includes expenditures on food consumed at home and in restaurants. For food stamp users, money spent for the stamps is included in the expenditure figures but not the bonus value of the stamps.

though differences among the intermediate strata are not as great and there are individual reversals of the general pattern, it is nonetheless true that the bottom half of income earners had to increase their expenditures on food more sharply than did the top half of income earners during this period of rapidly rising food prices.

Since the lower strata spend a greater share of their income on necessities and since the cost of necessities has been rising faster than the price of non-necessities, lower-income groups are obviously hit unequally hard by inflation. Forced to spend a disproportionately increasing share of their income on necessities, the lower strata are left with considerably less discretionary income for other consumer goods, thus actually widening the gap in living standards between themselves and higher strata.

If inflation since the 1970s has in fact hit the poor more severely than others, this represents a dramatic change in the impact of inflation over previous decades. In 1972 economists Robinson G. Hollister and John L. Palmer examined the effects on the poor of the moderate inflation in the postwar years 1947–67.[8] They constructed a "poor man's price index" based on the expenditure patterns of the poor and compared it with changes in the overall consumer price index. For this period their poor person's price index rose slightly more slowly than did the national consumer price index. This is not surprising since the prices of food, housing, and energy, three of the four basic necessities on which the poor spend the bulk of their income, rose more slowly during these decades than did the consumer price index itself. Moreover, inflation during the 1947–67 period was usually accompanied by a brisk economy, full employment, and tight labor markets, as predicted by the Phillips curve. Hollister and Palmer thus argued that what the poor might have lost to inflation was more than made up by lower unemployment rates, large-scale movement from part-time to full-time work, and a narrowing of wage differentials between the poor and the non-poor.

Generalizing from the 1947–67 experience, Hollister and Palmer wrote that "the poor as a whole must be gaining both absolutely and relatively in economic well-being during periods in which inflationary processes operate."[9] Inflation seemed to be consistent with a gradual trend toward class convergence.

The experience of the 1970s, however, marks a decisive break with earlier postwar inflation. First, as noted, because the inflation of the 1970s disproportionately hit basic necessities (on which the lower strata spend the bulk of their income), it is no longer true that prices for the poor are increasing more slowly than prices for everyone else. Second, while inflation might have benefited the poor in the earlier postwar period because it was usually accompanied by full employment, in the 1970s very high unemployment coexisted with very high inflation. Thus, whatever indirect benefits the poor might previously have derived from inflation are now gone. The peculiar perversity of the American economy since the 1970s, in fact, is that with the combination of hyperinflation in the necessities and general stagflation (high unemployment with inflation) the poor now suffer through *both* inflation and recession.

Actually, by the standards of Engel's Law alone, the level of living of most Americans may be said to have fallen. Engel's Law implies that the poor spend a greater share of their income on necessities than do the prosperous. Because the prices of such necessities as housing and energy are increasing much faster than most persons' income, and because most persons are consequently spending a much larger share of their income on these necessities, the majority of the population may be said to have become poorer.

Also, because of the sharp inflation of food prices in the 1970s, there was a widespread decline in the consumption of some high-status, high-priced foods. In 1975 the Harris Poll asked consumers whether they were buying more, less, or the same amount of a number of food products compared to five years earlier. Table

Table 32. "COMPARED TO FIVE YEARS AGO, ARE YOU NOW BUYING MORE, THE SAME, OR LESS OF THE FOLLOWING PRODUCTS?"

	Buying More	Buying the Same	Buying Less	Don't Buy	Total
Steak	14%	31%	46%	9%	100%
Hamburger	40%	39%	15%	6%	100%

SOURCE: Adapted from Louis Harris Poll, 1975.

32 shows that in the face of steeply rising costs of beef a large number of consumers underwent a kind of culinary downward mobility from more expensive steak to less expensive hamburger.

CLASS DIVERGENCE IN NON-NECESSITIES

In the 1970s a large number of anecdotal but significant indications of class divergence began to appear. I shall discuss some illustrative material first, then move to sociological evidence confirming a pattern of class divergence, and finally discuss what is perhaps the most crucial aspect of the emerging pattern of class divergence—the widening class gap in home ownership.

We have seen that the inflated price of necessities is widening the gap between social strata. Another component of class divergence is the unequal manner in which chronic inflation in the price of non-necessities affects the living standards of different strata. Under inflationary conditions the consumption of necessities tends to be relatively inelastic for all classes (even the poor must buy food, use gasoline to get to work, pay the rent, etc.), but the consumption of non-necessities is highly elastic. It is not equally elastic for all classes, however.

This aspect of the theory of class divergence is based upon the elementary principle of supply and demand. We know that the quantity of any item sold depends on its price. Generally, as the price of an item rises, fewer are sold; demand falls off. But why should this be true? It is true partly because as prices increase, a sector of the population can no longer afford to buy; and that part of the population first affected by rising prices is the poor. As prices rise, the lower strata are slowly priced out of the market; if prices continue to rise, the middle-income groups find themselves unable to buy; only if prices rise still further do the upper strata withdraw from the marketplace. To take a familiar example, at an auction the rich man can continue bidding long after the poor man has had to drop out. As the economists say, the demand curve of the poor is more elastic than the demand curve of the affluent.

In an inflationary economy the lower strata are much more

demand-elastic for many goods because, first, a greater share of their income goes for necessities, and second, they simply do not have the resources to pay inflated prices. Of course, if income is rising as fast or faster than prices, then price increases will not have this differential effect. In the current period, because prices for many goods are rising faster than income, the lower strata have been compelled to reduce their living standards much more sharply than the upper strata. This contributes to an additional widening of the gap between classes, creating a broad pattern of class divergence.

To continue the example used earlier, if the price of steak rises from $4 to $15 per pound, the rich may cut back slightly, but the rest of the population may have to switch from steak to hamburger (or spaghetti) altogether. This example bears investigation and will link class divergence in necessities and in non-necessities. In the 1975 Harris Poll presented in Table 32, a great many Americans reported that they were buying less steak than they had five years earlier. This reduction did not take place equally among all strata, however; lower-income groups reported a much greater reduction in steak purchases than did higher-income groups.* Table 33 reveals that 57 percent of the lower-income group reported buying less steak in 1975 than in 1970, compared to only 39 percent of the higher-income group. Moreover, 54 percent of the higher-income group reported buying as much or more steak than five years earlier, compared to only 26 percent of the lower-income group. If the pattern found here is typical, it suggests, first, that the traditional dietary differences between upper and lower strata are now widening, and second, that the greater elasticity of demand among the lower strata for non-necessities of all kinds is creating an overall pattern of growing inequality in American society.

This pattern can be seen in a variety of ways. If the price of a short European vacation increases, say, from $700 to $3,000, the

* The year 1975 was a time of both severe unemployment (8.5 percent) and of inflation (7 percent). It is possible that the class divergence seen here arose not so much from inflation as from the differential effects of recession. Data discussed later focus exclusively on the differential effects of inflation.

Table 33. SELF-REPORTED CHANGE IN STEAK PURCHASES, 1970–1975, BY INCOME

| | *1975 Gross Household Income* | | |
	Under $5,000	Over $15,000	Total
Reported buying more in 1975	6%	17%	14%
Reported buying the same in 1975	20	37	31
Reported buying less in 1975	57	39	46
Don't buy steak	12	7	9
Miscellaneous responses	5	—	—
TOTAL	100%	100%	100%

Source: Adapted from data provided by Louis Harris and Associates, New York, 1975.

rich will continue to fly first class, but the rest—even the middle class, formerly used to inexpensive charter flights to a Europe which was manageable on $5 a day—will be spending more vacations closer to home.

During the summer of 1974, a time of double-digit inflation and high unemployment, when the University of Michigan's Survey Research Center index of consumer sentiment was heading toward an all-time low and when many Americans were taking shorter and cheaper vacations than ever before—or none at all—travel agents specializing in vacations for the rich claimed it was business as usual—or better. "They are not cutting back," said one agent that year, noting that his clients were routinely spending $4,000 to $8,000 for a summer vacation for two. In a report on the expensive Mauna Kea Beach Hotel in Hawaii, owned by Laurence Rockefeller, where at the time a suite cost $270 a night and a family of four could easily spend $2,000 for a week, not including air fare to the island, the manager claimed that 1974 was the hotel's best summer ever. According to the report, "While most of the nation's travel industry has been experiencing a slump, apparently due largely to public anxiety about high prices, the Mauna Kea has frequently had to turn away business."[10] While inflation for the rich often merely means slightly larger subtraction problems in their checkbooks, for the lower strata, already afflicted with unavoidable higher prices for necessities, it means drastic cutbacks in living standards.

Ford Drives a Lincoln

The pattern of automobile sales in the mid-1970s also illustrates how high rates of inflation can increase class inequality. The 1973 model year was the best in the history of the U.S. auto industry to date, with sales of more than 11,350,000. The Yom Kippur War of October 1973, however, created havoc in Detroit. Not only did gasoline prices rise after the Arab oil embargo, but with gas lines and shortages it was uncertain whether gasoline would be available at any price. Worse yet, as part of the general inflationary spiral in 1974, Detroit raised automobile prices very sharply, not only at the beginning of the model year—the usual practice—but several times during the year itself, establishing what has now become a common pattern. Accordingly, auto sales in 1974 fell 18 percent from 1973.

Bad as auto sales were in 1974, they were worse in 1975. In that year, Detroit raised prices both in dollar and percentage terms more sharply than at any other time in the history of the industry. As a consequence, auto sales in 1975 declined another 20 percent over 1974. Yet by 1975 some things had changed. The flow of oil from the Mideast had resumed, the lines at the gasoline stations had disappeared, and gasoline supplies were assured, although at a much higher price. In 1975, then, guaranteed an ample supply of fuel, potential car buyers were deterred only by the extraordinarily high price of new automobiles compared with their cost just two years earlier. If we examine the pattern of automobile sales for the inflationary year 1975 and compare the sales of *luxury cars* with *non-luxury cars,* we can get some sense of the way in which high rates of inflation widen the gap between classes and generate greater inequality. Table 34 reveals that at General Motors, Chevrolet sales fell more than 23 percent from 1974 to 1975, while Cadillac sales increased 9 percent. At Ford Motor, the sale

Table 34. CLASS DIVERGENCE: 1975 DO-
MESTIC AUTO SALES AS A PERCENT-
AGE OF 1974 SALES

	1975/1974 Model Year
General Motors	
Chevrolet	−23.8%
Cadillac	+9.3
Ford Motor	
Ford	−28.6
Lincoln	+8.4
All U.S. Luxury Cars	+7.0
All U.S. Non-luxury Cars	−20.9
TOTAL DOMESTIC SALES	−19.7%

SOURCE: Adapted from *Automotive News,* April 28, 1977, pp. 23–24.

of Fords decreased nearly 29 percent while the sale of luxury Lincolns rose over 8 percent. During a year when total domestic auto sales declined more than 20 percent, luxury car sales increased 7 percent, even though the price of luxury cars at this time had increased to $10,000 and more.* Despite inflation, then, the affluent were undeterred and continued to buy, despite the general retrenchment in automobile sales.

Sales of foreign cars showed the same pattern in 1975. Although sales of imports increased in 1975 because of public de-

* Obviously, from year to year there are discrepancies between the sales of luxury and ordinary cars, but there have virtually never been differences of this magnitude. Is it possible, however, that the 1975 gain in luxury car sales simply made up for a steeper fall in sales of these cars during the energy crisis of 1974 and that the 1975 increase merely represented normal recovery? This hypothesis is not borne out. While luxury car sales did decline somewhat more than all others in 1974, 22 percent compared to 18 percent, the sales difference in 1974 is not sufficient to explain the much larger discrepancy in 1975.

mand for economical transportation and improved gasoline mile-age, the high priced luxury imports made greater gains than the economy imports, even though the former had increased tremen-dously in cost (see Table 35). While foreign cars in operation increased less than 13 percent in 1975, BMWs increased more than 29 percent, Mercedes more than 18 percent, and Rolls Royce more than 19 percent (although the total number of the latter was obviously small). The affluent continued to buy and were ap-parently impervious to dramatic price increases; in the mid-1970s, for example, Mercedes were selling for as much as $22,000. These figures are, of course, merely suggestive. But they do seem to in-dicate that the higher-income groups have great resiliency of de-mand and that the high rates of inflation afflicting the American economy require much greater retrenchment among lower-income groups, thus widening the gulf in living standards between higher and lower strata.

There are, however, other possible explanations for the di-vergence in sales between luxury and non-luxury cars in 1975. That year was one not only of inflation but of recession, unem-ployment, and uncertainty, which affected the working class and the poor disproportionately. Yet recession was not necessarily the major reason for the difference between sales of luxury and non-luxury automobiles. For example, during the five previous post-

Table 35.   CLASS DIVERGENCE: 1975 FOR-EIGN CARS IN OPERATION IN THE U.S. AS A PERCENTAGE OF 1974 FOREIGN CARS IN OPERATION

	1975/1974 Model Year
BMW	+ 29.4%
Jaguar	+ 12.8
Mercedes Benz	+ 18.2
Rolls Royce	+ 19.1
ALL FOREIGN MAKES	+ 12.7%

SOURCE: *Automotive News*, April 28, 1976, p. 54.

war recessions the spread between the sales of luxury and non-luxury cars was only a fraction of the spread in 1975.

While it is true that the sale of non-luxury cars fell in 1975, the sale of these cars in 1976 caught up with and exceeded the sale of luxury cars (see Table 36). Some of the decline in auto buying in 1975 was thus made up in 1976. It appears that a portion of the non-buying of the lower strata during inflationary periods is a *temporary postponement* of purchases (as the auto market in 1976 indicates). According to the traditional view, however, rapid inflation prompts people to buy immediately, before inflation carries prices still higher. Yet George Katona of Michigan's Survey Research Center has observed that chronic inflation creates economic confusion, insecurity, and malaise, which often result in the postponement of purchases and the felt need to save in uncertain times.[11] Thus, some of the car purchases that might have been made in 1975 were temporarily postponed to the following year.

After people live with the reality of inflation for a time, psychological accommodation to higher prices occurs and spending patterns rebound. Does this mean that inflation creates only *temporary* class divergence and that after a period of psychological adjustment, the lower strata resume their customary spending? For a brief time, possibly. Among low-income groups, however, there are obvious arithmetical limits to psychological adjustments to inflation. Persons in the lower strata cannot adjust to spiraling

Table 36. CHANGE IN SALES OF U.S.-BUILT LUXURY AND NON-LUXURY CARS, 1976 AND 1977

| | Model Year | |
	1976/1975	*1977/1976*
Luxury cars	+ 15.6%	+ 26.7%
All others	+ 28.0%	+ 12.1%
TOTAL	+ 27.1%	+ 12.9%

SOURCES: *Automotive News,* April 27, 1977, p. 42; *Automotive News, 1978 Market Data Book Issue,* p. 42.

prices for everything—housing, cars, food, energy, travel. At some point, they must cut back permanently, as income simply becomes insufficient for all these price increases. It is not surprising, then, that in 1977, when auto price increases were the fourth largest in the last twenty years, the growth of sales of luxury cars again far outpaced all others.

Suit Yourself

In the men's clothing industry another pattern of class divergence seemed to be emerging in the late 1970s. With the price of men's suits increasing 8–10 percent annually, a significant purchasing pattern developed. Sales of expensive custom-made suits and the higher priced mass-produced suits—ranging in price from $400 to $800—held firm. Affluent men, undaunted by price, continued to fill their closets. Sales of medium-priced suits fell, however. Middle-income buyers, unable to keep pace with inflation, were forced to move down a notch to lower-priced suits, sales of which increased markedly. In 1978 the executive director of the Menswear Retailers of America summed up what could be seen as still another example of the widening gap between classes.

At the Cadillac level—the Hickey Freeman and the Oxxford suits—and at the truly custom-made level, sales haven't been hit as hard by price pressures. Business is holding up in them, but there is no explosive sales trend. The business that may have been hurt most is that which includes men's suits selling for $275 to $375, sold basically in specialty stores and in many department stores. The lower range of $100 to $175 . . . is the best movement in unit sales.[12]

SOCIOLOGICAL SUPPORT FOR CLASS DIVERGENCE

The evidence supporting a theory of class divergence has so far been somewhat conjectural, but confirmation of the theory lies with David Caplovitz's important recent study of the effects of inflation on American families.[13] In 1976 interviewers spoke to some 2,000 persons in New York City, Atlanta, Detroit, and San Francisco to determine how families were coping with the stagflation of the mid-1970s. Caplovitz found that inflation was beginning to cut deeply into the fabric of American life. Fifty-nine percent of his respondents said that they were worse off financially than they had been two years earlier; 35 percent reported that they had been compelled to cut back their living standards; and a similar proportion acknowledged that the economic events of the previous years had caused them to lose confidence in the American dream.[14] Caplovitz's most important finding was that inflation affects classes unequally, and his conclusions dramatically support our argument that chronic inflation is increasing inequality and creating class divergence in American society:

> The people who are most affected by sharply rising prices are those toward the bottom half of the income distribution. Wealthy families and particularly those who enjoy rising income are able to weather the storm of inflation. On the basis of these data we can conclude that inflation is a force contributing to the economic cleavage of American society— between the haves and the have nots.[15]

Table 37 highlights some of Caplovitz's findings; virtually all validate the theory of class divergence. Lower-income groups are far more likely than higher-income groups to report being financially worse off now than they were earlier, to be suffering consciously from inflation, and to have to deny their children necessities as a consequence of economic conditions. More than this, we know that the economics of class almost invariably penetrates the social and psychological fabric of life. Thus, it is not surprising that Caplovitz found that the disproportionate economic hardship suffered by lower-income groups made them most vulnerable to mental strain—worry, irritation, depression, and anger—which they directly attributed to their economic problems, and to marital problems directly traceable to economic conditions. In sum, Caplovitz's study provides the most convincing evidence to date that unless inflation is soon brought under control, class divergence may be the model which for the foreseeable future best describes the dynamics of the American class structure.

Table 37. CLASS DIVERGENCE: EFFECTS OF INFLATION/ RECESSION ON VARIOUS INCOME GROUPS, 1976

	Family Income, 1976				
	Under $7,000	_$7,000– $12,000_	_$13,000– $19,999_	_$20,000 and Over_	_Total_
1. "Over the past couple of years, has your income kept up with the rising cost of living or has it fallen behind?"					
Income better now	3%	8%	15%	33%	16%
Income the same now	17	23	28	29	25
A little worse now	39	40	43	30	37
A lot worse now	42	29	14	8	22
2. Extent to which respondents report suffering consciously from inflation[a]					
Low (little suffering)	9%	14%	20%	38%	23%
Medium low	14	21	27	33	25
Medium high	26	24	24	18	22
High	51	41	29	11	30
3. Deprived Children: percent reporting their children had been denied things wanted or needed because of high cost of living	68%	n.a.[c]	n.a.	27%	43%

OBJECTIONS

Some have argued that the arbitrary distinction between necessities and non-necessities is a bit simplistic, and that a reconsideration of these may find the poor not the major losers after all. First, outside the four areas considered the basic necessities are such things as clothing and automobile expenses other than gasoline on which consumers spend a great deal and which might also

| | *Family Income, 1976* | | | |
	Under $7,000	*$7,000– $12,000*	*$13,000– $19,999*	*$20,000 and Over*	*Total*
4. Mental strain: percent undergoing high mental strain attributed by respondent to financial pressures[b]	44%	32%	18%	10%	24%
5. Impact of economic pressure on marriage: percent reporting that economic conditions had some negative effects on their marriage	47%	n.a.	n.a.	22%	33%

SOURCE: Assembled from David Caplovitz, *Making Ends Meet: How Families Cope with Inflation and Recession* (New York: Institute for Research on Human Affairs, Graduate School of the City University of New York, 1977), mimeograph, pp. 15, 23, 48, 50, 108, 117, 127–28, 134, 147. Subsequently issued by Sage Publications, Beverly Hills, Calif., 1979.

[a] An index based on such questions as whether inflation is making money worthless, causing respondent to go without necessities, preventing respondent from saving, causing him to dip into savings, etc.

[b] An index based on such questions as whether recent financial pressure has caused respondent worry, irritation, depression, or anger.

[c] n.a. = data not available from published report.

be considered necessities. Second, within the four basic necessity sectors prices are rising at different rates, and some highly inflated items in the necessity sectors are more often found in the budgets of the affluent than in the budgets of the poor. For example, the costs of home ownership have been rising faster than rents, and the price of restaurant meals has recently outpaced the price of food at home. Some economists have contended, therefore, that an analysis of the budgets for all income groups shows that the cost of living has been increasing at approximately the same rate for the poor as for everyone else.[16]

Even if it could be conclusively demonstrated that inflation has hit the non-poor as much as it has hit the poor, the latter would still emerge as the greatest losers today. This is easily illustrated. When the price of home heating oil rises over 60 percent in one year, as it did between winter 1978 and winter 1979, this across-the-board increase appears to strike all users equally, rich and poor. Yet it is obvious that the rich and the poor are not affected equally. To pay the added cost of heating oil, the affluent are able to allocate more from current income, draw from savings, cut out a few theater tickets, or forgo a few dinners on the town. The poor, on the other hand, have no such cushion in their budgets. Because they spend virtually all of their income on necessities (however defined), any large increase in the cost of these necessities cuts immediately into subsistence needs. In fact, it was generally acknowledged across the political spectrum that with the tremendous increase in the cost of home heating oil at the end of the 1970s, the poor might have to choose between "heating and eating." Caught in the inflationary squeeze, the poor are like an army making a last ditch defense of their capital; they have no defense in depth. Viewed in another way, if two persons are suspended above a lake, the first just one foot above the water, the other ten feet above the water, and if both are lowered exactly two feet, their "equal" descent will obviously have very unequal consequences. The first will drown, the second will be only slightly closer to the surface. As economists John L. Palmer and Michael C. Barth have written of the current period, "Even small losses in purchasing power can result in major hardships for lower income households already on the margin of subsistence. Equal percentage losses in purchasing power across different income levels . . . result in a very unequal distribution of hardship."[17]

Galbraith and most other economists who have addressed the question of the effects of contemporary inflation on distribution argue that sustained inflation has set off a competitive scramble for economic survival and that the process generally tends to redistribute income from the weak to the strong, from those unable to control their income (or prices) to those who can, from the unorganized to the organized, from the elderly to those in their productive middle years. In a study published in 1979, however, economist Joseph J. Minarik of the Brookings Institution argued that upper-income groups are the big losers to inflation. Minarik analyzed a Brookings computer data base which combined responses to the Census Bureau's Current Population Survey for 1970 and a sample of 100,000 IRS tax returns. To assess the impact of inflation, Minarik developed an income concept that went beyond wages, salaries, interest, dividends, rent, and the other forms of income used by the Current Population Survey. The more comprehensive income measure he constructed included, besides census income, miscellaneous income-in-kind, balance sheet changes (such as "depreciation of the cash value of bonds, the lagging of corporate retained earnings, and appreciation in home values"), and the effects of all federal, state, and local taxes.

Minarik studied both the impact of inflation over one year and the effect of a sustained rate of inflation over many years. Of the two, the latter seems closer to actual economic reality. To examine the consequences of sustained inflation Minarik analyzed the effect on 1970 incomes "of a simulated 2 percent increase over the actual inflation rate each year from 1965 to 1970." Results from this sustained simulated inflation during 1965–70 suggest that losses from inflation increase gradually with income. In general, most low-income households are found to be slightly improved under inflation and middle-income households are mainly unaffected, but the upper-income groups lose ground, due mainly to "greater real income taxes, lagging corporate retained earnings, and especially the depreciation of the face value of dollar-denominated interest-bearing securities. . . ."[18]

From the point of view of the sociologist, there are two problems with Minarik's simulation. First, his conclusion that upper-income groups are the big losers and that lower-income groups are for the most part "slightly better off" under inflation is contradicted by the testimony of the participants themselves—American families living through the inflation of the 1970s. In opinion research by Caplovitz, upper-income groups in fact reported that they had been hurt *less,* not more, by inflation than lower income groups.* According to the pattern of responses, as income falls,

---

* It is true that Minarik found the greatest losses in households with incomes exceeding $100,000. There were few of these households in Caplovitz's sample, and those few were included in the $20,000-and-over category, which might have concealed their distinctive views. There is a remote possibility that the decreasing hardship Caplovitz found at higher income levels might be reversed above $100,000.

losses from inflation increase, and the groups at the bottom report greater hardship than all others.

The second problem with Minarik's model is that even if his conclusion that the rich are the chief losers from inflation is nominally correct, the huge discretionary income of the rich easily offsets their greater percentage loss. For example, according to Minarik's simulation of sustained inflation from 1965–70, families earning $2 million a year stood to lose a larger share of their income than any other group—slightly under 10 percent in the final year of the inflation model. Thus, their annual income would be reduced from $2 million to "only" $1,800,000. By the standards of the sociologist this loss does not constitute a decline in class position, nor does it entail any necessary modification in style of life. Actually, smaller losses at lower income levels, where families live closer to subsistence, are much more likely to produce harm than large losses at higher income levels, where those whose income so vastly exceeds their expenses can easily absorb what might seem a significant loss. This occurs frequently to top corporate executives, for example. In bad years, the bonuses of chief executives may decline $200,000 to $300,000 or even more from the previous year. They are not noticeably injured.

HOME SWEET HOME?

> "Certainly the day is close at hand when almost anybody with a job can afford to own a house."
>
> The Editors of *Fortune*, 1955

No element is so central to the American dream as the hope and promise of home ownership. America is indeed unique in that respect, for in no other country in the modern world has universal home ownership been even remotely possible. If nothing else, the dream of universal home ownership is a contemporary symbol of American economic exceptionalism. And Americans take this dream seriously. In a poll taken in the mid-1970s, 92 percent of young Americans considered home ownership as either a necessity or "highly important." [19] Since the 1930s, the dream has been translated into national policy, with the creation of a diverse network of financial institutions (such as the Federal Housing Administration, Federal Home Loan Bank Board, and Federal National Mortgage Association) to make home mortgages widely available to American families. The U.S. tax structure also encourages and subsidizes home ownership, and in 1975 tax benefits to homeowners amounted to nearly $7.5 billion.

It was the spread of home ownership in the immediate postwar years, in fact, especially in the new suburbs, that seemed to confirm the vision of class convergence theorists. Home ownership, it was widely believed, would guarantee workers a middle-class standard of living. A new home in the suburbs would not only cut workers off from previous working-class ties to family and neighborhood but would expose them to middle-class culture, values, and behavior, absorbing them into the middle class. William H. Whyte, for example, as part of the postwar celebration of class convergence and working-class embourgeoisement, called the home-owning suburbs the "second great melting pot." [20]

The point I shall argue here is not, as with Bennett Berger, Herbert Gans, and other stability theorists that the working class retains its distinctive culture in a suburban home-owning milieu. Rather, I shall argue that the very possibility of home ownership itself is quickly disappearing for millions of working-class and even middle-class Americans. The 1970s was a great watershed, as the dream of home ownership for every family began to disintegrate before our eyes. While the upper strata are relatively untouched, the vast majority of American families are in a qualitatively worse position vis-à-vis home ownership than they were only a few years ago. What is so remarkable is not merely that it is happening, but that it is happening so quickly.

In a crucial analysis of the costs of home ownership in the U.S. from 1970 to 1976, the MIT–Harvard Joint Center for Urban Studies documented by just how much the costs of home ownership have outstripped the rise of income (see Figure 4). During this period, while both median family income (before taxes) and the overall consumer price index increased 46–47 percent, the median

Figure 4. HOUSING COSTS RISE FASTER THAN INCOME, 1970–1976

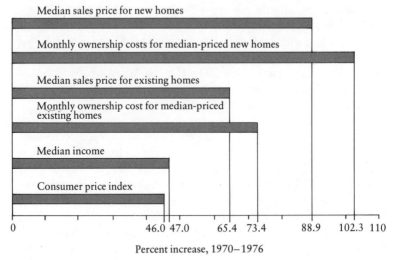

Median sales price for new homes

Monthly ownership costs for median-priced new homes

Median sales price for existing homes

Monthly ownership cost for median-priced existing homes

Median income

Consumer price index

0   46.0 47.0   65.4 73.4   88.9   102.3 110

Percent increase, 1970–1976

SOURCE: Bernard J. Frieden and Arthur P. Solomon, *The Nation's Housing: 1975 to 1985* (Cambridge, Mass.: Joint Center for Urban Studies of MIT and Harvard University, 1977), p. 119.

cost of a new home rose 89 percent, and the cost of an existing home rose 65 percent. Moreover, monthly ownership costs (including mortgage payments, insurance, maintenance, and utilities) rose 102 percent for a new home and 73 percent for an existing home in the same period. What these figures suggest is that in the early 1970s millions of middle-income Americans joined the poor in being priced out of the housing market. The speed and extent of this deterioration of working-class and middle-class purchasing power is shown dramatically in Figure 5.

As the price of new homes skyrocketed, the proportion of American families able to afford them declined sharply. In 1970, the MIT–Harvard Center calculated that about 46 percent of American families could afford to purchase a median-priced new home; by 1976, however, because the cost of housing so rapidly outstripped the rise of income, only 27 percent of American fami-

Figure 5. THE NARROWING MARKET FOR NEW HOUSES, 1970–1976

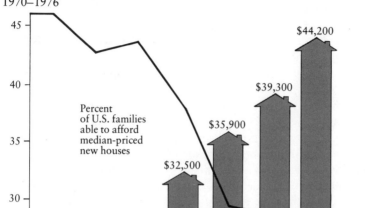

Percent of U.S. families able to afford median-priced new houses

$23,400
$25,200
$27,600
$32,500
$35,900
$39,300
$44,200
27.0

1970 1971 1972 1973 1974 1975 1976

■ Median sales price of new houses

Source: Bernard J. Frieden and Arthur P. Solomon, *The Nation's Housing: 1975 to 1985* (Cambridge, Mass.: Joint Center for Urban Studies of MIT and Harvard University, 1977), p. 125.

lies could afford to purchase a new home (following the brokers' rule of thumb that a family can afford to buy a home that costs 2–2.5 times its gross annual income). The situation with respect to existing homes was only slightly better. Ironically, after a postwar generation of rising incomes, a smaller proportion of American families were able to afford a house than at any time since the end of World War II.

The economic and social consequences of this unprecedented increase in housing costs are enormous. As a growing number of American families are squeezed out of the housing market, a fundamental class cleavage is developing between those who can still afford to purchase a house and those who cannot. In housing, then, the most basic form of class divergence is emerging. Until recently, families purchasing homes were not appreciably more affluent than others, illustrating a kind of democratization of home buying in the United States. In the mid-1960s, when the median income of all families was about $7,000 annually, for example, one survey revealed that the median income of families buying new homes was $8,000, only 15 percent higher than the national median.[21] By 1976–77, however, new home buying became far more highly concentrated among higher income groups. While median family income was $15,000 in 1976, the median income of new home buyers, according to a survey of the National Association of Home Builders, was more than $22,000, or nearly 50 percent higher than the national median.[22]

This rapid transformation of new housing from a mass market to a luxury market is clearly shown in Table 38. Between the mid-1960s and the mid-1970s, the share of new homes bought by middle- and low-income families decreased dramatically, while the share of all new homes purchased by the upper-income 25 percent increased sharply. True, the earlier period was one of boom, and the later period was one of recession in which the affluent might

Table 38. CLASS DIVERGENCE IN HOME BUY-
ING: FROM MASS MARKET TO LUXURY MAR-
KET IN 10 YEARS

Income Group	Share of All New Homes Bought	
	1965–1966	1975–1976
Top Quarter	31%	58%
Middle Income	53	38
Lower Third	17	4
TOTAL	100%[a]	100%

Source: Bernard J. Frieden and Arthur P. Solomon, *The Nation's Housing: 1975 to 1985* (Cambridge, Mass.: Joint Center for Urban Studies of MIT and Harvard University, 1977), p. 130.

[a] Percentages do not add to 100 due to rounding.

be expected to recover more quickly. Yet a comparison of the two periods at most merely exaggerates a trend that is clearly under way toward an increasing concentration of home buying among the upper strata.

While those families who already own houses can ride the escalator of inflated equity on their homes to purchase others, the first-time home buyer is obviously in trouble. Until recently, first-time buyers comprised about 50 percent of all buyers; by the late 1970s they numbered only about 35 percent. Are we thus moving rapidly toward an era in which only persons *with* houses will be able to *buy* houses? In the period of postwar expansion, the difference between the affluent and the non-affluent was often simply the difference between a large, expensive house and a smaller, more modest one. If the costs of home ownership continue to rise so much faster than income, are we heading toward a society of much greater inequality where the difference between the affluent and the non-affluent will be the difference between a class of entrenched homeowners on the one hand and a class of eternal apartment renters on the other?

In the Alice-in-Wonderland nightmare world of current housing costs, little boxes that sold for $25,000 just a few years ago are now seriously put on the market and quickly sold for $70,000, $80,000, and even $90,000. In a desperate effort to become homeowners before rising prices carry the opportunity forever beyond their grasp, many families are seriously overextending their budgets by paying a much larger share of their income for housing than has ever been considered prudent. According to the traditional bankers' rule, a family should spend no more than 25 percent of its gross income on housing expenses (including mortgage, utilities, etc.). Nevertheless, a study made by the National Association of Home Builders in 1976–77 found that 38 percent of new home buyers had to spend at least 25 percent of their income on housing.[23] And as Table 39 illustrates, middle- and low-income families have been especially hard hit. In this study, over 70 percent of families earning under $15,000 spent at least 25 percent of their income on housing, and many of these families were risking serious financial problems by spending considerably more than 25 percent. Of those earning less than

Table 39. ANNUAL MORTGAGE AND UTILITY COSTS OF NEW HOME AS PERCENTAGE OF FAMILY IN-COME, SAMPLE OF NEW HOME BUYERS, 1976–1977

Family Income	Less than 25%	25–29.9%	30–34.9%	35–39.9%	40–49.9%	50% and over
Less than $10,000	28.6%	17.1%	0%	11.4%	17.1%	25.7%
$10,000–14,999	23.4	16.7	17.8	20.0	15.6	6.8
$15,000–19,999	35.0	38.8	20.6	4.3	1.4	0
$20,000–24,999	65.9	25.9	6.8	0	0	1.3
$25,000–34,999	88.9	9.7	1.4	0	0	0
$35,000–49,999	94.9	5.2	0	0	0	0
$50,000 and over	100.0	0	0	0	0	0
TOTAL	61.7%	21.2%	8.7%	3.5%	2.6%	2.1%

Source: Michael Sumichrast et al., *Profile of a New Home Buyer: Survey of New Home Owners* (Washington, D.C.: National Association of Home Builders, 1978), p. 41.

Percentages may not add to 100 due to rounding.

$10,000, 54 percent were spending 35 percent or more of their income on housing expenses, as were 42 percent of those earning $10,000–$15,000 annually. Most affluent families, on the other hand, had no trouble keeping housing costs within the 25 percent boundary, as Table 39 shows.

It is clear that many middle-income families buying modest homes today are "overhoused" or house-poor in terms of present costs, if not in terms of actual accommodations. Although many new home buyers are young and will have higher earnings in later years, enormous and continuing inflation in housing costs is seriously straining the financial resources of many families, requiring sacrifices in virtually every other area. A family that buys a home today for the first time must cut back its living standards elsewhere—vacations, automobiles, food, clothing, entertainment, and even furniture for the new house. In 1977 *Time* published a photograph of a family sitting on the floor of their empty new house—too house-poor to furnish it. Moreover, in this market a permanent working wife is a virtual necessity for aspiring homeowners, with obvious long-range consequences for female labor force participation, birth rates, and family size. There is now, in fact, a convincing economic argument for polygamy: with the cost of housing today a homeowner needs not just one working spouse but several. On the other hand, the single-income blue-collar or lower white-collar family may soon be priced out of the housing market forever.

Some writers claim that the MIT–Harvard study is too pessimistic, that millions of families have growing equity in their homes, that half the houses for sale are priced below the median, and that first-time buyers can find lower priced, run-down houses to renovate or new, less desirable no-frills or attached houses. Nevertheless, as housing costs rise much faster than income, each passing year puts millions of potential first-time buyers further behind in their ability to afford a single-family home. In this wildly inflationary situation, increases in housing costs are so quickly outdistancing increases in income that the decline of living standards is occurring with amazing rapidity. It is clear, for example, that many families who purchased homes just ten years ago could not afford to purchase their own homes if they were buying them today. Five years ago a family with an income of $20,000 could buy a far better home than could a family with an equivalent income today, but the family buying today will undoubtedly be better housed than will a family buying five years hence.

With such a rapid deterioration of purchasing power in the housing market, how well one is housed depends almost more on when one bought than upon how much one earns, and families with similar incomes are progressively more poorly housed with each succeeding year. This is creating strange "class" cleavages between earlier home buyers and later home buyers. Ironically, earlier home buyers with low incomes may actually be better housed than later home buyers with higher incomes. Seen in another way, there is now a rapid downward mobility in housing, where, for example, young first-time buying college professors are forced to buy homes in working-class neighborhoods. In short, much of the middle class can no longer afford middle-class housing. Or, as an astonished family read on the "For Sale" sign in a recent Herblock cartoon: "Nice middle-income house for high-income family."

Aside from its effect on individual families, the soaring cost of private homes is beginning to create whole new ecological patterns in American cities. According to the traditional process of invasion and succession as it operated in urban areas during this century, minority ethnics and the poor slowly filtered into more affluent neighborhoods, displacing the white middle class into other more desirable areas of the city and eventually into the new suburbs. This pattern of invasion and succession was a genuine form of upward mobility, as the poor and minorities gradually inherited older middle-class neighborhoods, and the middle class moved onward and usually upward. Today we find precisely the reverse—downward rather than upward residential mobility. In cities across the country the young middle class, no longer able to afford middle-class housing in the suburbs or in the more prosperous areas of the city, is forced to enter rundown areas of the inner city, purchasing homes in working-class or even lower-class ethnic neighborhoods.[24]

By the end of the 1970s what had happened to the cost of buying a home was beginning to happen to the cost of renting an apartment. Downward residential mobility of homeowners was paralleled by downward residential mobility of apartment dwellers. During the early 1970s the cost of apartment rentals rose more slowly than the overall cost of living and much more slowly than the costs of home ownership. By the late 1970s, however, an acute national apartment shortage was developing as a consequence of shrinking supply and growing demand, driving rents up sharply. On the supply side, by the late 1970s U.S. rental construction had declined drastically—50 percent from the early 1970s—because of hyperinflation in the costs of land, money, material, construction, and what builders alleged was the fear of rent control. The furious pace of conversions to condominiums and co-operatives aggravated the rental shortage. As a consequence, in the late 1970s the U.S. was running an annual net loss of rental housing of about 2 percent a year, which the chief economist of the National Association of Home Builders called not only unprecedented but "frightening."

Meanwhile, over 1.5 million new households were formed annually in the 1970s. The children born during the baby boom were coming of age, the divorce rate was high and increasing, and growing numbers of elderly people were living on their own rather than with their children. With the supply of apartments stagnating and demand growing, the national rental vacancy rate in the late 1970s was the lowest it had been in decades. Because the baby boom ended in the 1960s, there will be fewer young adults after the mid-1980s; whether and by how much this will mitigate the apartment shortage is not clear. But it is apparent that a serious problem will persist at least well into the 1980s.

As the apartment shortage developed in the late 1970s, rents began to increase faster than income, especially in the major metropolitan areas. One study of New York City, for example, found that between 1975 and 1978 median rents increased more than 23 percent, while the median household income of renters rose only 7 percent. Because of such trends, the proportion of the average New Yorker's household income spent on rent increased steadily, from 21 percent in 1968 to more than 28 percent in 1978.[25] By the late 1970s, as with middle-class home buyers, middle-class apartment renters were finding it difficult to remain in middle-class neighborhoods. To do so, single persons living in the city often had to double or triple up with friends or strangers to pay the rent. Those who were unable or unwilling to pay a larger proportion of their income for rent or who refused to share were inexorably bumped from middle-class into declining neighborhoods. While some urban areas were upgraded by the middle-class invasion, this pattern created potential confrontation between the aged, poor, and minorities, on the one hand, and young middle-class whites, on the other hand, who began to uproot these traditional residents.

This situation became a political issue in San Francisco in the late 1970s. A 1977 firebombing incident in Philadelphia highlighted a dispute between Puerto Ricans and middle-class whites who moved into an inner-city neighborhood. Middle-class whites in Chicago, no longer able to afford suburban homes or housing in the expensive Gold Coast or Lincoln Park areas, moved into a North Side area around DePaul University that had been previously inhabited largely by persons of Latin descent. In Washington, D.C., according to the Urban League, middle-class whites were renting apartments and buying houses for $100,000 in neighborhoods "where even the police were afraid to go two years ago." In New York many persons who could no longer afford ordinary East Side apartments whose rents were rapidly approaching quadruple digits moved to previously run-down areas of the West Side. Many West Siders, unable to afford the skyrocketing rents even in that "grotty-chic ambiance" where in the late 1970s a small apartment in a brownstone might rent for $500 a month or more, were forced to move out of Manhattan altogether.[26] Other middle-class New Yorkers, wedded to Manhattan, who in better times might have settled in Greenwich Village, were priced out of the neighborhood and found themselves residentially downwardly mobile and compelled to locate in such less desirable areas as Chelsea or Murray Hill.

Some optimists view the return of a segment of the young middle class to the central city, where they restore declining neighborhoods, as heralding the end of the urban crisis.[27] While this white-collar influx obviously has positive elements, such writers basically have what has been called a tourist-eye view of the city and equate the establishment of a few chic middle-class restaurants, coffeehouses, antique shops, health-food stores, and book shops in certain select downtown areas with overall urban renaissance. They ignore the continued deterioration of most of the central city, the decay of public services, the disintegration of the urban infrastructure, high urban unemployment, and continuing fiscal crisis.

As the aged, poor, and minorities are priced out of their own neighborhoods, where will they go? They will be forced to flee to other ghettos; but ghettos which are smaller and more densely packed and congested than ever before. While some ghetto homeowners may profit from the increased value of their property, bid up by real-estate speculators and the returning middle class, ghetto renters will inevitably be uprooted and suffer. The actual extent of this trend is not yet clear. A 1979 study by the Department of Housing and Urban Development found that while displacement of low-income families by the in-migrating middle class was not yet a widespread national problem, some cities had experienced considerable dislocations. Thus, in Seattle some 19 percent of all families who moved in recent years did so "involuntarily"—because of eviction or changed economic conditions.[28]

The pattern for this new urban transformation was created in Europe. In Paris, Amsterdam, London, and innumerable other cities, the middle class is displacing workers from their traditional neighborhoods and in some cases driving workers out of the cities entirely.[29] The process, known derogatorily as "gentrification" in Europe—from whence the term came to America minus its derogation—has stirred special resentment between uprooted European workers and the new middle-class in-migrants.

Following World War II, Europeans played catch up with American living standards and patterns of "classlessness." Now it appears that the process is being reversed. The displacement of European workers from the cities, a consequence of sharp class inequality in Europe, is now being repeated in the U.S. As American living standards fall, they begin to take on characteristics of the more highly stratified European model.

According to the MIT–Harvard study of U.S. housing:

If the [pricing] trends from 1971 to 1976 were to continue for another five years—and, given the extremely unusual circumstances over the last few years we do not predict they will—typical new homes in 1981 would sell for $78,000, and only the most affluent groups would be able to afford them. Should this exceptional inflation of house prices continue, however, the United States would become less and less a nation of homeowners and, despite the decades of federal encouragement and massive tax subsidies, the new single-family house would become a luxury item.[30]

Although the MIT–Harvard study found it almost inconceivable that housing prices would continue to rise as quickly in the late 1970s as they had in the early 1970s, in fact they rose much faster. The average purchase price of a new house had passed $74,000 by the end of the 1970s, according to the Federal Home Loan Bank Board; this was only a few thousand dollars less than the MIT–Harvard "worst-case" projection for 1981. In many metropolitan areas the average price was considerably more than that. In 1979 the price of an ordinary three-bedroom ranch house in a tract development in the San Francisco Bay area reached $100,000. Using the conventional brokers' rule of thumb, a family that spent $100,000 for the basic tract house in 1979 needed an income of at least $40,000; yet in 1979 median family income was less than half that. To this price, add unprecedented double-digit mortgage interest rates and the spiraling cost of gas, home heating oil, and electricity. By the end of the decade, Los Angeles and Washington, D.C. had also reached the $100,000 milestone for a basic 1500-square-foot house on a small plot. These cities were not somehow unique but were merely leading the way. Housing experts predict that by the early 1980s the average home in most metropolitan areas in the U.S. will cost $100,000. And a 1979 study by the Joint Economic Committee of Congress estimated that the cost of an average house in the U.S. could reach $151,000 by 1988.

Just as huge sections of the middle class (and below) are now finding it difficult to move to desirable areas of the *city,* such persons are also finding it difficult to move to desirable areas of the *country.* Spiraling real estate costs now constitute an enormous obstacle for older persons who wish to retire to attractive areas of California; they are simply being priced out of these areas if not out of the state. Even younger persons may find it difficult to take jobs in such regions, unable to afford the inflated costs of home ownership. Thus, choice areas of the country favored by climate or geography may ultimately become the almost exclusive preserve of those who are already there or who have sufficient pecuniary strength to afford what the hyperinflated real estate market is asking.

Mobility has always been central to the American conception of freedom—social mobility, the freedom to move up, and physical mobility, the freedom to move out. From the frontier to the renowned transience of the postwar suburban generation, Americans have always been on the move. In fact, part of the class convergence literature (William H. Whyte's *The Organization Man,* for example) was based on the freewheeling postwar mobility of the American corporate middle class. In these early postwar years Americans played an elaborate game of musical chairs, with families constantly on the move from city to city, city to suburb, state to state, and region to region. Now, in that game of musical chairs the final strains of that cheerful postwar music are dying out and Americans are scrambling for the closest chair, where they will find themselves under great pressure to remain lest they be bumped down to something worse. As housing costs increase ever faster than income, the fabled mobility of the American people may be radically diminished and replaced by a new kind of rootedness, with perhaps a certain marginal advantage of community offset by stagnation and the decline of what has been a key component of American freedom.

Perhaps the comment of *Time* magazine most aptly symbolized this sudden and remarkable crystallization of class divergence in America. For the entire postwar era *Time* wrote the scripture on the affluent society and the class convergence it was creating. But in 1977, sobered by the events of the previous years and observing the rapid transformation of the housing market in the U.S., *Time* cautioned:

Americans have come to look on a home of their own—and a pretty big, detached, single-family home at that—as not just a desire but a need and almost a right. *They are being unrealistic.* To shelter the entire nation in spaced-out, single-family houses near metropolitan centers would be a physical impossibility; to house a substantial portion that way is turning out to be enormously expensive.[31]

If Time Inc. is beginning to hedge on the American dream, then, indeed, how far we must have fallen.

CHAPTER SIX

America Transformed

During the post-war boom which has recently been so rudely terminated, *The Times* together with leading politicians regularly assured us that class struggles and crises were things of the past, that a new society was emerging, that, with properly run government, prosperity and expansion were assured. Academics discussed the post-industrial and affluent societies, television programs began to cover the so-called "leisure problem." Economists were cheery, optimistic men. . . .

All of that jocular bulldog confidence now seems to have evaporated. It has been replaced by accusations of social irresponsibility and greed . . . and by a mood of growing pessimism and despair.

> Social scientists Andrew Gamble and Paul
> Walton writing about Great Britain in 1976 [1]

Of course it would be premature on the basis of trends of no more than a decade and a half to be caught up by the moment and conclude that our present condition represents the inevitable future of inequality in America. During the Great Depression, many writers, prisoners of their age, believed that American economic growth had peaked and begun an inevitable decline.[2] In that dismal decade even the dean of American economics, Harvard professor Alvin Hansen, forecast permanent stagnation for the American economy. And in the postwar world, sociologists, economists, demographers, and political scientists, attempting to forecast the future—even a future lying only two or three years ahead—have been wrong so many times about so many things that their errors ought to humble even the most immodest social scientists possessed by a vision of the future.[3]

And yet, it is important to consider the possibilities. While prosperity may be right around the corner, it is essential to examine the possibility that American capitalism has now entered a period of long-term stagnation and decline.

The events of the 1970s seemed to involve not merely rapid social change or even the acceleration of social change but a radical discontinuity or break in the direction of social change from the earlier postwar era. And this discontinuity has begun to make fundamental changes in the traditional class structure of the United States. Although the exact dimensions and characteristics of these changes need to be further explored, it seems likely that we are moving generally toward something that might be called the Europeanization of the American class system, with lower levels of living, a more rigid structure, and greater inequality. After a generation of moving up that inclined plane, the mass of Americans now find themselves, in a great many dimensions of social class, including jobs, income, housing and living standards, being *locked in or bumped down*. If for postwar Americans there was always room at the top, there now seems ominously to be ample room at the bottom.

In any case, in its major assumptions the dominant theory of class in postwar America, for all intents and purposes, now seems dead. The theory of class convergence is now in fact mainly of interest from the point of view of the sociology of knowledge—how a group of basically patriotic intellectuals, living through a period of unprecedented prosperity and American hegemony, proceeded to spin out a near-utopian vision of classlessness, abundance, and social harmony.

The relative decline of American power has struck the class structure with especial force, and that has been our major focus in this book. Yet this decline has implications that go beyond social class. In a real sense we are witnessing the transformation of American society itself. It is indeed true that the America we have always known is disappearing before our eyes. Fast-moving events are touching the very center of American life and values and affecting the prospects for social order and consensus. It is to some of these issues that I wish to turn in this final chapter.

THE END OF POSTINDUSTRIAL SOCIETY

After the Second World War a great many sociological prophets heralded the end of industrial society and the birth of a new, affluent, postindustrial world. I suspect that underlying the celebrated thesis that we now inhabit a postindustrial world—or postmodern, postcapitalist, postscarcity, postmaterialist, and every other possible post except Post Toasties—were two motives: first, the impulse to be sociologically avant garde and fashionable; second, the urge to dismiss Marxism by arguing that contemporary society has been totally transformed from the world described by Marx. Whatever the motives, the notion of a postindustrial society suggests more than a social system where knowledge is central and employment is concentrated in the services. The thesis that American society has evolved from an industrial to a postindustrial form also clearly implies that the problems of the previous industrial epoch have been solved, that American society has in effect gone beyond—transcended—its industrial phase.

Ironically, however, despite the glowing vision of those who see industrial society giving way to postindustrial society, the recent stagnation of American capitalism suggests just the opposite—that we are actually moving *back* from a postindustrial *to* an industrial society—for the perennial problems of industrial capitalist society—scarcity, poverty, inequality, inflation, and unemployment—are with us anew, and in forms more virulent and intractable than ever. Much to the dismay of the postindustrialists, the clock of history seems to be turning counterclockwise. And if it is true that in a society of growing shortages, diminishing resources, and stagnating living standards we are moving back from postindustrial to industrial society, then obviously all of the assumptions of the postindustrialists which were based on their expectations of growing abundance and declining material scarcity must be thoroughly reexamined if not repudiated altogether.

FIGHTING OVER THE PIE

Many convergence theorists argued that even if wealth and income were not becoming distributed much more equally in the postwar period, class conflict over redistribution was prevented because of absolute gains for everyone. In the postwar generation relative class harmony was achieved by rapidly rising productivity and economic expansion. Because the size of the pie was constantly increasing, a larger slice for one group miraculously meant a larger slice for other groups as well. In 1958, amid the full flush of the affluent society, John Kenneth Galbraith described the postwar American answer to the class struggle:

. . . it has become evident to conservatives and liberals alike that increasing aggregate output is an alternative to redistribution or even to the reduction of inequality. The oldest and most agitated of social issues [equality], if not resolved, is at least largely in abeyance, and the disputants have concentrated their attention, instead, on the goal of increasing productivity.[4]

But what was true in the 1950s was no longer true by the 1970s. With the rapid international decline of American capitalism, alarming slowdowns in productivity growth, especially compared to other industrial nations, and the ensuing stagnation of domestic living standards, the United States has entered a period in which growth is no longer an alternative to redistribution. As the size of the pie remains relatively constant, a larger slice for one group now necessarily means a smaller slice for everyone else.

The Hobbesian implications are apparent in a zero-sum game where many groups are competing for fixed and scarce rewards. Add to this explosive economic cauldron the disturbing American cultural traditions of violence and the kind of communal sense best embodied in the American expression discussed below, "taking care of number one." Will the most apt symbol of the coming period indeed be the photograph of the Los Angeles gas-station attendant with a revolver strapped to his hip to keep "order" in the gas lines?

We saw in Chapter 1 that in the postwar era of naive abundance some enthusiastic convergence theorists forecast the "withering away of the strike" as a natural concomitant of affluence and the end of scarcity. Now, however, it is likely that we shall see just the reverse. As economic growth atrophies, as the only way one class can increase its living standards is at the expense of others, what we shall likely see is not the withering away of the strike but what used to be called the "intensification of the class struggle." Those U.S. manufacturers increasingly pressed by foreign imports may attempt to meet the competition by cutting costs, imposing speedups, and increasing productivity in ways which directly attack working conditions in the plant. Where American unions are weakened by foreign competition, the intensification of the class struggle may ironically take the form of a new trade union docility in the context of a general corporate offensive against unions and the gains that have previously been made.

Where unions remain strong and militant, on the other hand, recent British industrial experience may provide a disconcerting model. The extraordinary labor unrest in Britain in the late 1970s offers an instructive and perhaps prophetic example for the United States of how a declining economy, low productivity growth, hyperinflation, and falling living standards can intensify the class struggle. Between 1975 and 1978 the precarious wage-price restraint in Britain managed to reduce inflation from 26 percent to 8 percent annually. But in 1979 the dikes gave way when workers, frustrated by years of declining living standards, walked out. A wave of authorized and wildcat strikes swept the nation, creating widespread chaos in private industry, municipal services, schools, and hospitals, as workers tried to recoup some of the ground they had lost to inflation. The success of some unions increased the determination of others. Besides its economic dimension, the desperation and extent of the struggles threatened to burst the venerable bonds of British civility. Britain seemed to be dissolving into fratricidal anomie.

Theorizing about the social dynamics of a no-growth society, economist Robert Heilbroner argues that class conflict will pit not only the working class against the corporate rich but each class against all. We have already noted the potential white-collar antagonism toward unionized blue-collar workers whose income gains have wiped out the traditional superiority enjoyed by white-collar workers. More generally, Heilbroner observes,

> . . . when growth slows down, we must expect a struggle of redistribution on a vast scale—a confrontation not just between a few rich and many poor, but between a relatively better-off third of the nation and a relatively less well-off slightly larger working class. And fighting against both will be the bottom 20 percent—the group with most to gain, the least to lose.[5]

Indeed, America's raging inflation is itself a kind of impersonal class struggle, as each class and sub-class battles others by raising prices or wages to protect and enhance its own real income at the expense of others.

But intensification of the class struggle is not the only conflict that will develop in a society of scarcity. If not offset by countervailing forces, the stagnation of American capitalism will almost inevitably increase the overall level of social nastiness in American society. Wherever there are fissures or cleavages in America, scarcity will aggravate them, creating social conflict amid a general scramble for self-aggrandizement. And there are currently many cleavages in American society that scarcity may deepen.

Racial.   In the current situation, continuing conflict is almost inevitable, for blacks and other minorities aspire to mobility at a time of growing scarcity. Minorities now enter the marketplace not in the affluent fifties or sixties but in the austere seventies and eighties. The abundance of terms suggests the intensity of the struggle over jobs: quotas, affirmative action, tokenism, reverse discrimination, quality vs. equality, meritocracy, etc. The *Bakke* case was, of course, the prime symbol in the late 1970s of the conflict between whites and blacks over scarce and desirable positions. Falling living standards in Britain have led to virulent scapegoating of black immigrants. Whether American society is capable of renewed and intensified scapegoating of blacks, or whether that historical gambit has now finally been exhausted, remains to be seen.

Sexual.   Because the contemporary women's movement did not need to wage a struggle for civil rights or the vote, as did blacks, economic issues have been paramount from the very first. Women continue to enter the labor force in growing numbers seeking a piece of the economic action—but not since the end of World War II has there been so little action. More women are moving into graduate and professional schools and into the business and professional careers for which their training prepares them. Yet, as with racial minorities, the scarcity of good jobs has created conflicts in affirmative action and other hiring situations, and if scarcity intensifies, tensions between men and women in the marketplace will continue as each self-righteously claims to be suffering discrimination at the hands of the other.

The steadily growing proportion of teenage white girls who have entered the labor force in recent years have bumped black teenagers out of jobs they might have held and contributed to the extraordinarily high unemployment rates among young blacks. In the adult labor force, as women and black men move out of their respective occupational ghettos and into the labor-force mainstream, they will more frequently collide, each group invoking its own distinctive ideology of past oppression in its bid for present compensation.

Educational. There are now more college graduates than there are college-level jobs. Graduates confront each other in a paper chase more relentless than ever. Competition, always rigorous, intensifies as the intellectual reserve army grows.[6] College graduates, forced to take jobs for which no college training is necessary, bump high-school graduates and dropouts out of these jobs into lower positions, increasing those rivalries and resentments.

Generational. As younger graduates seek the jobs of older persons occupying these positions, generational conflict develops. The university offers a prototype of this condition in which young Ph.D.s confront a desperate shortage of academic jobs. The resentment of younger faculty who feel their qualifications match or exceed those of their entrenched elders and who feel cheated by the sheer accident of the date of their birth, and the defensiveness of the tenured faculty, has created a potentially divisive conflict of generations within the academy that may be a model of the generational resentment in the economy at large.[7]

An angry young law-school graduate, frustrated at his fruitless eighteen-month search for a job in a law firm and forced to take a demeaning position as a government clerk, described the envy and resentment he felt for his successful elders on the Op-Ed page of the *New York Times:*

The whole experience [of looking for a job with a law firm] has left me with a growing anger and resentment toward anybody 50 years old or older.

I am jealous of the 30 years of unlimited prosperity they took for granted, of entire communities built on plentiful wood and brick and unlimited farmland, cheap cars and No. 2 heating oil warming a house at 17.2 cents a gallon. I'm livid at the virtual unlimited opportunity they enjoyed—for job entry and advancement, to buy a home for $250 down, and to live in a world marked by building booms, baby booms, expanding civil rights and social programs. But most of all, I resent the denial of the full use of my talents and the perpetuation of the American dream for a generation that has reaped the benefits for so long.

Where is my ticket *into* the system? . . . Sandbagged into a dead-end job, working as a clerk for the Federal Government, going for months without even getting an interview for a job I was trained to do, I must be considered a failure. Yet, I can't be. I haven't even had a chance to compete. I can't even get my foot in the door.

I am still waiting my turn.[8]

This poignant complaint drew many heated replies from *Times'* readers over fifty.

Regional. Regional conflicts are nothing new in American history, but scarcity may increase them now as the Northeast sinks and the Sun Belt prospers. The struggle for federal assistance, projects, and jobs becomes crucial for the depleted Snow Belt. Energy shortages may exacerbate regional conflicts, illustrated by the compassionate Sun Belt slogan, "Let them freeze in the dark," coined during the energy crisis of 1973–74.

Within regions, growing scarcities of all kinds (of desirable land in cities and suburbs, for example) intensify social conflict. Most remaining vestiges of the urban and suburban frontier fill up, suburbs develop no-growth philosophies supported by zoning laws and other ideological and legal fences, and costs soar as crowds compete for the meager remaining turf.

POLITICS IN AN AGE OF DECLINE

However serious, the crisis in America has nothing to do with revolution, contrary to the expectations of the vulgar Marxists. In an exercise in Marxist wish-fulfillment, for example, sociologist Albert Szymanski forecasts nothing less than revolutionary consciousness among American workers arising from these developments. Noting the serious problems of the American economy, Szymanski argues that "The natural inference from all this is that the long overdue socialist working-class consciousness can be expected to develop and the revolutionary struggle of American workers commence. It may yet turn out that American workers play a leading role in the world revolutionary struggle." [9] More realistic observers understand that while serious recession and inflation have created social and personal malaise, basic commitment to the system remains high. This is reflected both in the politics of our era and in available opinion research. In his 1976 study, for instance, David Caplovitz found that although the United States was enduring its worst economic times since the Great Depression only a small minority of respondents (9 percent) believed both that capitalism was not the best economic system and that socialism was preferable. [10]

Not only is the vulgar-Marxist vision of revolutionary consciousness for the American working class ridiculous in the present context, but continued stagnation of U.S. living standards has actually strengthened right-wing political elements who have capitalized on the frustrations arising from poorly understood forces of economic decline. Indeed, the conservative tax revolt of the late 1970s, whose major symbol was the overwhelming victory of California's Proposition 13, grew directly out of many of the forces we have already discussed:

1. Living standards for most citizens have stagnated or declined, creating public frustration, anger, and confusion.

2. The values of American capitalism extoll the privatization of consumption, while the public sector languishes.

3. Much of the public has swallowed the corporate ideology that government is parasitic, wasteful, inefficient, bureaucratic, and corrupt. In this view, tax money is largely squandered and all

virtue and wisdom reside in the marketplace and in the business sector.*

4. Housing costs have soared and as a consequence property taxes have risen sharply.

5. Desperate to boost sagging living standards, citizens realize that some ballast must be thrown overboard. During most of the postwar period living standards rose out of the dynamism and productivity of the economy. This no longer works. Thus, the only way to preserve accustomed living standards now is to cut "unnecessary" expenses, viz. taxes. But what fueled Proposition 13 was not so much high taxes as stagnating incomes. Opinion polls in recent years have not shown taxes to be a fundamental obsession of Americans; because of declining incomes attention has focused on taxation as a means of reducing expenses and lifting family fortunes. As one reluctant supporter of Proposition 13 said in a study of California voters, "I felt I had to get money from somewhere."

Public goods and services must therefore be sacrificed upon the altar of private consumption. If schools, parks, libraries, mass transit, hospitals, museums, and all the other public amenities which constitute the bedrock of a civilized society must suffer to ensure the continued flow of Cuisinarts, color TVs, and electric toothbrushes into the home, then so be it. The priorities are clear. Enter Proposition 13 and all the efforts that have followed at local, state, and national levels to reduce taxes or limit government spending.

The seizure of American hostages by Iranian students and the Soviet invasion of Afghanistan in 1979 illustrate additional right-wing possibilities of America's changed position in the world. The relative decline of American international influence may invite

---

* Opinion polls regularly show that Americans think much of their tax money is wasted by government. A 1978 Gallup Poll, for example, found that the median public estimate was that the federal government wastes about 50 percent of all the tax monies it receives, state governments waste a third, and local governments waste one quarter (*New York Times,* November 19, 1978).

growing Soviet adventurism and real or imagined assaults to U.S. interests by Third World countries. The U.S. may respond by a revival of the Cold War mentality, bigger military budgets and acceleration of the arms race, the draft, attacks on civil liberties, and a new belligerence in an effort to "restore international respect for the U.S." or demonstrate that "Uncle Sam cannot be pushed around in the world any more," as political figures of the day expressed it. Leftist author Stanley Aronowitz has predicted, in fact, that as American power wanes, its bellicosity will increase. Indeed, renewed U.S. international machismo serves several functions. It is both a catharsis for a population frustrated by economic problems at home and perceived threats abroad and a natural vote-getting issue for political candidates. President Carter's dismal standing with the public in the late 1970s changed dramatically with the national unity growing out of the crisis in Iran and Afghanistan. Ironically, then, despite America's grave economic problems, public attention may well be diverted to foreign affairs and military bread and circuses for an increasingly frustrated population.

On the other hand, economic problems at home may simply be too great and persistent to ignore. Foreign affairs may then become only a temporary interlude, following which the urgency of economic issues will require center stage. If this, in fact, occurs, the moderate political left has a chance to make genuine gains.

Sociologist Seymour Martin Lipset observed many years ago that blue-collar workers are politically more liberal on economic issues than they are on social issues. For obvious reasons, workers tend to be more receptive to labor law reform, wage and hour legislation, occupational health and safety laws, federal job creation, and national health insurance than they are to such social issues as busing and affirmative action, drug-law reform, the Equal Rights Amendment, and, during the 1960s, the youth movement and anti-war protest. This political characteristic of the American working class has been reflected in the last four Presidential elections. In those elections in which economic issues were paramount, workers were more likely to vote Democratic than in elections fought mainly over social issues. When social issues prevailed, the moderate or conservative social inclinations of many workers drew large numbers into the Republican camp.

The 1964 election between Lyndon Johnson and Barry Goldwater was a classic battle over the economic issues of the New Deal, Keynesianism, and laissez-faire capitalism. As Table 40 shows, the working-class vote for the Democratic candidate was very high, and class cleavage in voting patterns was quite pronounced (14 percentage points separated the blue- and white-collar vote for Johnson). In the 1976 election, inflation, recession, and high unemployment were crucial economic issues that drew strong blue-collar support for the Democrats again. In both 1968 (Nixon vs. Humphrey) and 1972 (Nixon vs. McGovern), such social issues as the student movement, black big city riots, Vietnam, the women's movement, drug reform, homosexual rights, and abortion reform—all these effectively tapped the social conservatism of the working class. Republicans exploited these issues; Nixon and Agnew appealed to the law-and-order mentality and were able to move large numbers of socially conservative blue-collar workers into the Republican columns.

Some years ago, Kevin Phillips, a leading Republican ideologist and one-time speech writer for Nixon, wrote a very unprophetic book called *The Emerging Republican Majority*.[11] Phillips's argument was based in part on the notion that in an affluent society economic issues recede, and as they do, social issues become more important. As this happens the Republican party should thus be

Table 40. CLASS VOTING: PERCENTAGE VOTING FOR THE DEMOCRATIC PRESIDENTIAL CANDIDATE, 1964–1976, BLUE- AND WHITE-COLLAR WORKERS

	1964	1968	1972	1976
Blue-collar workers	71%	50%	43%	59%
White-collar workers	57%	41%	36%	50%
BC–WC	14	9	7	9

SOURCES: Miscellaneous Gallup and Harris polls, 1964–76.

able to win the white working-class vote back from the Democrats by appealing to the essential social conservatism of workers.

If the analysis made here is accurate, however, Phillips's expectations may be realized in the reverse. Persistent economic problems—unemployment, inflation, the declining value of the dollar, huge trade imbalances, the growing non-competitiveness of U.S. industry, class stagnation, and class divergence—may create a more class-based politics than ever before. With economic issues again paramount and potentially large working-class majorities for Democratic and left-liberal candidates, if the left can articulate the public malaise and outflank the growing conservative mood, the prospects may be favorable for long-term economic reform along the lines of European social-democratic parties.

In the 1960s, when such social issues as civil rights and the antiwar movement prevailed, most observers argued that trade unions had become conservative and were no longer in the vanguard of reform. In the 1980s, however, as class politics again emerges, labor may play a larger role and, as in the 1930s, become a central force for change. This has, in fact, already begun to happen. The crisis of American capitalism is also a crisis of American labor: wages stagnate and prices soar; unions represent a shrinking portion of the labor force; corporations resist health-and-safety programs; a Democratic Congress defeats fundamental labor law reform despite labor's lobbying efforts; corporate consulting firms using lawyers, psychologists, and public relations experts attempt to create a "union-free environment." In such a context labor needs all the help it can get from the left. By the late 1970s coalition politics for a broad range of economic reform had become central to the agenda of organized labor. In 1978, for example, the United Automobile Workers (UAW), along with the Machinists (IAM), the state, county and municipal employees (AFSCME), and nearly a hundred other liberal trade unions, civil rights groups, women's organizations, and consumer groups organized a national political coalition—the Progressive Alliance—to work for a liberal economic program that a Democratic Congress had ignored, defeated, or watered down. Besides organizing the Progressive Alliance, liberal trade unions provided money and manpower for a wide range of coalitions such as the

Full Employment Action Council, the Citizen/Labor Energy Coalition, the Leadership Conference on Civil Rights, the Democratic Agenda, the Consumer Coalition for Health, and many more.

As U.S. capitalism falls on hard times, the most progressive sections of the American trade-union movement are gradually being pushed in a social democratic or even socialist direction. As economic conditions in America begin to take on a more austere European pattern, the traditional American trade-union antipathy toward socialism seems also to be diminishing. As American economic exceptionalism disappears, so ultimately may American political exceptionalism. By the late 1970s Michael Harrington's Democratic Socialist Organizing Committee (DSOC) had close ties with the key leadership of the UAW, the Machinists, the Clothing & Textile Workers, AFSCME, and even the traditionally-conservative building trades department of the AFL-CIO. And socialism had its first important trade-union spokesman in decades in William Winpisinger, president of the Machinists. By the end of the 1970s, also, the mounting energy crisis had made the conflict between private profit and public interest ever more visible to organized labor. In 1979 the AFL-CIO executive council called for the nationalization of the oil industry if it could not properly serve the public interest, and the International Union of Electrical Workers (IUE) urged the nationalization of all domestic energy resources, arguing that this wealth "should be regulated in the interest of all Americans and not for the profit of a few."

For generations, the principle of "managerial prerogative" prevailed in American industry. This meant essentially that management retained for itself the exclusive right to run the company as it saw fit, and the union, taking an adversarial role, bargained with management on a narrow range of issues restricted to the job area—wages, hours, and conditions. This seemed to work fairly well as long as American capitalism was dynamic, expanding, and affluent. In that context managerial prerogative meant more factories, more jobs, and with union prodding, higher wages. Today, with the economy in the doldrums, managerial prerogative often means closed plants, international runaways, and front-end technology transfers. And these policies are ultimately as important to workers as wages, hours, and working conditions. Because managerial prerogative in an age of economic decline may do more damage to workers than ever before, American trade unions may be increasingly drawn into that sacred preserve, through either collective bargaining or political action. Labor's growing pressure for state and federal laws to regulate plant closings and to protect worker and community interests is a prime example of the way trade unions may be forced to encroach upon managerial prerogatives in order to defend the economic interests of their members. Moreover, as the exercise of managerial prerogative in such areas as investment, plant location, and technology transfer begin to impinge on workers as much as decisions in the job area, it is apparent that some trade unions, along with others on the left, will try to bring the structure of corporate management itself under more democratic control.

In companies that have been weakened, management may be either willing or compelled to yield ground on the principle of absolute managerial sovereignty. In this context, the symbolic importance of the UAW's victory in securing a seat on Chrysler's Board of Directors can hardly be exaggerated. Although Douglas Fraser's power will of course be small and although Chrysler tried to make clear that Fraser was chosen as an able man, not as a union representative, this event establishes a crucial precedent for the democratization of corporate governance in the U.S. Fraser himself explained that membership on the Chrysler board was just the beginning, the first step toward implementing the principle that workers should have a greater voice in their own economic destiny. And he made it clear that he hoped ultimately to extend worker representation to the boards of both General Motors and Ford.

While socialism is still an alien ideology for most Americans, democracy and pluralism are central to the American tradition. If the movement for the democratization of corporate governance gains strength—and it does seem to be an idea whose time is coming—it will grow not directly out of socialist ideology but will be a logical extension of the American democratic tradition. Indeed, appeals to democratize the corporation strike a responsive chord primarily because they represent a very natural enrichment of the American democratic heritage.

There is another element as well. An enormous body of both theoretical work and empirical evidence over the years has convincingly demonstrated that direct worker participation in management not only enhances job satisfaction but also generally increases productivity.[12] With America's competitive economic edge disappearing, productivity growth lagging, and the work ethic among Americans allegedly disappearing, U.S. corporations may be more willing than in the past to cooperate with the growing movement for job enrichment and various forms of worker participation. Corporations will undoubtedly seek to hold these experiments tightly in check, to limit their power and extent, and to deny that they constitute any precedent for encroachment upon managerial control. However, in the context of the gradual enrichment of American democracy, these experiments will undoubtedly have a democratic dynamic that may prove impossible to control in the long run.

The new austerity does not predetermine an inevitable turn to the political left or to the political right. Much depends on unforeseeable events and on which political forces are best able to channel the national mood. One pattern, nonetheless, seems probable. In an age of decline, the party in power—whatever party it happens to be—is likely to be held responsible for the country's woes. As voters blame incumbent parties and politicians for the nation's increasing problems, they will turn to others in search of remedies. Thus, we are entering a period in which incumbents may be turned out of office frequently; unable to solve the structural problems of decline, one party, one elected official, will be voted out in favor of others, creating a rapid-fire political turnover.

The national political leadership is especially vulnerable here, symbolizing as it does the entire society. At the presidential level forces of continuing decline may strengthen the opposition, making reelection—or even renomination—of an incumbent president difficult. This pattern developed quite clearly during the Carter Administration in the late 1970s. We noted earlier that foreign crises provoked by America's diminished influence may actually aid incumbents as Americans rally 'round the flag and the officials who have draped themselves in it. But this can operate two ways.

President Carter, presiding over the acclerated decline of American power, was held responsible and accused of a failure of leadership, although the forces underlying this decline had been developing for years if not decades and most were clearly beyond the responsibility of one man, one party, or one administration. Nonetheless, because his presidency coincided with America's declining economic power and waning international influence, Carter was blamed for these developments. With Carter weakened, Edward Kennedy and Governor Jerry Brown of California took the unusual step of challenging an incumbent president's renomination.

TAKING CARE OF NUMBER ONE

> "Years ago a person, he was unhappy, didn't know what to do with himself—he'd go to church or start a revolution—*something*. Today you're unhappy? Can't figure it out? What is the salvation? Go shopping.
>
> "If they would close the stores for six months in this country there would be from coast to coast a real massacre."
>
> Mr. Solomon in Arthur Miller's *The Price*

If, indeed, the best times for the American economy now lie behind us, if incomes continue to fall or stagnate, then American society may face not only an economic crisis but a social and moral crisis as well. For as David M. Potter has argued in his influential book *People of Plenty*, one of the most powerful forces shaping American civilization for nearly four hundred years has been the fact of abundance.[13] The abundance of land, resources, wealth, opportunity, and the ability and determination to exploit this bounty has been crucial to the American experience and to the shaping of the American national character. If this abundance, which Americans have simply taken for granted for centuries, is now diminishing, what vast consequences may this have for American society? Abundance has been, after all, a primary social glue that bound this country together. Without it, will the center hold?

While material abundance has been America's blessing, it has also been its curse, for the worship of abundance has dominated the moral landscape for so long that it has crowded out the development of other more spiritual, communal, or collective goals. By what wild stretch of the imagination could the Chinese motto, "Serve the people," or any other theme stressing collective welfare or communal concern ever prevail in America as we know it? In America both radicals (Herbert Marcuse et al.) and conservatives (most convergence theorists) have observed that the good life is defined essentially as the endless private accumulation of material goods; and progress is taken as synonymous with increasing levels of personal consumption even at the expense of the deterioration of the public sector. John Kenneth Galbraith's observation of the 1950s that postwar America was living in private opulence amid public squalor is even more true today than it was twenty-five years ago. Underlying this strange imbalance in American society is the total privatization of life and the fallacious corollary that if private living standards can be maintained in the face of the collapse of the public sector, then one's personal level of living is safeguarded and will not be diminished. We have seen that the Proposition 13 movement epitomizes this view. With private living standards falling, the only conceivable way to arrest their descent was to throw overboard the dispensable ballast of public services. And, of course, the values that stress voracious privatized self-aggrandizement over social reconstruction have been effectively cemented into the national mind by the most powerful economic force of our time, the national corporation, and its ubiquitous voice, modern advertising.

Historian Christopher Lasch has called ours a "culture of narcissism," and sociologist Richard Sennett has written of the "fall of public man" and the reign of private man in contemporary society. For a small but influential stratum of young people the political activism of the 1960s temporarily papered over the privatization of American life. But after its exhaustion in the 1970s that privatization appeared once again in the guise of what came to be called the "Me Decade." Its major feature, according to journalist Tom Wolfe who coined the term, was a personal obsession with "remaking, remodeling, elevating, and polishing one's very *self* . . . and observing, studying, and doting on it (Me!)." [14] The Me Decade was best caricatured—perhaps intentionally—by the New Left guru Jerry Rubin. In the 1970s Rubin discovered that politics couldn't solve every problem. So, turning inward to a search for self, Rubin, in the few short years between 1971 and 1975, managed to find time to drink deeply of "Est, gestalt therapy, bioenergetics, rolfing, massage, jogging, health foods, tai chi, Esalen, hypnotism, modern dance, meditation, Silva Mind Control, Arica, acupuncture, sex therapy, Reichian therapy, and More House. . . ."[15]

The social organization of the contemporary family intensifies the privatization of life. The small size of the modern nuclear family promotes a kind of trivialized, inward-looking social provincialism. That this tiny nuclear family is also the primary unit of consumption, social class, and social mobility also encourages a narrow social vision and a self-absorbed material ambition and creates what Arthur Miller has called that "hermetic seal around the American family." One's social interests and social responsibilities stop at the front door.

While the nuclear family is a privatizing structure, the breakdown of marriage and the rising divorce rate promote even further isolation. The number of single-person households in the U.S. increases as the legions of the separated and divorced join the delayed-marriage singles and the growing numbers of widows and widowers. While we spoke earlier of rising rents and increased apartment sharing, this is still mainly a big-city phenomenon concentrated among younger singles. Despite it, there has probably never been a society where so many people have lived by themselves. By the end of the 1970s nearly a quarter (22 percent) of all households in the U.S. were occupied by only one person—17 million people living alone. These isolated millions are left to spin out the implications of their own solipsism. Meanwhile, manufacturers respond with products for people living alone—soup for one, a banquet. In a society with a growing number of people living alone, taking care of number one becomes a reality out of default: there *is* only one.

Modern technology and architecture also contribute to the privatization of contemporary life. Sociologists such as Georg Simmel and Louis Wirth, writing earlier in the twentieth century, observed that in the large city social relationships become superficial, anonymous, and transitory. While this is now obvious, twentieth-century technology is going one step beyond that and making human contact of any kind increasingly superfluous. Sociologist Phillip Slater, in fact, has written that the whole force of modern urban life often seems to be directed toward making it unnecessary for anyone to speak to anyone else. Superficial contact with bank tellers is replaced with machines—some of which are given human names and human form—that take deposits and hand out money. Personal telephone conversations with human beings are replaced with recorded messages and answering machines. Automatic elevators replace elevator operators. Cartoonist Jules Feiffer creates an immediately recognizable character whose best friend is his television set, which he talks to intimately. Meanwhile, as public mass transit languishes, the one-family (or one-person) automobile—the prime symbol of privatized consumption in America—becomes the major means of transportation.

In the modern apartment building each individual or family is nested away in its own human file drawer, meeting "neighbors" only briefly and accidentally in the elevator, lobby, or laundry room. And landlords have read their Marx. Should they restore a little *Gemeinschaft* and provide a comfortable communal meeting room for all residents where they can socialize, share common grievances, and form a tenants' union? Divide and conquer.

In his classic essay on socialism Albert Einstein wrote of man's dual nature: as a solitary being pursuing self-interest, and as a social being recognizing the interdependence of human welfare and responding to altruistic motives. Some balance of these dual impulses is essential in any civilized society. Yet the pathology of capitalism, Einstein wrote, is that "the egotistical drives of his [man's] make-up are constantly being accentuated, while his social drives, which are by nature weaker, progressively deteriorate." [16] Nowhere has the atrophy of man's social feeling and the triumph of egotistical feeling been more complete than in the American ethos of privatized material consumption. If, as Einstein implied, life takes meaning only through personal transcendence of narrow egotistical drives, then the American ethos encouraging the endless accumulation of personal possessions has always failed to provide meaning; and the end of abundance may leave our spiritual cupboard more bare than ever before, unless it is replaced by something more substantial.

Some years ago Buick ran an expensive advertising campaign: "Buick—something to believe in." And why not? If God is dead, then why not an automobile? The rise of Sunday store openings in America is also no accident, for Sunday, after all, is the day of worship; and what better place to worship than in the shopping center? Worship or therapy? As Arthur Miller observed, shopping is now the great American psychotherapy—something to do when depressed, to lift the spirits and give meaning.

Driving east from New York City on the Long Island Express-way, just before leaving Queens and entering Nassau County, there is a pleasant rise in the land just south of the highway, a hill that overlooks the highway and all the surrounding area. On such a point in the Middle Ages a magnificent cathedral would have risen. But today, a more secular age, there stands instead Kor-vettes, the great discount department store. In the Middle Ages, standing in the shadow of that stately cathedral might have been peasants' huts, grouped around in silent obeisance. Today, stand-ing beneath Korvettes and encircling it from below are its twen-tieth-century counterparts, tacky one- and two-family tract houses paying their obeisance to this national shrine.

But Americans have demonstrated their devotion to consuming in still another way. One can reasonably argue, I believe, that the ultimate form of privatized consumption is overeating. If so, it is no wonder that obesity is one of the nation's major public health problems.

Cross-cultural research on national values confirms the impres-sion that "Americans more than Europeans aspire toward material goals, higher incomes, occupational status and increasing con-sumption. . . ." [17] Not only do Americans have higher material expectations for the future than Europeans, but they are also not prepared to accept frustration of these expectations. In 1972 the University of Michigan's Survey Research Center found that 40 percent of their national sample said they would be either some-what disappointed or quite disturbed if their living standards had not increased five years later—as indeed they did not. [18] And David Caplovitz found that although the recession and inflation of the mid-1970s had not radicalized the public, fully 35 percent of his respondents said they had lost faith in the American dream—a substantial desertion from the kingpin of American values.[19]

Wartime experience suggests that for a legitimate national cause Americans are prepared to sacrifice, temporarily at least, the living standards to which they have become accustomed. It is far more unlikely, however, that Americans will stoically accept declining living standards for no national cause at all, especially if it is due to meaningless drift and decline of the economic system.

Periodic opinion research since the 1960s has confirmed what seems to be apparent—that there has been a crisis of legitimacy in American society, and that there is little basic trust in the fundamental political, economic, and religious institutions of that society.[20] Such an anomic atmosphere is not conducive to a national spirit of mutual sacrifice in the face of stagnating living standards. Moreover, because of the elevation of private acquisitiveness to a socially sanctioned ethic, the stagnation of American capitalism may engender a fierce personal struggle to salvage oneself and one's family, a national temper reminiscent of that collective psychology of the early 1960s when people stored guns in their bomb shelters to keep unwanted neighbors out amid the nuclear debris.

If it finally comes down to it, it is possible that Americans will resist the end of empire and the stagnation of their living standards far more ferociously than have the British. The greater violence of American society (compare, for example, the history of labor violence here, the astronomically higher American homicide rate, or the incidence of political assassinations) and the greater stress in this country upon personal, material well-being suggest that the American response to decline may be far more turbulent and uncontrolled, far more likely to resemble a war of each against all than the dignified resignation of a people to its role as a declining economic power.

AMERICAN CHARACTER RECONSIDERED: BLUE JEANS AND BARGAINS, CHALLENGE AND RESPONSE

But are we perhaps selling America short? Is American society, although preoccupied with material abundance, not flexible and complex enough to nourish other values as well? As the heritage of material abundance diminishes, America's central challenge in the 1980s and beyond will be to call forth values pertaining to the quality of American life rather than merely the quantity of life which can give renewed meaning to the American experience.

America is in fact so diverse and so rich ideologically that it is impossible to make a definitive judgment about the American future based on the tradition of material acquisitiveness alone. While the institutions of social class and the materialism based upon it undoubtedly have deep roots here, there is also the strong American ideological tradition of classlessness and equality which really disdain the kind of materialism often associated with America. There are, in short, within American society interweaving and often conflicting strands of both class and classlessness, of materialism and antimaterialism. There are, in the U.S., as in all class societies, forces of class competition manifested in materialistic striving, conspicuous display, and invidious ranking. But these characteristics clash head-on with other qualities of American society: the unpretentiousness, the plain-folks tradition, the frugality, the practicality, and the rough-and-ready informality of American life. There is, in fact, probably less sheer stuffiness and class snobbery in America than in any other stratified society.

In all class societies there are impulses to display costly material goods in order to demonstrate one's pecuniary prowess; yet in America what one might call the "bargain psychology" is just as highly developed—the impulse to boast about how cheaply and economically one was able to acquire something rather than how dearly. It is no accident, moreover, that the prime American fashion symbol to the world is not furs or jewels or other expensive ornaments befitting an affluent society, but blue jeans; that fact alone speaks volumes about the basic informality and unpretentiousness of American life. And yet, with the appearance of "status jeans"—high-priced designer jeans—we see the interweaving themes of class and classlessness, of pretense and practicality.

More seriously, did not Americans (or at least groups of Americans) develop the world's first, strongest, and most militant movement for environmental protection and ecological concern, many of whose objectives run directly counter to the established principles of conspicuous consumption, privatized acquisitiveness, and unabashed materialism? In short, are there not within the American national character sufficient habits of thrift, practicality, sobriety, informality, and conservation to see us through—ideologically as well as materially—a long period of austerity or even decline?

We must also recognize that the challenges facing America in the 1980s and beyond are custom-made for American national character and constitute an almost classic illustration of Toynbee's theory of challenge and response. If national character alone could solve a nation's problems, then America's would be solved. Besides death and taxes, Americans are resigned, passive, and fatalistic about almost nothing. The national spirit has always been extraordinarily activist and energetic and Americans as a people completely convinced that any challenge—at home, abroad, or in space—could be met. Perseverance in the face of adversity and ingenuity under duress are intrinsic to the American experience. It is true that under the impact of recent events American optimism has been waning among the general public (as we shall see) as well as in the business community; nonetheless, an underlying tenacious spirit remains. With energy shortages and the crisis of U.S. capitalism, America's problems in the next generation will be technological and economic. But technology and economics have always been America's forte. It would be a serious error, then, to ignore the inevitable struggle to develop innovations in technology, production, financing, and social and economic organization to keep the houses and all the wonted consumer durables flowing, in order to maintain and enhance the proverbial American standard of living.

THE SILENT STRUGGLE IN AMERICAN SOCIETY: THE STAGNATION OF AMERICAN CAPITALISM VS. THE ENRICHMENT OF AMERICAN DEMOCRACY

As American capitalism endures its most serious and intractable crisis since the Great Depression, raising the threat of social conflict, intolerance, and disorder, something equally momentous is also happening to American society which has the potential to do the exact opposite. Far-reaching social and political changes are enriching American democracy and creating a more mature, civil, and tolerant society. Both in terms of personal freedom and political liberty, by the late 1970s American society had become more open, more genuinely pluralistic, and less repressive than at any time in this century. For the first time in its modern history, in fact, American society seemed to be running out of witches to burn. Not only was American society becoming more permissive toward the usual political scapegoats, but the public was becoming increasingly tolerant of, or at least acclimated to, an extraordinary range of social and cultural diversity.*

By the 1970s the anti-communist hysteria that had gripped the country for generations had pretty much burned itself out and probably could be resurrected only by a major international confrontation with the Soviet Union. Not since the Russian Revolution itself had America been so unconcerned with the "threat" of domestic communism and so willing to grant communists, socialists, and other radicals their basic Constitutional rights. A replication in the 1970s of Samuel Stauffer's famous postwar opinion study *Communism, Conformity, and Civil Liberties* showed a striking and unmistakable rise in public respect for the specific First Amendment rights of free speech, free press, and assembly for communists, socialists, and other ideological dissenters.[21] This is ironic in a sense because by the late 1970s communism had spread further and Soviet military power had grown stronger than ever before. Yet whether out of political maturity or sheer political boredom, Americans could no longer be whipped up into the same witch-hunting fervor so common in previous decades, and demogogic office-seekers could no longer run their campaigns on fear of communism and a spirit of persecution.

Following Watergate, public revulsion against government wiretapping increased enormously.[22] And by the mid-1970s, in the wake of Watergate, Vietnam, and secret and illegal activities at

---

*I am not arguing T. H. Marshall's convergence thesis (see Chapter 1) that the enrichment of citizenship has mitigated class differences; there has actually been little impact on class as such. Rather, I am merely arguing that the enrichment of democracy has made America a freer and more civil society.

home and abroad, it was not the Socialist Workers party or even the Communist party that felt publicly harassed, legally restricted, and victimized by a hostile press, but the FBI and the CIA. Even for a democracy, this was quite extraordinary. It is true that by the end of the decade, growing U.S. vulnerability to Arab oil and Soviet military power created great public and Congressional sentiment to "unleash" the CIA once again, but the somber lessons of previous covert operations made it unlikely that the intelligence agencies would have as free a hand in the future as they had in the past.

Meanwhile, loyalty oaths and blacklists are becoming historical relics that parents tell their uninterested children about. A quarter of a century ago leftists in Hollywood were hounded, purged, and driven from their professions. Today, radical activist Jane Fonda wins an Academy Award for her performance in the anti-Vietnam War film *Coming Home*.* In 1950 Howard Fast went to prison for refusing to cooperate with the House Committee on Un-American Activities. Now his novel *Freedom Road* is dramatized for prime-time TV. The Freedom of Information Act now provides public access to government files, occasionally with devastating effect. William Shawcross, the British journalist who wrote a withering attack on U.S. policy in Cambodia in his book *Sideshow: Kissinger, Nixon and the Destruction of Cambodia,* readily admitted he could not have written that indictment of U.S. policy without access to the files of the U.S. Department of Defense and of State provided under the Freedom of Information Act. In fact, Shawcross acknowledged that if he had tried to write such a book in democratic Britain, with that nation's Official Secrets Act, he would probably have landed in jail.

Petty censorship is still brought to bear in the public schools of many small towns across America. Yet the secular decline in censorship over the decades can hardly be doubted. *Ulysses,* after all, is available at most bookstores. Sociologists (and others) who regard contemporary America as particularly repressive should recall that as late as 1935 Robert and Helen Lynd, in their classic

---

* Asked in the late 1970s whether the political climate had changed, Fonda herself quipped, "Well, I'm working and Nixon isn't."

re-study of "Middletown" (Muncie, Indiana), noted that the omnipotent Ball family had successfully removed Bertrand Russell's *Marriage and Morals* (a book whose revolutionary proposal was that young people might wish to live together for a time before marrying) not merely from the local high school, but from the library of the local state-supported *college*.[23]

Some of the changes in America have been very gradual and thus have gone unnoticed by those who live here day in and day out. Perhaps the country's drift is more evident to someone who has been away for many years and then returns. The expatriate leftist writer Clancy Sigal moved from the United States to England in 1957. Returning to America for a lengthy visit after twenty-two years, Sigal observed:

Coming back to the U.S. now is like my dreams come true—it almost seems as if everybody's [politically] left. It must seem an absolutely daft statement to anyone who lives in the States, but I'm coming back reaping the benefit of the struggle in the '60s and '70s, and now it seems to me the left is much more accepted and acceptable than ever before.[24]

Even the ever-vigilant, never-complacent American Civil Liberties Union said on its sixtieth anniversary in 1980 that ". . . it is fair to say that we have won many important victories and established many new rights during our first sixty years. There is more liberty today than there was in 1920, and more people have more rights now than they did then."[25]

Other changes reflect the slowly growing civility of American society. The decline of capital punishment in the U.S. over the last several decades is a striking example.* True, in the late 1970s there were a number of executions when capital punishment was resumed after a moratorium beginning in 1967, followed by the restrictive 1972 Supreme Court *Furman* decision. Yet despite the

---

* Prisoners executed in the U.S.:

1930–39:	1,667
1940–49:	1,284
1950–59:	717
1960–69:	191
1970–79:	3

resumption of capital punishment, it is almost impossible to imagine a climate under which the number of executions could ever again reach the level of the 1930s. What is important here, as elsewhere, is not what appear to be temporary reversals but the long-term secular direction of change.

In another area, the Supreme Court overturned all state anti-abortion laws in 1973; thus, in one stroke American women were freed from the nightmare of criminal abortion. Victory came so fast in fact that the major abortion rights organization, the National Association for the Repeal of Abortion Legislation, had to change its name only four years after its founding in 1969. Although legalized abortion is under attack by right-to-life groups, is it not a significant advance from their point of view that for the first time those who *favor* the right of abortion now represent the legal status quo?

While an enormous amount of race prejudice certainly persists in America, what is important again is the long-term direction of change. Opinion research since the early 1960s shows increasing moderation in white attitudes.[26] White stereotypes of blacks (blacks have less ambition than whites, have less native intelligence, are inferior, etc.) are declining sharply. Compared to the 1960s, whites expressed less race prejudice by the late 1970s and were less likely to insist on traditional racist forms of social distance from blacks in public accommodations, housing, schools, jobs, and social relations. These are not abstract attitudes unconnected to behavior, for whites reported more contact and communication with blacks in the late 1970s than in the 1960s at work, school, as neighbors, and elsewhere.

The enormous edifice of Jim Crow institutions was built up in the South over a period of three quarters of a century, and many felt that it would take that long to bring it down. Yet under the combined impact of civil rights activism, legislation, and court decisions in the 1960s, the entire structure of Jim Crow collapsed with a speed that laid to rest once and for all the received conservative wisdom from Burke to Buckley that social change cannot be achieved by government action. While the array of legislation, court decisions, and executive orders relating to voting rights, fair employment, fair housing, and affirmative action obviously have not achieved the final goal of equality, the legal and perhaps more important moral claims have clearly established the national agenda.

The spirit of every age is captured by the kinds of persons who are thrust into public prominence. By the late 1970s Southerners with the views of James Eastland and George Wallace were fading fast from the American scene and being rapidly replaced by Southern moderates. And civil rights activist Andrew Young had gone from the picket line in the 1960s to the United Nations in the 1970s, and from there had become a kind of younger elder statesman.

In 1963 Martin Luther King, Jr., called Birmingham "probably the most thoroughly segregated city in the United States." There, Bull Conner turned dogs and firehoses on civil rights workers, police assaulted peaceful demonstrators, and four black girls were killed in a church bombing. In 1979, although race relations were still far from ideal, a black man was elected mayor of Birmingham, joining such other Southern cities as Richmond, Atlanta, and New Orleans which had also elected black mayors in the 1970s. And by the late 1970s there were more elected black officials in the South than most optimistic civil rights workers had thought possible a decade and a half earlier.

As blatant racism recedes, the problems of blacks become more than ever problems of social class—jobs, income, education, and housing—which they share with the poor of all races. Without for a moment denying the magnitude of black poverty and unemployment, a balanced view requires recognition that economic forces and diminished racism have led many blacks into main-line unionized blue-collar jobs in manufacturing and into white-collar jobs as well. Between 1960 and 1978, for example, the proportion of white workers employed in white-collar jobs increased only from 47 percent to 52 percent; in the same period, the proportion of non-whites working in white-collar occupations rose from 16 percent to 36 percent.[27]

Although the long-term trend in racism is undoubtedly down, the recent revival of the Ku Klux Klan, cross burnings in the North, and white resistance to affirmative action threaten recent gains and highlight the national frustration that is linked to the economic crisis and the stagnation of living standards, about which I shall have more to say below.

Along with the secular decline of race prejudice is a concomitant decline in religious prejudice as well. In 1960 when John F. Kennedy ran for the highest political office in the land, many wondered whether a Catholic could—or should—be elected president of the United States. By 1980 when Edward Kennedy ran for the same office (and even by 1968 when Robert Kennedy ran for president), the Catholic issue was not merely declining, it was dead.

Prejudice is declining not only against the usual ideological minorities—political, racial, religious—but against what might be called normative minorities as well. Homosexuals are a normative rather than an ideological minority, for their behavior violates the most fundamental social morality. Bigotry against normative minorities is more difficult to eradicate than any other because its historical roots run so deep. Communism may be subversive, but homosexuality is immoral, which, in the public mind, is far worse. In many respects, William Graham Sumner was right: the inertia of morality can hardly be exaggerated.

Yet by the late 1970s homosexuals in America were out of the closet and into the streets and meeting halls, demanding that sexual preference be treated as any other form of free choice. Obviously, homosexuals are still stigmatized, as the celebrated Anita Bryant campaign to repeal a homosexual rights law in Dade County, Florida aptly demonstrated. Yet that a legal battle for homosexual rights could be openly waged at all is testimony to the advance of civil rights. Once again, what is crucial is the direction of change in public attitudes, and here we see an unmistakable rise in public tolerance. In 1978 California voters defeated an initiative that would have permitted the dismissal of homosexual schoolteachers, an issue that in previous times would have sent the public into paroxysms of self-righteous sexual persecution. In San Francisco, avowed homosexuals had won high political office by the late 1970s, and politically active homosexuals were becoming major power brokers in the city.

In an extraordinary sociological spectacle, homosexuals, one of history's most stigmatized minorities, were emerging in San Francisco as "perhaps the most powerful voting bloc in the city," according to the *New York Times*. Ironically, homosexual pressure-group politics in San Francisco were assuming a marked similarity to ethnic-group and immigrant politics in American cities in earlier generations.

And of course the media responded. Before the 1970s homosexuals were rarely portrayed on television in any context; by the late 1970s they were seen in a number of serious roles, neither stereotyped nor ridiculed, and network documentaries treated them openly and frankly. And Hollywood as well as Broadway began presenting more homosexuals and homosexual themes in serious dramatic context.

In general, by the late 1970s there had been a sweeping de-stigmatization of all forms of sexuality in American life which was both transmitted and exploited by the media. Violence on television was becoming unfashionable and sex, therefore, was its natural replacement. Both in front of and behind the television camera divorce has become almost the future tense of marriage. Spotless monogamy is no longer a *sine qua non* for ambitious politicians. Adultery and illegitimacy hardly excite public attention any more, and celebrities are frequent role models (compare, for example, the public response to Ingrid Bergman a generation ago with celebrities in the same situation today). Premarital sex, abortions, consensual unions, infidelity, prostitution, sex among the aged have all become the daily fare of afternoon and prime-time television. Even incest, the "last taboo," is talk show material. On television, of course, these serious themes are often run through the mass-culture gin mill, emerging as barely concealed titillation. In the 1960s capitalism learned how to turn the cultural revolution to good profit, boosting ratings or enlarging the bottom line. The unanticipated consequence of this, however, has been to increase public exposure and thus tolerance for a wide range of cultural styles and consequently to change the climate of American life.

What sociologist Herbert Gans called the equality revolution swept away not only the most obvious ideological and normative minorities, but revived and strengthened a dormant feminism and stirred senior citizens to action. And by the late 1970s the new movement to enrich American democracy had penetrated even to one of society's most forgotten minorities—the handicapped and disabled—who were demanding and slowly receiving their own version of equality of opportunity.

The Role of Education

Several forces underlie the growing openness, tolerance, and civility of American life. First, the political ideology of American democracy itself contains the dynamic for its own expansion. If democracy is defined as a good, then in terms of the logic of the system more democracy is even better. As an ideal type, democracy resembles a perpetual motion machine, constantly regenerating, replenishing, and building upon itself. The dynamic is clearly seen in the essential *contagiousness* of liberation movements since the 1960s. The civil rights movement and black liberation set in motion a chain reaction that produced women's liberation, gay liberation, senior citizens' liberation, handicapped liberation, and more.

Second, changes in the social characteristics of the American population are also responsible for changing public attitudes. In his unforgettable phrase, Marx spoke of the "idiocy of rural life," and at least since that time it has been well known that city life generates a more tolerant state of mind. As America's rural areas are relentlessly depleted, and as the urbanization and metropolitanization of America continues apace, Americans become, literally and figuratively, more cosmopolitan.[28]

Third, and even more important than urbanization, is the growth of higher education. The relationship between formal education and general social and political tolerance has been well known for decades. Twenty years ago sociologist Seymour Martin Lipset wrote that ". . . *the most important single factor differentiating those giving democratic responses from others has been education. The higher one's education, the more likely one is to believe in democratic values and support democratic practices.*"[29] What produces this liberal drift is not so much the status- or class-conferring properties of education, but the substantive content of education itself. Education, like travel, is broadening; it acquaints people with a wide variety of political and cultural per-

spectives and re-familiarizes them with the ideals of American democracy. Conservatives are quite right, higher education in the
U.S. has been a liberalizing force; but it is not, as many conservatives imply, the result of a liberal conspiracy.

The liberalizing effects of education can be seen clearly in the
1973 replication of the Stauffer study which measured public support for the civil liberties of communists, socialists, and atheists (see
Table 41). As educational attainment rises, political tolerance also
rises; those with college experience are far more likely than others
to support the Constitutional rights of ideological minorities.
Also, between 1954 (the date of the original Stauffer study) and
1973 the proportion of Americans rated "more tolerant" rose
from under a one third (31 percent) to over half (55 percent).
Growing public support for basic civil liberties, reflected both in
public opinion research such as this and in obvious changes in the
political climate, are at least partly attributable to the level of educational achievement in the nation.

We have written at length about class stagnation and class divergence. And while these patterns have in fact developed within
crucial economic dimensions and have washed over into innumer-

Table 41. POLITICAL TOLERANCE AND
EDUCATION, 1973

Education	% Rated "More Tolerant"
College graduate	84%
Some college	75
High-school graduate	58
Some high school	40
Grade school	19
TOTAL	55%

SOURCE: Clyde Z. Nunn, Harry J. Crockett, Jr., and
J. Allen Williams, Jr., *Tolerance for Nonconfor-
mity: A National Survey of Americans' Changing
Commitment to Civil Liberties* (San Francisco:
Jossey-Bass, 1978), p. 60.

able social and psychological areas, one must recognize that at the same time the educational level of the American people has been rising. Both convergence and stability theorists noted the growth of education, and on this one point they are obviously correct; the major difference between them was not whether educational expansion had occurred, but whether it had narrowed the gap between classes. Whatever the case, it must be granted that by the late 1970s the number and proportion of Americans who had attended college was completely unprecedented, compared both to all other nations of the world and to American society in the past.

In 1940 there were less than 3.5 million college graduates over the age of 25 in the U.S. By 1950 the figure had grown to about 5.5 million. But by the late 1970s, there were 18.5 million college graduates over 25 years of age, more than 20 million college graduates of all ages, and over 43 million persons who had at least one year of college.[30]

We spoke earlier of the career problems of this college-educated mass, and these must not be forgotten. Yet what is crucial in this context is not the vocational implications of education but the unanticipated social, cultural, and political implications of a society where more than 43 million persons have received at least some higher education. Inevitably, the intellectual level of publics, audiences and electorates rises, however gradually. The tone, feel and climate of American culture and politics have undoubtedly changed.

This growing maturity is reflected in many ways. In his book on popular culture and high culture, Herbert Gans argued that the general level of mass taste had risen since the end of World War II. If it is an exaggeration to speak of a "cultural explosion" in America, then perhaps the more measured phrase cultural expansion is apt, with rising attendance at the theater, ballet, opera, concert hall, and museum. Public television has blossomed, and its cultural programming creates new audiences for the performing arts. At the same time, Congress finally discovered that government subsidy for the arts is not tantamount to Bolshevism, and although the level of federal aid is still small by European standards, the funds available to the National Endowment for the Arts and the National Endowment for the Humanities grew by about ten-fold in the 1970s.[31]

Commercial television is still largely the vast waste land described years ago by Newton Minow, but oases of literacy are beginning to form even there. By the late 1970s even ratings-wise television executives were surprised that the CBS news documentary program, *60 Minutes,* was one of the most popular prime-time shows on television. And underlying the great (and unexpected) popularity of the *Mary Hartman, Mary Hartman* series in the mid-1970s were the changing American demographics of an increasingly educated and sophisticated viewing public.

Daytime television has always been directed at women, for whom TV executives have shown particular contempt, treating them like fools or children or both. As educational levels rise, however, this becomes more difficult to do; and the popularity of the literate Phil Donahue show, which treats women as mature adults, reflects the growing sophistication of this traditionally most insulted sector of the viewing public.

As the educational level of film audiences rises, a growing number of Hollywood films have themes relevant to the experience of college-educated persons, and more films have protagonists who are college-educated themselves. In recent years Hollywood has become less the "dream factory" described by anthropologist Hortense Powdermaker in the 1940s and more a reality factory.* By the 1970s the best American films had achieved—especially for a popular medium—a remarkable maturity and seriousness of purpose. In the last year of the decade, for example, among the five films nominated in Hollywood for best picture of the year were *Kramer vs. Kramer,* a sensitive portrait of a divorce and child custody battle set in the context of the changing role of women and the disintegration of modern American family values; *Apocalypse Now,* an indictment of epic proportions of American policy in Vietnam; and *Norma Rae,* a sympathetic account of a struggle to organize textile workers in the South.

---

* If one accepts the premise that in some way life in New York City represents reality and life in Los Angeles represents fantasy, then there is some significance in the recent renaissance of filmmaking in New York.

Mass-culture cynics who are used to dismissing popular taste *in toto* are beginning to have a hard time of it with the rising educational level of middle-class audiences.

A growing national sophistication is reflected even in the development of American humor. As late as the 1940s or 1950s, the major appeal of American humorists was not to a college-educated audience. The most popular comics themselves were either not college educated or lacked general intellectual sophistication: the slapstick of Abbott and Costello or Laurel and Hardy; the inanities of Jerry Lewis; the apolitical comedy of such radio personalities as Jack Benny or Fred Allen. Compare a later generation of brainy, urban comics whose humor appeals to a college-educated audience and is more social or political in content: Mort Sahl, Lenny Bruce, Woody Allen, George Carlin, Robert Klein, Dick Cavett. Indeed, a society in which Woody Allen's comedy *Annie Hall* wins an Academy Award for the best picture of the year is obviously a society of growing cultural sophistication.

Rising levels of education, plus the changing patterns of industrial employment, are also creating a discernible shift in the dominant American personality type. Millions of professionals and other college-educated white-collar employees now work in nonprofit, noncapitalist sectors of the economy. By the late 1970s about 16 million persons worked for federal, state, and local government, compared to only 6.5 million in 1950. Countless millions more work for private cultural, religious, educational, and charitable organizations. Their work in the nonprofit sector has not fostered the usual business-minded, bottom-line mentality so typical of capitalist enterprise. Their education, especially in the social sciences and humanities, has also created a kind of value system and orientation which is different from, if not directly hostile to, the typical business values and business personality. In any case, as millions of educated workers are now employed in the vast and growing nonprofit, non-business sector, much of the traditional Babbitry is going out of American life. The dominance of the business personality as such is declining. Although the extent of the change is still moderate and should not be exaggerated, there seems nonetheless to be a perceptible drift in American values away from money and business toward culture and intellect.

One senses, for example, that the kind of politics and personality represented by John Connally—the archetypal old-fashioned plutocrat—is fading fast from the American scene.

Woodstock Nation

It is naive, of course, to view education alone as the explanation of and the prescription for the good society. An educated population by itself is an insufficient guarantor of liberty. After all, the level of education and culture in Nazi Germany was among the highest in Europe; and how many Nazi atrocities were committed to a musical background of Bach, Beethoven, or Wagner? On the domestic scene, moreover, Americans had attained a higher level of education in the 1950s than in the 1930s; yet it was in the 1950s that McCarthyism flourished. And it is clear that the greater political tolerance today compared to the 1950s is not due solely to increasing levels of education. Surveys in the 1950s and the 1970s have shown that not only has political tolerance increased in the country as a whole, but that even at similar levels of education there is now more support for civil liberties than there was two decades ago. Thus, 84 percent of college graduates in 1973 were rated politically "more tolerant," compared to only 65 percent of this group in 1954; in 1973, 58 percent of high-school graduates were considered more tolerant, compared to just 40 percent in 1954.[32] Obviously, what has opened America up in the last two decades has not been rising educational levels alone, but the changing spirit of American society itself.

The lasting impact of the 1960s is central to the new climate of tolerance in American society. In the 1960s America became nothing less than a sociological bazaar. A most extraordinary crazy quilt covered the country, not only of politics, but also of fashion, sex, religion, theater, music, and general *Weltanschauung,* challenging every imaginable American institution. Moreover, while that equality revolution which swept the country did not achieve all its aims, it successfully staked its claims and laid out the political agenda for minorities of all kinds in the decades ahead. Equally important, this new political and cultural pluralism was not confined to an isolated backwash of American society but was picked up by the media and spread across the land. The intentions of the media were journalistic at best and commercial and exploitative at worst, but again the unanticipated consequence of the media treatment of the 1960s was that even in the most remote areas Americans became familiar with—and ultimately tolerant of or at least resigned to—an enormous variety of political and cultural styles. Unquestionably, the 1960s pushed American society to the left in the sense of legitimizing dissent and modes of life radically different from and often hostile to the typical Norman Rockwell standard American.

The public was comparatively receptive to the new political and cultural pluralism of the 1960s and early 1970s because it arose at a time of crisis in American society, when confidence in major American institutions had been shaken as never before in modern history. The military was tainted by Vietnam, politics corrupted by Watergate, corporations damaged by pervasive white-collar crime, civil order threatened by urban race riots, religion weakened by the secularization of American society, universities crippled by an enraged student body, and the family undermined by the epidemic of divorces which by the mid-1970s exceeded one million annually for the first time. In this vacuum of faltering public confidence in established institutions, new ideas gained a lasting foothold.

When we consider all the trends sketched here, is it possible to conclude that American society is undergoing a fundamental change? Is it possible that while America is becoming a less affluent society, it is at the same time becoming one which is more humane, civil, sophisticated, and democratic? Is it possible that in an era of scarcity, the national obsession with material abundance will give way to a society of enriched and deepened democracy? But herein lies the central irony: all these democratic gains are now jeopardized by economic stagnation and the hardening of the class structure. As we have seen, the crisis of American capitalism threatens to unleash forces of social conflict, intolerance, conservative fundamentalism, and a Hobbesian war of each against all at home and international bellicosity abroad. On the other hand, the forces which have led to the enrichment of American democracy tend to diminish conflict and violence, promote order and restraint, reduce intolerance and bigotry. Thus the major conflict of American society in the remaining years of this century may well be between the disintegrative forces arising out of the stagnation of American capitalism and the integrative forces deriving from the expansion of American democracy.

This dialectic does not hold perfectly, however. Social forces driving to expand democracy can themselves create social conflict. The struggle for trade unionism and later for civil rights created enormous social upheaval. Yet it could also be argued that once the organizing rights of workers and the civil rights of blacks are secured, society achieves a higher degree of integration and social peace than when previous injustices prevailed.

While the crisis of American capitalism can be expected to raise the level of social nastiness and social conflict, we have seen that it could also conceivably increase demands for further democratization. We discussed earlier, for example, how the economic crisis may stimulate efforts by labor, consumer groups, local communities, and others to democratize the corporations and for economic reform generally.

With these qualifications in mind, it is nonetheless true that the forces of democracy will generally tend to promote social justice and integration while the forces of declining capitalism will tend to promote social conflict and disorder. Both of these forces will surely coexist in the coming years. But the climate and feel of American life in the years ahead may well be determined by which of these two forces—in the struggle between them—can prevail.

THE REVOLUTION OF FALLING EXPECTATIONS

> "We've always believed in something called progress. We've always had a faith that the days of our children would be better than our own.
> "Our people are losing that faith."
>
> Jimmy Carter, Address to the nation, July 15, 1979

Despite the growing vitality of American democracy, a pall hangs over the nation, for public faith in continuous material improvement has been shaken. For generations, American parents have hoped and believed that their children would have it easier than they. First-generation immigrant parents especially worked and saved to make a better life for their native-born children. Native-born parents, echoing the American faith in progress, also believed that the younger generation would have it better and that living standards would naturally improve almost by some divine law with each succeeding generation. Children would live better than their parents, it was believed, just as parents were living better than grandparents.

Now there is the real possibility that this entire scenario will be turned around and that today's children will actually have it worse, not better, than their parents and that we will all look back nostalgically to the mid-twentieth century as a time of carefree but transient abundance.

Beginning in the 1970s, public opinion research revealed a gathering cloud of pessimism throughout the land.[33] The unprecedented darkening of the national *Zeitgeist* was so noticeable toward the end of the decade, in fact, that it became central to President Carter's appraisal of the American condition.

One of the most useful measures of the public outlook involves the use of a so-called ladder scale in which interviewers show respondents a picture of a ladder with steps numbered from 0 to 10. Respondents are told to assume that the top step of the ladder (10) represents the best possible situation for the country and the bottom step (0) represents the worst possible situation. Interviewers then ask where on the ladder America ranks presently, where it ranked five years ago, and where it will probably rank in five years. Table 42, presenting the results of these studies over a twenty-year period from 1959 to 1979, reveals an unmistakable pattern of deepening national pessimism. In the two earliest surveys (1959 and 1964), Americans demonstrated their traditional optimistic spirit: America's past was good, its present was better, and its future would be an improvement over even the rosy present. Then between 1971 and 1976, public pessimism rose: the past was good, the present was not as good as the past, but much or all of the ground that had been lost would be made up in the future. The latest surveys, taken in 1978 and 1979, were clearly

Table 42. RATINGS FOR THE NATION, 1959–1979

	Five Years Ago	*Today*	*Five Years From Now*	
1959	6.5	6.7	7.4	———— 10
1964	6.1	6.5	7.7	
1971	6.2	5.4	6.2	
1972	5.6	5.5	6.2	
1974	6.3	4.8	5.8	———— 5
1976	6.0	5.5	6.1	
1978	5.8	5.4	5.3	
1979	5.7	4.7	4.6	———— 0

SOURCES: 1959–78: Albert H. Cantril and Susan Davis Cantril, *Unemployment, Government and the American People: A National Opinion Survey* (Washington, D.C.: Public Research, 1978), mimeograph, p. 16; 1979: Patrick H. Caddell, "Crisis of Confidence: I, Trapped in a Downward Spiral," *Public Opinion*, October/November 1979, p. 5; 1979 data are from the 1st quarter.

the most pessimistic: not only was the present worse than the past, but for the first time the public felt the future looked even darker than the present. In short, while the earlier surveys suggested continuous progress, the most recent surveys suggest continuous decline.

These same questions have been used in at least twenty-one countries, both in developed and developing nations, and in only two other instances has the public predicted a decline from the present to the future.[34] The 1979 American survey was unique in another respect: the public ranked both America's present and the prospects for its future lower than they had ever been ranked before, considerably lower than in the sanguine fifties and sixties, and lower even than in 1974, a dreary year of energy shortages, double digit inflation, and high unemployment, not to mention Watergate and the resignation of a president.*

* In a crude way, these surveys also seem to capture the emerging national nostalgia of the seventies. In 1974 Americans gave that year an average rank of only 4.8. But in 1979 the public, looking backward five years,

Some have argued that while Americans have become increasingly pessimistic about the prospects for the nation, they remain optimistic about their own personal lives. Table 43 seems to confirm this view, with two important qualifications. First, Americans were less optimistic by the end of the 1970s about their own personal future than in any of the previous studies. Second, the 1979 survey produced the flattest curve in two decades of questioning, i.e., the smallest change from past to future. If by the end of the 1970s Americans were not pessimistic about their personal lives, they certainly were decreasingly optimistic.

Table 43. AMERICANS APPRAISE THEIR PERSONAL LIVES, 1959–1979

	Five Years Ago	Today	Five Years From Now	
1959	5.9	6.6	7.8	
1964	6.0	6.9	7.9	
1971	5.8	6.6	7.5	
1975	6.1	6.3	7.0	
1976	5.8	6.4	7.4	
1977	5.6	6.1	7.2	
1978	5.5	6.2	6.9	
1979	6.1	6.4	6.7	

SOURCE: Patrick H. Caddell, "Crisis of Confidence: I, Trapped in a Downward Spiral," *Public Opinion*, October/November 1979, p. 6; the 1975–79 studies were done in the 1st quarter of the year.

recalled that year much higher, 5.7, while the present and future seemed much bleaker. In the fifties and sixties, on the other hand, Americans looked forward to a rosy future and were less likely to romanticize the past. In 1959, for example, Americans gave the present an average rank of 6.7. Five years later, in 1964, the public in retrospect recalled that year at 6.1, while both the present and future looked brighter.

THE MUTABILITY OF FORTUNE

Can it be true, then, contrary to all our American presuppositions, that our children are growing up into a poorer society with energy and material shortages, chronic inflation, crowding, the continued Howard Johnsonization of the land, the decay of social services in the cities, and increasing difficulties of employment, from which not even highly educated college graduates will be protected? As I suggested earlier, insofar as the values of private accumulation and consumption have been ascendant in America and given life its meaning, unless democratic and other values are continuously strengthened, the stagnation of American capitalism may pull the props out from under the society's main belief system and provoke a crisis of meaning, purpose, and personal identity that will end in anomie and collective malaise.

In his classic work, historian J. B. Bury examined the idea of progress in Western civilization.[35] Nowhere has this idea of unilinear progress based on faith in technological improvement and an inevitable increase in living standards been more uncritically accepted than in the United States. But how naive is this idea of progress, how historically bound to the optimism of the bourgeois (and now communist) era. And in the light of recent developments in American society, how reasonable now in contrast seems the ancient Greek view of history. The Greeks derived their interpretation of history from the rhythm of nature and never considered history to be a record of continuous progress or improvement.[36] Observing the endless alternations of day and night, the recurring patterns of growth and decay, the periodic cycles of moons and seasons, the Greeks saw in history the "mutability of fortune"—the endless rise and fall, capriciousness and changeability of fortune, even for the mightiest of civilizations.

Notes

Introduction: The End of the American Era

1. The literature of America's decline in the 1970s is growing apace and is not confined to any one political perspective. For a recent sample, moving roughly from political left to right, see *U.S. Capitalism in Crisis* (New York: Union for Radical Political Economics, 1978), especially Arthur MacEwan, "The Development of the Crisis in the World Economy," pp. 45–54; Albert Szymanski, "The Decline and Fall of the U.S. Eagle," *Social Policy* 6 (March/April 1974), pp. 5–13; Robert L. Heilbroner, "Boom and Crash," *The New Yorker,* August 28, 1978, pp. 52ff; Robert Gilpin, *U.S. Power and the Multinational Corporation* (New York: Basic Books, 1975); Daniel Yergin, "Order and Survival," *Daedalus* 107 (Winter 1978), pp. 263–87; Andrew Hacker, *The End of the American Era* (New York: Atheneum, 1971); Charles P. Kindleberger, "An American Economic Climacteric?" *Challenge* 17 (January/February 1974); "The Decline of U.S. Power," *Business Week,* March 12, 1979.
2. Gilpin, *U.S. Power*.

Chapter 1   Theories of Class in Postwar America

1. Charles Page, quoted in Kurt Mayer, "Diminishing Class Differentials in the United States," *Kyklos* 12 (1959), p. 605.
2. Milton Gordon, quoted in Mayer, "Diminishing Class Differentials", p. 606.
3. George Chapman and John Marston, *Eastward Ho,* quoted in David

     M. Potter, *People of Plenty: Economic Abundance and the American
     Character* (Chicago: University of Chicago Press, 1954), p. 78.

 4. Engels to Florence Kelley Wischnewetsky, June 3, 1886, in *Selected
     Correspondence of Karl Marx and Frederick Engels: 1846–1895*
     (New York: International Publishers, 1942), p. 449.

 5. Engels to Wischnewetsky, January 7, 1886, *Selected Correspondence,*
     p. 443.

 6. Engels to H. Schlüter, March 30, 1892, Ibid., p. 497.

 7. Werner Sombart, *Why Is There No Socialism in the United States?*
     (White Plains, N.Y.: M. E. Sharpe, 1976). For excerpts, see John
     H. M. Laslett and S. M. Lipset, eds., *Failure of a Dream? Essays in
     the History of American Socialism* (Garden City, N.Y.: Doubleday
     Anchor Books, 1974).

 8. Kingsley Davis and Wilbert E. Moore, "Some Principles of Stratifi-
     cation," *American Sociological Review* 10 (April 1945), pp. 242–49.
     This piece has probably been reprinted more often than any other ar-
     ticle in sociology published since the end of the war.

 9. For a comprehensive bibliography of the controversy which even
     now continues to swirl around the Davis-Moore thesis, see Leonard
     Broom and Robert G. Cushing, "A Modest Test of an Immodest
     Theory: The Functional Theory of Stratification," *American Socio-
     logical Review* 42 (February 1977), pp. 157–69.

10. The Editors of *Fortune, The Changing American Market* (Garden
     City, N.Y.: Hanover House, 1955).

11. For a sample of some of the best works supporting class convergence,
     see Robert A. Nisbet, "The Decline and Fall of Social Class," *Pacific
     Sociological Review* 2 (Spring 1959), pp. 11–17, reprinted in Paul
     Blumberg, ed., *The Impact of Social Class* (New York: T. Y. Cro-
     well, 1972), pp. 49–61; Harold L. Wilensky, "Class, Class Con-
     sciousness, and American Workers," in William Taber ed., *Labor in
     a Changing America* (New York: Basic Books, 1966), pp. 12–28;
     Wilensky, "Mass Society and Mass Culture: Interdependence or In-
     dependence?" *American Sociological Review* 29 (April 1964), pp.
     173–97; Kurt B. Mayer, "The Changing Shape of the American Class
     Structure," *Social Research* 30 (Winter 1963), pp. 460–68, reprinted
     in Bertram Silverman and Murray Yanowitch, eds., *The Worker in
     "Post-Industrial" Capitalism* (New York: Free Press, 1974), pp.
     117–22; Mayer, "Diminishing Class Differentials in the United
     States," *Kyklos* 12 (1959), pp. 605–26; Peter Drucker, "The New
     [Middle-Class] Majority," *The Listener* (a BBC publication), October
     23 and 30, 1958, reprinted in Edgar Schuler et al., *Readings in Soci-*

ology, 4th ed. (New York: T. Y. Crowell, 1971), pp. 286–92; Paul Blumberg, "The Decline and Fall of the Status Symbol: Some Thoughts on Status in a Postindustrial Society," *Social Problems* 21 (Spring 1974), pp. 480–94. The latter contains a bibliography of works based on postindustrial society theory, and the essay is a final attempt to interpret the postwar American class structure in terms of a class convergence model. For a class convergence position from a European perspective, see Raymon Aron, *Progress and Disillusion: The Dialectics of Modern Society* (New York: Praeger, 1968). Additional works in the class convergence tradition are mentioned in Gavin Mackensie, *The Aristocracy of Labor: The Position of Skilled Craftsmen in the American Class Structure* (Cambridge: at the University Press, 1973). For the final work of the 1970s in this general tradition, see Irving Kristol, *Two Cheers for Capitalism* (New York: Basic Books, 1978).

12. See Peter Steinfels, "Neoconservatives and the Fear of Equality," *Dissent* (Spring 1979), pp. 169–82; Steinfels, *The Neoconservatives: The Men Who Are Changing America's Politics* (New York: Simon and Schuster, 1979).

13. Nisbet, "Decline and Fall of Social Class," 1959.

14. Mayer, "Changing Shape of American Class Structure," in Silverman and Yanowitch, eds., *Worker in "Post-Industrial" Capitalism,* p. 118.

15. Wilensky, "Class, Class Consciousness, and American Workers."

16. Simon Kuznets, *Share of Upper Income Groups in Income and Savings* (New York: National Bureau of Economic Research, 1953). Kuznets's findings were later disputed by radical historian Gabriel Kolko in *Wealth and Power in America* (New York: Praeger, 1962).

17. John Kenneth Galbraith, *The Affluent Society* (Boston: Houghton Mifflin, 1958), p. 323.

18. Editors of *Fortune, Changing American Market,* p. 67.

19. For a discussion of this claim, see Michael Harrington, "Hiding the Other America," *The New Republic,* February 26, 1977, pp. 15–17, and Sheldon Danziger, "The War on Poverty Revisited," *The Wharton Magazine* (Fall 1979), pp. 60–64. See also Chapter 2 of this book.

20. For statistical details on the diffusion of this standard package, see Blumberg, "Decline and Fall of the Status Symbol" cited in n. 11 above.

21. Editors of *Fortune, Changing American Market,* pp. 215–16.

22. Quoted in Blumberg, "Decline and Fall of the Status Symbol," p. 483.

23. David Riesman, *Abundance for What? and Other Essays* (Garden City, N.Y.: Doubleday Anchor Books, 1965), p. 289.

24. See Bell's excellent discussion of scarcity in *The Coming of Post-Industrial Society* (New York: Basic Books, 1973), pp. 456–75. While Bell believes that "the possibility of [material] abundance is real," he argues that economic scarcity will simply be replaced by other forms—scarcities of time, and scarcities arising out of the soaring costs of information and coordination in complex postindustrial society.

25. William H. Whyte, Jr., *The Organization Man* (Garden City, N.Y.: Doubleday Anchor Books, 1957), pp. 353, 331.

26. Drucker, "New Majority," p. 286, cited in n. 11. For a wide-ranging debate on the nature of this group and whether they constitute a new class, see the essays in *Society* 16 (January/February 1979). See also Barbara and John Ehrenreich, "The Professional-Managerial Class," *Radical America* (March/April 1977), pp. 7–31; "The New Left: A Case Study in Professional-Managerial Class Radicalism," *Radical America* (May/June 1977), pp. 7–22.

27. Drucker, Ibid., p. 287.

28. Bell, *Coming Post-Industrial Society,* p. 125. Curiously, only eight pages later, Bell seems to contradict himself, writing that "Richard Bellman, the Rand mathematician, has often been quoted as predicting that by the year 2000 only 2 percent of the labor force will be required to turn out all the necessary manufactured goods, but the figure is fanciful and inherently unprovable" (p. 133).

29. Drucker, "New Majority," p. 290.

30. Wilensky, "Mass Society and Mass Culture," p. 178.

31. Drucker, "New Majority," pp. 289–90.

32. Wilensky, "Mass Society and Mass Culture," pp. 193–94.

33. Robert K. Burns, "The Comparative Economic Position of Manual and White-Collar Employees," *Journal of Business* 27 (October 1954), pp. 257–67. See also this book, Chapter 2.

34. Mayer, "Changing Shape of American Class Structure," p. 119.

35. Ibid., p. 121.

36. Richard Centers, *The Psychology of Social Classes: A Study of Class Consciousness* (Princeton, N.J.: Princeton University Press, 1949).

37. Wilensky, "Class, Class Consciousness, and American Workers," p. 454.

38. Charles W. Tucker, "A Comparative Analysis of Subjective Social

Class: 1945–1963," *Social Forces* 46 (June 1968), pp. 508–14; Robert W. Hodge and Donald J. Treiman, "Class Identification in the United States," *American Journal of Sociology* 73 (March 1968), pp. 535–47.

39. Seymour Martin Lipset, "The End of Ideology," in Chaim I. Waxman, ed., *The End of Ideology Debate* (New York: Funk & Wagnalls, 1968), p. 73. This volume offers a good collection of essays, as does M. Rejai, ed., *Decline of Ideology?* (Chicago: Aldine, Atherton, 1971).

40. Arthur M. Ross and Paul T. Hartman, "The Withering Away of the Strike," in *Changing Patterns of Industrial Conflict* (New York: John Wiley, 1960), pp. 42–61.

41. Ibid., p. 4.

42. T. H. Marshall, "Citizenship and Social Class," in *Class, Citizenship, and Social Development* (Garden City, N.Y.: Doubleday Anchor Books, 1965), originally published in 1950.

43. Ibid., p. 127.

44. For a sample of works which generally share a class stability framework, see S. M. Miller and Frank Riessman, "Are Workers Middle Class?" *Dissent* (Autumn 1961), pp. 507–16; Herbert J. Gans, *Popular Culture and High Culture: An Analysis and Evaluation of Taste* (New York: Basic Books, 1974); Richard F. Hamilton, "The Behavior and Values of Skilled Workers," in Arthur B. Shostak and William Gomberg, eds., *Blue-Collar World* (Englewood Cliffs, N.J.: Prentice-Hall, 1964), pp. 42–57; Hamilton, "The Marginal Middle Class: A Reconsideration," *American Sociological Review* 31 (April 1966), pp. 192–99; Andrew Levison, *The Working-Class Majority* (New York: Penguin Books, 1974); Patricia Cayo Sexton and Brendan Sexton, *Blue Collars and Hard-Hats: The Working Class and the Future of American Politics* (New York: Random House, 1971); Richard Parker, *The Myth of the Middle Class* (New York: Liveright, 1972); Stanley Aronowitz, *False Promises* (New York: McGraw-Hill, 1973), and *Food, Shelter and the American Dream* (New York: Seabury Press, 1974); Lillian Breslow Rubin, *Worlds of Pain: Life in the Working-Class Family* (New York: Basic Books, 1976); James W. Rinehart, "Affluence and the Embourgeoisement of the Working Class: A Critical Look," *Social Problems* 19 (Fall 1971), pp. 149–61; J. H. Westergaard, "The Withering Away of Class: A Contemporary Myth," in Perry Anderson and Robin Blackburn, eds., *Toward Socialism* (Ithaca, N.Y.: Cornell Univ. Press, 1966), pp. 77–108; and the indispensable anthology, Maurice Zeitlin, ed., *American Society,*

Inc.: Studies of the Social Structure and Political Economy of the United States, 2nd ed. (Chicago: Rand McNally, 1977). Finally, the embourgeoisement thesis is examined (and rejected) for affluent British workers in the well-known, pioneering study by John H. Goldthorpe, David Lockwood, Frank Bechhofer, and Jennifer Platt. See *The Affluent Worker in the Class Structure* (Cambridge: at the University Press, 1969); *The Affluent Worker: Industrial Attitudes and Behavior* (Cambridge: at the University Press, 1968); *The Affluent Worker: Political Attitudes and Behavior* (Cambridge: at the University Press, 1968).

45. Daniel W. Rossides, *The American Class System* (Boston: Houghton Mifflin, 1976), p. 30.

46. Morgan Reynolds and Eugene Smolensky, "The Fading Effect of Government on Inequality," *Challenge* 21 (July/August 1978), p. 33; Reynolds and Smolensky, *Public Expenditures, Taxes, and the Distribution of Income* (New York: Academic Press, 1977). Kolko, *op. cit.,* in fact, argued that there had been little redistribution since about 1910.

47. Paul A. Samuelson, *Economics,* 6th ed. (New York: McGraw-Hill, 1964), p. 113.

48. See Paul Blumberg, "Another Day, Another $3,000," *Dissent* (Spring 1978), pp. 157–68.

49. James D. Smith and Stephen D. Franklin, "Concentrations of Personal Wealth, 1922–1969," in Maurice Zeitlin, ed., *American Society,* pp. 70–79.

50. John Strachey, *Contemporary Capitalism* (New York: Random House, 1956), Chapter 7.

51. Tom Wolfe, *Mauve Gloves & Madmen, Clutter & Vine* (New York: Farrar, Straus and Giroux, 1976), p. 136.

52. On salaries for new M.B.A.s and beginning lawyers, see Michael Knight, "Harvard M.B.A.: A Golden Passport," *New York Times,* May 23, 1978; Tom Goldstein, "Business and the Law," *New York Times,* May 19, 1978.

53. Paul Blumberg, "The Decline and Fall of the Status Symbol," p. 487; U.S. Bureau of the Census, *Statistical Abstract of the United States: 1978* (99th ed.) Washington, D.C., 1978, p. 474.

54. Levison, *Working-Class Majority,* cited in n. 44 above.

55. Harry Braverman, *Labor and Monopoly Capital: The Degradation of Labor in the Twentieth Century* (New York: Monthly Review Press, 1974).

56. Ibid., p. 427.

57. Bell, *Coming Post-Industrial Society,* p. 137.
58. *Statistical Abstract: 1978,* pp. 419–20.
59. See, e.g., Braverman, *Labor and Monopoly Capital,* Chapter 10. On the reduction of skill in one postindustrial occupation, see Philip Kraft, *Programmers and Managers: The Routinization of Computer Programming in the United States* (New York: Springer-Verlag, 1977).
60. See Robert Heilbroner, "Economic Problems of a 'Postindustrial' Society," *Dissent* (Spring 1973), pp. 163–76, reprinted in Silverman and Yanowitch, eds., *Worker in "Post-Industrial" Capitalism,* pp. 96–111.
61. James Bright, *Automation and Management* (Cambridge, Mass.: Harvard University Press, 1958). See also Paul Blumberg, *Industrial Democracy: The Sociology of Participation* (New York: Schocken Books, 1969), Chapter 4.
62. See, e.g., Karl Kaysen, "The Social Significance of the Modern Corporation," *American Economic Review* 47 (May 1957), pp. 311–19.
63. Maurice Zeitlin, "Corporate Ownership and Control: The Large Corporation and the Capitalist Class," in Zeitlin, ed., *American Society,* pp. 233–79; Lawrence Pedersen and William K. Tabb, "Ownership and Control of Large Corporations Revisited," *Antitrust Bulletin,* 21 (Spring 1976), pp. 53–66.
64. Paul Blumberg, "Another Day, Another $3,000."
65. An excellent summary of the research on the impact of social class upon education can be found in Rossides, *American Class System,* Chapter 6. See also Christopher Jencks et al., *Who Gets Ahead? The Determinants of Economic Success in America* (New York: Basic Books, 1979); Richard H. deLone, *Small Futures: Children, Inequality, and the Limits of Liberal Reform* (New York: Harcourt Brace Jovanovich, 1979).
66. Ivar Berg, assisted by Sherry Gorelick, *Education and Jobs: The Great Training Robbery* (New York: Praeger, 1970).
67. See Paul Blumberg and James M. Murtha, "College Graduates and the American Dream," *Dissent* (Winter 1977), pp. 45–53.
68. Rossides, *American Class System,* pp. 216–18; Randall Collins, "Functional and Conflict Theories of Educational Stratification," *American Sociological Review,* 36 (December 1971), pp. 1002–19.
69. Herbert Gans, *Popular Culture,* cited in n. 44 above.
70. Stanislaw Ossowski, *Class Structure in the Social Consciousness* (New York: Free Press, 1963).

71. For an aging but still perceptive discussion of the ambiguities of class consciousness in the U.S., see Joseph A. Kahl, *The American Class Structure* (New York: Holt, Rinehart & Winston, 1957).

72. E. M. Schreiber and G. T. Nygreen, "Subjective Social Class in America: 1945–68," *Social Forces* 48 (March 1970), pp. 348–56.

73. See, e.g., Robert R. Alford, *Party and Society* (Chicago: Rand Mc-Nally, 1963); A. M. Guest, "Class Consciousness and American Political Attitudes," *Social Forces* 52 (June 1974), pp. 496–510.

74. Michael Harrington, *Socialism* (New York: Bantam Books, 1973), p. 307.

75. John Goldthorpe et al., "The Affluent Worker and the Thesis of *Embourgeoisement:* Some Preliminary Findings," in Paul Blumberg, ed., *Impact of Social Class*, pp. 61–82.

76. I am following Goldthorpe's discussion here.

77. Ralph Nader, Mark Green, and Joel Seligman, *Taming the Giant Corporation* (New York: W. W. Norton, 1976), pp. 145–48.

78. Peter M. Blau and Otis Dudley Duncan, *The American Occupational Structure* (New York: John Wiley, 1967).

79. Bennett M. Berger, *Working-Class Suburb: A Study of Auto Workers in Suburbia* (Berkeley: University of California Press, 1960); William M. Dobriner, *Class in Suburbia* (Englewood Cliffs, N.J.: Prentice-Hall, 1963).

80. Miller and Riessman, "Are Workers Middle Class?"

81. Gerald Handel and Lee Rainwater, "Persistence and Change in Working-Class Life Style," in Shostak and Gomberg, *Blue-Collar World*, pp. 36–41; Miller and Riessman, "Are Workers Middle Class?"; Mackensie, *Aristocracy of Labor*.

82. Norval D. Glenn and Jon P. Alston, "Cultural Distances among Occupational Groups," *American Sociological Review*, 33 (June 1968), pp. 365–82.

83. Ibid., p. 381.

84. Joan Talbert Dalia and Avery M. Guest, "Embourgeoisement among Blue-Collar Workers?" *The Sociological Quarterly* 16 (Summer 1975), pp. 291–304.

85. Mackensie, *Aristocracy of Labor,* cited in n. 11 above. Convergence theorists, however, examining Mackensie's comparison between his sample of skilled, affluent blue-collar workers and his peculiarly depressed, seemingly atypical lower white-collar workers, could make a good case for the embourgeoisement thesis here; the two groups are very similar. In any case, for a view similar to Mackensie's of the af-

fluent, skilled workers as a separate stratum, see Richard F. Hamilton, "The Behavior and Values of Skilled Workers," in Shostak and Gomberg, eds., *Blue-Collar World,* pp. 42–57.

86. Milton M. Gordon and Charles H. Anderson, "The Blue-Collar Worker at Leisure," in Shostak and Gomberg, eds., *Blue-Collar World,* pp. 407–16.

87. Lillian Breslow Rubin, *Worlds of Pain,* cited in n. 44 above. Other studies of working-class marriage and family life with implicit or explicit contrasts to middle-class patterns include Lee Rainwater, Richard P. Coleman, and Gerald Handel, *Workingman's Wife: Her Personality, World and Life Style* (New York: Oceana Publications, 1959) and Mirra Komarovsky, *Blue-Collar Marriage* (New York: Random House, 1962).

88. See, e.g., Mackensie, *Aristocracy of Labor,* cited in n. 11 above. Despite the objective similarities between the affluent, skilled blue-collar workers Mackensie studied and a contrasting sample of lower-middle-class clerks, there was virtually no friendship or association across the blue-collar/white-collar line. See also Chapter 7.

89. C. Wright Mills's *White Collar* (New York: Oxford University Press, 1951) still offers the single most eloquent description of the contemporary status crisis of the new (salaried) middle class.

90. See Richard B. Freeman, *The Overeducated American* (New York: Academic Press, 1976); Paul Blumberg and James M. Murtha, "College Graduates."

91. A brief account of the historic controversy, whither white-collar workers, is given by Sandra J. Coyner and Martin Oppenheimer, "Scholars and White Collars: A Social History of the Great Debate," paper presented at the 71st Annual Meeting of the American Sociological Association, New York City, September 1976. For a brief summary of the historic German debate on this question, see Bell, *Coming Post-Industrial Society,* pp. 66–72.

92. Postwar stability theorists tended to support elitist and Marxist rather than pluralist theories of power and thus felt comfortable with the ways in which local and national power were analyzed by C. Wright Mills, Floyd Hunter, G. William Domhoff, and, earlier, Robert and Helen Lynd.

Chapter 2   Stagnation: Up the Down Escalator

1. For a technical description of the Bureau of Labor Statistics surveys, see *Employment and Earnings* 25 (November 1978), pp. 142–48.

2. On the growth of part-time employment, see William V. Deuter-

mann, Jr. and Scott Campbell Brown, "Voluntary Part-Time Workers: A Growing Part of the Labor Force," *Monthly Labor Review* 101 (June 1978), pp. 3–10. The Department of Labor defines as part-time workers those who are gainfully employed 1–34 hours weekly.

3. On the increase of women in the labor force, see U.S. Bureau of the Census, *Statistical Abstract of the United States: 1977* (98th ed.) Washington, D.C., 1977, p. 387.

4. "LRA Real Spendable Wages," *Economic Notes* 46 (December 1978), p. 5 (Published by the Labor Research Association).

5. For this argument, see *Employment and Earnings* 25 (October 1978).

6. *Economic Report of the President, 1978,* U.S. Government Printing Office, Washington, D.C., 1978, p. 147, makes this same argument with respect to the alleged impact of the increasing labor-force participation of women upon falling productivity growth in the U.S.

7. See, e.g., Gilbert Burck, "A Time of Reckoning for the Building Unions," *Fortune,* June 4, 1979, pp. 82–96.

8. Robert K. Burns, "The Comparative Economic Position of Manual and White-Collar Employees," *Journal of Business* 27 (October 1954), p. 261.

9. Paul Blumberg and James M. Murtha, "College Graduates and the American Dream," *Dissent* (Winter 1977), pp. 45–53; Blumberg, "Lockouts, Layoffs, and the New Academic Proletariat," in Arthur S. Wilke, ed., *The Hidden Professoriate* (Westport, Conn.: Greenwood Press, 1979).

10. *New York Times,* February 13, 1978.

11. According to *Current Population Reports,* "Individual income amounts greater than or equal to $100,000 are recorded as $99,999 in the Current Population Survey." Series P-60, No. 118, "Money Income in 1977 of Families and Persons in the United States," U.S. Government Printing Office, Washington, D.C., 1979, p. 268. For the items on income in the CPS facsimile questionnaire, see p. 288.

12. See also *Dollars and Sense* #29 (September 1977), pp. 12–13. Economists for *Dollars and Sense* also argue that the systematic underreporting by the rich of their complete income is inadequately treated by the Current Population Survey and thus further underestimates the total income of higher-income groups.

13. U.S. Dept. of Health, Education, and Welfare, *The Measure of Poverty,* U.S. Government Printing Office, Washington, D.C., 1976.

14. Quoted in Leonard Beeghley, *Social Stratification in America* (Santa Monica, Calif.: Goodyear, 1978), p. 125.

15. Beeghley, *Social Stratification,* p. 127.
16. U.S. Dept. of Health, Education, and Welfare, *Measure of Poverty,* Chapter 5.
17. U.S. Bureau of the Census, *Current Population Reports,* Series P-60, No. 119, "Characteristics of the Population Below the Poverty Level: 1977," U.S. Government Printing Office, Washington, D.C., 1979.
18. Quoted in Sheldon Danziger, "The War on Poverty Revisited," *Wharton Magazine* (Fall 1979), p. 60.
19. Quoted in Michael Harrington, "Hiding the Other America," *New Republic,* February 25, 1977, p. 16.
20. Danziger, "War on Poverty," p. 63.
21. Harrington, "Hiding Other America," p. 17.
22. Ibid.
23. From *The Wealth of Nations,* quoted in U.S. Dept. of Health, Education, and Welfare, *Measure of Poverty,* p. 22.
24. Victor R. Fuchs, "Redefining Poverty and Redistributing Income," *The Public Interest* #8 (Summer 1967), pp. 88–95.
25. U.S. Dept. of Health, Education, and Welfare, *Measure of Poverty,* p. 108.
26. This paradox is discussed by Robert Stobaugh and Daniel Yergin, eds., *Energy Future* (New York: Random House, 1979), p. 4.
27. Charles P. Kindleberger, "An American Economic Climacteric?" *Challenge* 17 (January/February 1974), pp. 35–44.

Chapter 3   Decline: I

1. *New York Times,* May 13, 1978. Each OECD annual yearbook is based on figures gathered two years earlier; as trends have continued and even intensified, by the late 1970s the U.S. had fallen even further behind the position suggested by the figures.
2. For an analysis of the ways in which fluctuating exchange rates distort international comparisons of per capita income and a discussion of how real living standards might be compared internationally without relying on the distortions of exchange rates, see Irving B. Kravis, Alan W. Heston, and Robert Sommers, "The Affluence of Nations," *Wharton Magazine* 3 (Fall 1978), pp. 60–65.
3. For a perceptive analysis of the recent fate of the dollar, see Wendy Cooper, "Decline and Fall of the Dollar," *Nation,* May 12, 1979, pp. 533–36.
4. *Newsweek,* March 20, 1978, p. 52.
5. *U.S. News & World Report,* March 13, 1978, p. 45.

6. *New York Times,* July 25, 1978.
7. *U.S. Capitalism in Crisis* (New York: Union for Radical Political Economics, 1978), p. 345. Figures for 1979 are computed from Department of Commerce figures on GNP and imports.
8. Daniel Yergin, "The Real Meaning of the Energy Crisis," *New York Times Magazine,* June 4, 1978. See also Robert Stobaugh and Daniel Yergin, eds., *Energy Future* (New York: Random House, 1979).
9. Unless otherwise noted, this section is based on the excellent analysis of the American steel industry by Helen Shapiro and Steven Volk, "Steelyard Blues: New Structures in Steel," *NACLA (North American Congress on Latin America) Report on the Americas* 12 (January/February 1979).
10. The first quotation is from Walter Adams and Joel B. Dirlam, "Big Steel, Invention, and Innovation," *Quarterly Journal of Economics* 80 (May 1966), p. 175; the second two quotations are from Shapiro and Volk, "Steelyard Blues," p. 2.
11. See the studies cited by Shapiro and Volk and also Robert W. Crandall, "Competition and 'Dumping' in the U.S. Steel Market," *Challenge* 21 (July/August 1978), pp. 13–20.
12. John M. Blair, *Economic Concentration: Structure, Behavior and Public Policy* (New York: Harcourt Brace Jovanovich, 1972), p. 233.
13. On the basic oxygen furnace, see Adams and Dirlam, "Big Steel"; on continuous casting, see David Ault, "The Continuous Deterioration of the Competitive Ability of the U.S. Steel Industry: The Development of Continuous Casting," *Western Economic Journal* 11 (March 1973), pp. 89–97.
14. Crandall, "Competition and 'Dumping.' "
15. *Wall Street Journal,* August 3, 1977. U.S. Steel has also received technical assistance from Nippon Kokan and from Sumitomo Metal Industries.
16. Quoted in Shapiro and Volk, "Steelyard Blues," p. 11.
17. Bureau of Labor Statistics, *Productivity and the Economy,* Bulletin 1926, U.S. Government Printing Office, Washington, D.C., 1977, pp. 24–25, 96.
18. "Big Steel's Liquidation," *Business Week,* September 17, 1979, p. 89.
19. From the "MacNeil/Lehrer Report" on Public Television, March 1, 1978.
20. Edmund Faltermayer, "How Made-in-America Steel Can Survive," *Fortune,* February 13, 1978, pp. 122–30.
21. "Workers Occupy U.S. Steel Offices," *New York Times,* January 29, 1980.

22. "Big Steel's Liquidation," p. 84.

23. Henry Gittlen, quoted in Shapiro and Volk, "Steelyard Blues," p. 11.

24. Robert Gilpin, *U.S. Power and the Multinational Corporation* (New York: Basic Books, 1975), p. 90.

25. Herbert E. Meyer, "Those Worrisome Technology Exports," *Fortune,* May 22, 1978, p. 108.

26. *Electronic News,* October 3, 1977.

27. "Electronics: The Global Industry," *NACLA's Latin America and Empire Report* 11 (April 1977), p. 20.

28. Gene Bylinsky, "The Japanese Spies in Silicon Valley," *Fortune,* February 27, 1978, p. 75.

29. "Apparel's Last Stand," *Business Week,* May 14, 1979, pp. 60–70.

30. Lazare Tepper, *Women's and Children's Apparel and the Multifiber Textile Arrangement* (New York: International Ladies' Garment Workers Union, 1977), p. 15.

31. *New York Times,* February 11, 1978, p. 27 and December 28, 1978, p. D1.

32. Seymour Melman, *The Permanent War Economy: American Capitalism in Decline* (New York: Simon and Schuster, 1974), p. 93.

33. In 1977, of the ten leading U.S. exports to Japan—soybeans, logs and lumber, coal, corn, wheat, wood pulp, business machinery, cotton, tobacco, and grain sorghum—only one, business machinery, was a strictly industrial product. See *New York Times,* June 13, 1978.

34. *New York Times,* May 31, 1978.

35. Melman, *Permanent War Economy,* p. 74.

36. Jack Newfield and Paul DuBrul, *The Abuse of Power: The Permanent Government and the Fall of New York* (New York: Penquin Books, 1977), p. 1.

37. Brian Ketcham and Stan Pinkwas, "That's the Way the City Crumbles," *Village Voice,* September 18, 1978.

38. Grace Lichtenstein, "New York Bridges Aren't Falling, but Some Are Crumbling," *New York Times,* March 27, 1978.

39. Ibid.

40. Michael Sterne, "Garbage Problems Continue to Grow but Officials Try to Put the Lid On," *New York Times,* November 7, 1978.

41. John Herbers, "Beneath the Streets, Old Cities Crumble and Decay," *New York Times,* April 9, 1978.

Chapter 4   Decline: II

1. Seymour Melman, *The Permanent War Economy: American Capitalism in Decline* (New York: Simon and Schuster, 1974), p. 83.

2. *Economic Report of the President, 1979,* U.S. Government Printing Office, Washington, D.C., 1979, p. 68.

3. *Economic Report of the President, 1978,* U.S. Government Printing Office, Washington, D.C., 1978, p. 147.

4. See *Economic Report of the President, 1979.*

5. Bill Cunningham, "Bringing Productivity into Focus," *AFL-CIO American Federationist,* May 1979, p. 1. See also "Productivity Slowdown: A False Alarm," *Monthly Review* 31 (June 1979), pp. 1–12.

6. Bureau of Labor Statistics, *Productivity and the Economy,* Bulletin 1926, U.S. Government Printing Office, Washington, D.C., 1977, p. 22.

7. Sanford Rose, "The Global Slowdown Won't Last Forever," *Fortune,* August 14, 1978, p. 98.

8. National Science Board, *Science Indicators—1976,* U.S. Government Printing Office, Washington, D.C., 1977, p. 35.

9. See *The Permanent War Economy; Pentagon Capitalism* (New York: McGraw-Hill, 1970); *Our Depleted Society* (New York: Holt, Rinehart & Winston, 1965).

10. Albert Szymanski, "Military Spending and Economic Stagnation," *American Journal of Sociology* 79 (July 1973), p. 5.

11. Melman, *The Permanent War Economy,* p. 19.

12. Ibid., p. 24.

13. Hans Fantel, "How Long Can Japan Rule the World of Audio?" *New York Times,* June 11, 1978.

14. *Business Week,* March 27, 1978.

15. See Melman's letter to the *New York Times,* May 18, 1979.

16. Melman, *The Permanent War Economy,* pp. 34, 39. See also A. Ernest Fitzgerald, *The High Priests of Waste* (New York: W. W. Norton, 1972).

17. Delbert Tesar, "Mission-Oriented Research for Light Machinery," *Science* 201 (September 8, 1978), p. 880.

18. Melman, *The Permanent War Economy,* pp. 80–81.

19. National Science Board, *Science Indicators—1976,* p. 187.

20. Tesar, "Mission-Oriented Research for Light Machinery," p. 881.

21. Daniel Yergin, "Order and Survival," *Daedalus* 107 (Winter 1978), p. 266.

22. Quoted in Tesar, "Mission-Oriented Research," p. 884. Optimism, when expressed, was often guarded and defensive, as in the title of an article by Niles Howard with Susan Antilla in a leading business publication, "U.S. Innovation: It's Better than You Think," *Dun's Review* 113 (March 1979), pp. 55–58.

23. Robert Gilpin, "An Alternative Strategy to Foreign Investment,"

Challenge 18 (November/December 1975), pp. 12–18. This article is an adaptation of Chapter 8 of Gilpin's *U.S. Power and the Multinational Corporation* (New York: Basic Books, 1975).

24. Statement by the AFL-CIO to the House Committee on International Relations, Subcommittee on International Economic Policy Hearings on U.S. Multinational Corporations, March 5, 1976; United Electrical, Radio and Machine Workers of America (UE), *How Foreign Is "Foreign" Competition?* (New York: 1971).

25. Steve Babson, "The Multinational Corporation and Labor," *Review of Radical Political Economics* 5 (Spring 1973), pp. 19–36; Herbert E. Meyer, "Those Worrisome Technology Exports," *Fortune,* May 22, 1978, p. 108.

26. Jack Baranson, *Technology and the Multinationals* (Lexington, Mass.: D.C. Heath, 1978), p. 84. See also Baranson's *International Transfers of Industrial Technology by U.S. Firms and Their Implications for the U.S. Economy* (Washington, D.C.: U.S. Department of Labor, Bureau of International Labor Affairs, 1976). This section is based on Baranson's research in this area.

27. Meyer, "Those Worrisome Technology Exports;" William M. Bulkeley, "Concern Grows over Rising U.S. Exports of Skilled Technology to Overseas Firms," *Wall Street Journal,* July 5, 1979.

28. Baranson, *Technology and the Multinationals,* p. 149.

29. Ibid., pp. 55–56.

30. Baranson, *International Transfers of Industrial Technology,* p. 32.

31. National Science Board, *Science Indicators—1976;* National Science Board, *Science Indicators—1974,* U.S. Government Printing Office, Washington, D.C., 1976. A gloomy appraisal of the 1974 report, from the American viewpoint, is contained in Philip M. Boffey, "Science Indicators: New Report Finds U.S. Performance Weakening," *Science* 199 (March 12, 1976), pp. 1031–33.

32. Don Stillman, "The Devastating Impact of Plant Relocations," *Working Papers for a New Society* 6 (September/October 1978), pp. 42–53.

33. *Economic Report of the President, 1978.*

34. Statement of Andrew J. Biemiller, director of the Department of Legislation, AFL-CIO, before the Senate Subcommittee on Multinational Corporations of the Senate Committee on Foreign Relations on the Impact of Multinational Corporations on the U.S. Economy, December 10, 1975.

35. Gus Tyler, "The Threat of a U.S. without Factories," *AFL-CIO American Federationist* 83 (April 1976), pp. 9–12; Gilpin, "An Alternate Strategy," cited in n. 23 above.

36. Ibid.
37. Statement by the AFL-CIO to the House Subcommittee on International Economic Policy.
38. Statement of Andrew J. Biemiller to the Senate Subcommittee on Multinational Corporations.
39. See Robert Gilpin's excellent article, "An Alternate Strategy to Foreign Investment," cited in n. 23 above.
40. Peggy B. Musgrave, *Direct Investment Abroad and the Multinationals: Effects on the United States Economy,* prepared for the use of the Subcommittee on Multinational Corporations of the Committee on Foreign Relations, U.S. Senate, U.S. Government Printing Office, Washington, D.C., 1975, p. ix.
41. Resolution on Multinational Corporations adopted by AFL-CIO Convention, October 1975.
42. This discussion of U.S. electronics runaways is based on the excellent analysis by the North American Congress on Latin America (NACLA), "Electronics: The Global Industry," *NACLA's Latin America and Empire Report* 11 (April 1977), and "Hit and Run: U.S. Runaway Shops on the Mexican Border," *NACLA's Latin America and Empire Report* 9 (July/August 1975). The quotation from *Fortune* and the figures on imports of "American" consumer electronics products appears in "Hit and Run," p. 13.
43. "Changing Role of Southeast Asian Women: The Global Assembly Line and the Social Manipulation of Women on the Job," *Southeast Asia Chronicle* #66 (January/February 1979), and *Pacific Research* 9 (July/October 1978), special joint issue, p. 7.
44. "Electronics: The Global Industry," p. 16.
45. "Hit and Run," pp. 12ff.
46. "Changing Role of Southeast Asian Women."
47. Babson, "The Multinational Corporation and Labor."
48. "Electronics: The Global Industry," p. 15.
49. Tomarsz Hermanowski, "Industrial Cooperation between Poland and the USA," *Polish Economic Survey* (1975), p. 8.
50. "Electronics: The Global Industry," p. 21.
51. Ibid., pp. 22–23.
52. Raymond Vernon, "International Investment and International Trade in the Product Cycle," *Quarterly Journal of Economics 80 (May 1966), pp. 190–207.*
53. *Anticipating Disruptive Imports,* a study prepared for the use of the Joint Economic Committee, Congress of the United States, U.S. Government Printing Office, Washington, D.C., 1978, p. 9.
54. Ibid., p. 15.

55. Helen Shapiro and Steven Volk, "Steelyard Blues," *NACLA Report on the Americas* 13 (January/February 1979), p. 18.
56. Musgrave, *Direct Investment Abroad,* p. 69.
57. Quoted in Ibid., p. 70.
58. Robert Gilpin, *U.S. Power.* The following paragraphs are based on Gilpin's discussion, pp. 46ff.
59. Quoted in Musgrave, *Direct Investment Abroad,* p. 70.
60. Stillman, "The Devastating Impact of Plant Relocations."
61. Statement of Andrew J. Biemiller to the Senate Subcommittee on Multinational Corporations.
62. Ibid.
63. Melman, *The Permanent War Economy,* p. 103.
64. Cited in Stillman, "The Devastating Impact of Plant Relocations," p. 49.
65. Thorstein Veblen, *Imperial Germany and the Industrial Revolution* (New York: Viking Press, 1939), first published in 1915.
66. Ibid., p. 130.
67. Ibid., p. 131.
68. Gilpin, *U.S. Power,* pp. 89, 91.
69. Veblen, *Imperial Germany,* p. 131.
70. Robert W. Crandall, "Competition and 'Dumping' in the U.S. Steel Market," *Challenge* 21 (July/August 1978), pp. 14–15.
71. Melman, *The Permanent War Economy,* p. 82.
72. Gilpin, "An Alternate Strategy," p. 44; Raymond Vernon, "International Investment and International Trade in the Product Cycle"; Vernon, *Sovereignty at Bay* (New York: Basic Books, 1971); Charles P. Kindleberger, "An American Economic Climacteric?" *Challenge* 17 (January/ February 1974), pp. 35–44; E. H. Phelps Brown et al., "The 'Climacteric' in the British Economy of the Late Nineteenth Century: Two Interpretations," in Barry E. Supple, ed., *The Experience of Economic Growth* (New York: Random House, 1963), pp. 203–25.
73. Leonard Silk and David Vogel, *Ethics and Profits: The Crisis of Confidence in American Business* (New York: Simon and Schuster, 1976).
74. Ibid., pp. 21, 58, 72.
75. Ibid., p. 72.
76. Fred Charles Ikle, "What It Means to Be Number Two," *Fortune,* November 20, 1978; "The Decline of American Power," *Business Week,* March 12, 1979.

Chapter 5 Divergence

1. COIN (Consumers Opposed to Inflation in the Necessities), *There Are Alternatives: A Program for Controlling Inflation in the Necessities* (Washington, D.C., 1979), mimeograph, p. 4.

2. John M. Blair, *Economic Concentration: Structure, Behavior and Public Policy* (New York: Harcourt Brace Jovanovich, 1972), p. 406.

3. Leslie Ellen Nulty, *Understanding the New Inflation: The Importance of Necessities* (Washington, D.C.: Exploratory Project for Economic Alternatives, 1977).

4. For an exhaustive study of the trends and consequences of economic concentration, see Blair, *Economic Concentration,* cited in n. 2 above. A popular account of the modern corporation, with emphasis on the postwar formation of conglomerates, can be found in Richard J. Barber, *The American Corporation: Its Power, Its Money, Its Politics* (New York: E. P. Dutton, 1970).

5. Blair, *Economic Concentration,* p. 436.

6. Howard M. Wachtel and Peter D. Adelsheim, "How Recession Feeds Inflation: Price Markups in a Concentrated Economy," *Challenge* 20 (September/October 1977), pp. 6–13.

7. Institute for Social Research, University of Michigan, *ISR Newsletter* (Spring 1979).

8. Robinson G. Hollister and John L. Palmer, "The Impact of Inflation on the Poor," in Kenneth E. Boulding and Martin Pfaff, eds., *Redistribution to the Rich and the Poor* (Belmont, Calif.: Wadsworth, 1972), pp. 240–70.

9. Hollister and Palmer, "Impact of Inflation on the Poor," p. 270.

10. Robert Lindsey, "Rich Families Still Spend Freely for Vacations," *New York Times,* August 16, 1974.

11. George Katona, "The Psychology of Inflation," in Richard C. Curtin, ed., *Survey of Consumers: Contributions to Behavioral Economics* (Ann Arbor: Institute for Social Research, University of Michigan, 1976), pp. 9–19.

12. Isadore Barmash, "Men Buy Cheaper Suits, Hurting Some Makers," *New York Times,* July 6, 1978.

13. David Caplovitz, *Making Ends Meet: How Families Cope with Inflation and Recession* (New York: Institute for Research on Human Affairs, Graduate School of the City University of New York, 1977), mimeograph; also (Beverly Hills, Calif.: Sage Publications, 1979). Subsequent page references are to mimeographed version.

14. Ibid., pp. 15, 174.

15. Ibid., p. 32. Caplovitz later writes, "It is clear then that social class is a key determinant of a family's vulnerability to or immunity from the ravages of inflation. Those who are favored in social life are relatively immune to inflation; those who are underprivileged are especially likely to be victims of economic ills" (p. 53).

16. See *Dollars and Sense* #50 (October 1979), pp. 14–15.

17. Quoted in National Advisory Council on Economic Opportunity, *Eleventh Report* (Washington, D.C., 1979), p. 4.

18. Joseph J. Minarik, "Who Wins, Who Loses from Inflation?" *Challenge* 22 (January/February 1979), pp. 26–31. Also, Minarik, *The Size Distribution of Income During Inflation* (Washington, D.C.: Brookings Institution, 1979), mimeograph. On the ways in which inflation and the stagnation of the stock market in the last decade have eroded the endowments of both nonprofit foundations (such as Ford and Rockefeller) and some of our major private universities (Harvard, Yale, Stanford, Chicago) and have, by implication, reduced the similarly invested capital of wealthy individuals, see "Liberals and Inflation," *The New Republic,* January 20, 1979, pp. 5–6, 8–13.

19. Cited in Nulty, *Understanding the New Inflation,* p. 34.

20. William H. Whyte, Jr., *The Organization Man* (Garden City, N.Y.: Doubleday Anchor Books, 1957); Chapter 23, "Classlessness in Suburbia," cited in Gavin Mackensie, *The Aristocracy of Labor* (Cambridge: at the University Press, 1973), p. 5.

21. Bernard J. Frieden and Arthur P. Solomon, *The Nation's Housing: 1975 to 1985* (Cambridge, Mass.: Joint Center for Urban Studies of MIT and Harvard University, 1977), p. 128.

22. Median 1976 family income is taken from U.S. Bureau of the Census, "Money Income in 1976 of Families and Persons in the United States," *Current Population Reports,* Series P-60, No. 114, U.S. Government Printing Office, Washington, D.C., 1978. Median income of new home buyers is taken from Michael Sumichrast et al., *Profile of a New Home Buyer: Survey of New Home Owners* (Washington, D.C.: National Association of Home Builders, 1978), p. 11.

23. Sumichrast, *Profile of a New Home Buyer,* p. 41. These conclusions are confirmed by a large study conducted by the U.S. League of Savings Associations of 8,500 mortgage loans made during 1977, which found that 38 percent of buyers spent more than 25 percent of their income on housing expenses. And of all buyers, the lower-income groups were hardest hit: 72 percent of those earning less than $15,000 exceeded the 25 percent limit, compared to 51 percent earn-

ing $15,000–$19,000, 32 percent of those earning $20,000–$24,999, and 20 percent of those earning over $25,000. See *Wall Street Journal,* October 19, 1978, p. 5.

24. Robert Lindsey, "Urban Revival Poses Some Hard Choices: Middle-Class Interest in Older Housing Presses Poor," *New York Times,* April 21, 1978.

25. Peter Marcuse, *Rental Housing in the City of New York: Supply and Condition 1975–1978* (New York: Department of Housing Preservation and Development, 1979), mimeograph, pp. 5, 8.

26. Fergus M. Bordewich, "Real Estate: How High the Boom?" *New York,* December 11, 1978, p. 62.

27. T.D. Allman, "The Urban Crisis Leaves Town," *Harper's,* December 1978; Blake Fleetwood, "The New Elite and an Urban Renaissance," *New York Times Magazine,* January 14, 1979.

28. U.S. Department of Housing and Urban Development, Office of Policy Development and Research, *Displacement Report,* February 1979, mimeograph.

29. Jonathan Kandell, "Amsterdam Halts Decay in Center but Prices Workers out of Area," *New York Times,* June 11, 1978.

30. Frieden and Solomon, *Nation's Housing,* p. 116.

31. *Time,* September 12, 1977, p. 53 (emphasis added).

Chapter 6   America Transformed

1. Andrew Gamble and Paul Walton, *Capitalism in Crisis: Inflation and the State* (London: Macmillan, 1976), p. 1.

2. Richard Hofstadter, *The American Political Tradition* (New York: Random House, 1954).

3. On the errors of postwar social science, see Seymour Martin Lipset, "Growth, Affluence, and the Limits of Futurology," in Richard C. Snyder, ed., *From Abundance to Scarcity: Implications for the American Tradition,* The Hammond Lectures, No. 1 (Columbus: Ohio State University Press, 1978), pp. 65–108; Paul Blumberg, "Lockouts, Layoffs, and the New Academic Proletariat," in Arthur S. Wilke, ed., *The Hidden Professoriate: Credentialism, Professionalism, and the Tenure Crisis* (Westport, Conn.: Greenwood Press, 1979), pp. 33–58.

4. John Kenneth Galbraith, *The Affluent Society* (Boston: Houghton Mifflin, 1958), p. 97.

5. Robert L. Heilbroner, "Middle-Class Myths, Middle-Class Reali-

ties," *Atlantic Monthly,* October 1976, p. 41, quoted in Lipset, "Growth, Affluence, and the Limits of Futurology," pp. 95–96.

6. See Paul Blumberg and James M. Murtha, "College Graduates and the American Dream," *Dissent* (Winter 1977), pp. 45–53.

7. Paul Blumberg, "Lockouts, Layoffs, and the New Academic Proletariat."

8. Scott M. Olin, "Lawyer, 25, Wnts Job, Phila.; Drs Clsd," *New York Times,* April 29, 1978.

9. Albert Szymanski, "The Decline and Fall of the U.S. Eagle," *Social Policy,* March/April 1974, pp. 5–13.

10. David Caplovitz, *Making Ends Meet: How Families Cope with Inflation and Recession* (New York: Institute for Research on Human Affairs, Graduate School of the City University of New York, 1977), mimeograph, pp. 161ff; issued subsequently by Sage Publications, Beverly Hills, Calif., 1979.

11. Kevin P. Phillips, *The Emerging Republican Majority* (New Rochelle, N.Y.: Arlington, 1969).

12. Paul Blumberg, *Industrial Democracy: The Sociology of Participation* (New York: Schocken Books, 1969); Karl Frieden, *Workplace Democracy and Productivity* (Washington, D.C.: National Center for Economic Alternatives, 1980).

13. David M. Potter, *People of Plenty: Economic Abundance and the American Character* (Chicago: University of Chicago Press, 1954).

14. Tom Wolfe, "The Me Decade and the Third Great Awakening," in *Mauve Gloves & Madmen, Clutter & Vine* (New York: Farrar, Straus and Giroux, 1976), p. 143.

15. Jerry Rubin, *Growing (Up) at Thirty-Seven* (New York: M. Evans, 1976), p. 20.

16. Albert Einstein, "Why Socialism?" in *Out of My Later Years* (New York: Philosophical Society, 1950), p. 128.

17. Burkhard Strumpel, "The Future of Affluence: Social Indicators of Changes in Economic Welfare and Behavior," in Strumpel et al., *Survey of Consumers, 1972–73* (Ann Arbor: Institute for Social Research, University of Michigan, 1975), p. 74.

18. Ibid., p. 76.

19. Caplovitz, *Making Ends Meet,* p. 174.

20. On public distrust of basic American institutions, see periodic Harris polls.

21. Clyde Z. Nunn, Harry J. Crockett, Jr., and J. Allen Williams, Jr., *Tolerance for Nonconformity: A National Survey of Americans' Changing Commitment to Civil Liberties* (San Francisco: Jossey-Bass, 1978).

22. Ibid., p. 168.
23. Robert S. Lynd and Helen Merrell Lynd, *Middletown in Transition* (New York: Harcourt, Brace and World, 1937), p. 83.
24. *In These Times,* January 9–15, 1980, p. 16.
25. *Civil Liberties,* February 1980, p. 8.
26. For figures on the decline in white stereotyping and prejudice against blacks, see the survey conducted by Louis Harris, *A Study of Attitudes toward Racial and Religious Minorities and Toward Women* (New York: National Council of Christians and Jews, 1978), mimeograph, pp. 13ff. See also *Newsweek,* February 26, 1979.
27. U.S. Bureau of the Census, *Statistical Abstract of the United States: 1979* (100th edition), Washington, D.C., 1979, p. 416.
28. Nunn et al., *Tolerance for Nonconformity,* Chapter 6.
29. Ibid., p. 58 (italics in original).
30. For data on the educational attainment of the American people, see National Center for Education Statistics, *Digest of Education Statistics,* U.S. Government Printing Office, Washington, D.C., issued periodically; Kopp Michelotti, "Educational Attainment of Workers, March 1977," *Monthly Labor Review,* December 1977.
31. For figures on growing attendance at cultural events and funds granted to the National Endowment for the Arts and the National Endowment for the Humanities, see U.S. Bureau of the Census, *Statistical Abstract,* pp. 245–46.
32. Nunn et al., *Tolerance for Nonconformity,* p. 60.
33. See Patrick H. Caddell, "Crisis of Confidence: I, Trapped in a Downward Spiral," *Public Opinion,* October/November 1979.
34. Albert H. Cantril and Susan Davis Cantril, *Unemployment, Government and the American People: A National Opinion Survey* (Washington, D.C.: Public Research, 1978), mimeograph, p. 127.
35. J. B. Bury, *The Idea of Progress* (London: Macmillan, 1922); cf. Robert Nisbet, *History of the Idea of Progress* (New York: Basic Books, 1980).
36. See Karl Lowith, *Meaning in History* (Chicago: University of Chicago Press, 1949). I am grateful to Professor Reinhard Bendix for this reference and for acquainting me with the idea of the mutability of fortune.

Index